Creative Writing Studies

PEFC™

PEFC/16-33-111
CATG-PEFC-052
www.pefc.org

NEW WRITING VIEWPOINTS
Editor: Graeme Harper, *University of Wales, Bangor, Wales, Great Britain.*

The overall aim of this series is to publish books which will ultimately inform teaching and research, but whose primary focus is on the analysis of creative writing practice and theory. There will also be books which deal directly with aspects of creative writing knowledge, with issues of genre, form and style, with the nature and experience of creativity, and with the learning of creative writing. They will all have in common a concern with excellence in application and in understanding, with creative writing practitioners and their work, and with informed analysis of creative writing as process as well as completed artefact.

Other Book in the Series:
Power and Identity in the Creative Writing Classroom: The Authority Project
Anna Leahy (ed.)
Teaching Poetry Writing: A Five-Canon Approach
Tom C. Hunley

Other Books of Interest:
Constructing Cultures: Essays on Literary Translation
Susan Bassnett and André Lefevere
Contemporary Translation Theories (2nd edn)
Edwin Gentzler
Cultural Encounters in Translation from Arabic
Said Faiq (ed.)
Culture-Specific Language Styles: The Development of Oral Narrative and Literacy
Masahiko Minami
Frae Ither Tongues: Essays on Modern Translations into Scots
Bill Findlay (ed.)
Literary Translation: A Practical Guide
Clifford E. Landers
The Rewriting of Njáls Saga: Translation, Ideology, and Icelándic Sagas
Jón Karl Helgason
Theatrical Translation and Film Adaptation: A Practitioner's View
Phyllis Zatlin
Time Sharing on Stage: Drama Translation in Theatre and Society
Sirkku Aaltonen
Translating Milan Kundera
Michelle Woods
Translation and Religion: Holy Untranslatable?
Lynne Long (ed.)
The Translation of Children's Literature: A Reader
Gillian Lathey (ed.)
A Companion to Translation Studies
Piotr Kuhiwczak and Karin Littau (eds)

For more details of these or any other of our publications, please contact:
Multilingual Matters, Frankfurt Lodge, Clevedon Hall,
Victoria Road, Clevedon, BS21 7HH, England
http://www.multilingual-matters.com

NEW WRITING VIEWPOINTS
Series Editor: Graeme Harper

Creative Writing Studies
Practice, Research and Pedagogy

Edited by
Graeme Harper and Jeri Kroll

MULTILINGUAL MATTERS LTD
Clevedon • Buffalo • Toronto

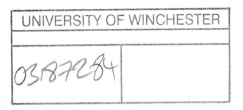
Library of Congress Cataloging in Publication Data
Creative Writing Studies: Practice, Research and Pedagogy / Edited by Graeme Harper and Jeri Kroll.
New Writing Viewpoints
Includes bibliographical references and index.
1. English language–Rhetoric–Study and teaching (Higher) 2. Creative writing (Higher education)–United States. 3. Creative writing (Higher education)–Great Britain. 4. Creative writing (Higher education)–Australia. I. Harper, Graeme. II. Kroll, Jeri
PE1404.C73 2007
808′.0420711–dc22   2007029775

British Library Cataloguing in Publication Data
A catalogue entry for this book is available from the British Library.

ISBN-13: 978-1-84769-020-3 (hbk)
ISBN-13: 978-1-84769-019-7 (pbk)

Multilingual Matters Ltd
UK: Frankfurt Lodge, Clevedon Hall, Victoria Road, Clevedon BS21 7HH.
USA: UTP, 2250 Military Road, Tonawanda, NY 14150, USA.
Canada: UTP, 5201 Dufferin Street, North York, Ontario M3H 5T8, Canada.

The policy of Multilingual Matters/Channel View Publications is to use papers that are natural, renewable and recyclable products, made from wood grown in sustainable forests. In the manufacturing process of our books, and to further support our policy, preference is given to printers that have FSC and PEFC Chain of Custody certification. The FSC and/or PEFC logos will appear on those books where full certification has been granted to the printer concerned.

Typeset by Wordworks Ltd.
Printed and bound in Great Britain by MPG Books Ltd.

Contents

The Contributors vii

Introduction
Graeme Harper and Jeri Kroll xi

1   Creative Writing in the University
    Graeme Harper and Jeri Kroll 1

2   The Novel and the Academic Novel
    Nigel Krauth 10

3   Let Stones Speak: New Media Remediation in the Poetry Writing
    Classroom
    Jake Adam York 21

4   That Was the Answer: Now What Was the Question? The PhD in
    Creative and Critical Writing: A Case Study
    Nessa O'Mahony 36

5   Six Texts Prefigure a Seventh
    Inez Baranay 48

6   Sleeping With Proust vs. Tinkering Under the Bonnet: The Origins
    and Consequences of the American and British Approaches to
    Creative Writing in Higher Education
    Stephanie Vanderslice 66

7   Workshopping the Workshop and Teaching the Unteachable
    Kevin Brophy 75

8   Creating an Integrated Model for Teaching Creative Writing: One
    Approach
    Nigel McLoughlin 88

9   Gonzo-Formalism: A Creative Writing Meta-Pedagogy for Non-
    Traditional Students
    Nat Hardy 101

10 Acting, Interacting and Acting Up: Teaching Collaborative
    Creative Practice
    Jen Webb 117

11 Writer as Teacher, Teacher as Writer
    Aileen La Tourette. 130

12 The Ladies and the Baggage: Raymond Carver's Suppressed
    Research and the Apologetic Short Story
    Rob Mimpriss 141

13 A Translator's Tale
    Gregory Fraser 152

Afterword
David Fenza. 165

Index 168

The Contributors

Inez Baranay's latest novel and ninth book *With The Tiger* will be published by HarperCollins India in 2007. Other novels include *Neem Dreams, Sheila Power, Pagan, The Edge of Bali* and *Between Careers*. Her non-fiction books include *Rascal Rain: A Year in Papua New Guinea* and *sun square moon: writings on yoga and writing*. Her short stories and essays have been published in many journals and collections. She has taught and commented on Creative Writing in Australia and internationally since 1989 and was awarded a Doctor of Philosophy in Writing from Griffith University.

Kevin Brophy is the author of ten books: four collections of poetry, three novels, a short fiction collection and two books of essays on Creativity and Creative Writing. He is Associate Professor and lecturer in Creative Writing in the School of Culture and Communication at the University of Melbourne. His latest collection of poetry is *Life Size* (Five Islands press).

David Fenza received an MA degree from Writing Seminars of Johns Hopkins University and an MFA degree from Writers' Workshop of the University of Iowa. He has taught creative writing, literature, and composition at Johns Hopkins University, Old Dominion University, Essex Community College and Goucher College, and has served as editor for numerous literary magazines. He has served on the boards of Share Our Strength and the Fall for the Book Literary Festival and is the author of a book-length poem, *The Interlude*. He was awarded a Fellowship in Poetry from the National Endowment for the Arts for his work on a novel in verse. He joined the staff of The Association of Writers and Writing Programs (AWP) in 1988 as Publications Manager and became Executive Director of AWP in 1995.

Gregory Fraser has published poetry in the *Southern Review,* the *Paris Review,* the *Chicago Review,* and many other literary journals. A two-time finalist for the Walt Whitman Award, Fraser's first book of poems, *Strange Pietà*, was published in 2003 by Texas Tech University Press. The recipient of a grant from the National Endowment for the Arts, he teaches creative writing, literature, and critical theory at the University of West Georgia, outside Atlanta.

Nat Hardy is Assistant Professor of Creative Writing and Literature in the Department of Liberal Arts at Savannah State University. A former editor-in-chief of the *New Delta Review*, Nat has served on the editorial staffs of the *Exquisite Corpse*, the *Cimarron Review*, and is currently an editor with the *Nimrod International Journal of Poetry and Prose* and *New Writing: The International Journal for the Theory and Practice of Creative Writing*. Nat also edits for the textbook divisions of Multilingual Matters, Penguin's Academic Series, W.W. Norton & Co, Pearson-Longman,Thomson-Wadsworth, and Cambridge University Press. His creative and scholarly work has appeared in journals in the US, Canada, Italy, the Netherlands, the UK, Algeria, and the Czech Republic.

Graeme Harper is Professor of Creative Writing at Bangor University and Director of the National Institute for Excellence in the Creative Industries.™ He is Editor-in-Chief of the journal *New Writing: The International Journal for the Practice and Theory of Creative Writing*, and his most recent creative works are: *Small Maps of the World* (Parlor, 2006) and *Moon Dance* (Parlor, 2007). His most recent critical book in the field of Creative Writing is *Teaching Creative Writing* (Continuum, 2006). In the wider academic community, Graeme is the Creative Writing member of Great Britain's Arts and Humanities Research Council (AHRC) Steering Committee on Practice-led Research and an honorary visiting Professor of Creative Writing at the University of Bedfordshire. A Fellow of the Royal Geographical Society (RGS) and of Royal Society for the Encouragement of Arts, Manufactures and Commerce) (RSA), his awards include the NBC Award for New Fiction (Aust.).

Nigel Krauth is Head of the Creative Writing program at Griffith University, Gold Coast, Australia. His publications include the novels *Matilda, My Darling* (co-winner of the Australian/Vogel Literary Award), *JF Was Here* (winner of the New South Wales State Literary Award) and *Freedom Highway*. His books have been published in the US, the UK and Germany. He has also written stories, plays, reviews and essays, edited collections, and judged national literary awards. Nigel is co-editor (with Jen Webb) of the international on-line creative writing teaching journal *TEXT* (http://www.griffith.edu.au/school/art/text). His most recent publication (2006) is *Creative Writing: Theory Beyond Practice*, edited with Tess Brady (http://www.snodger.com.au/bookstore).

Jeri Kroll completed her PhD at Columbia University and taught in the US and England before moving to Australia. She is Professor of English and Program Coordinator of Creative Writing at Flinders University and immediate past President of the Australian Association of Writing Programs. Her publications cover children's literature, Samuel Beckett, contemporary poetry and the pedagogy and theory of creative writing. She has published more than 20 books for adults and young people, including poetry, picture books (two Children's Book Council Notable Awards), novels and anthologies, released both in Australia and overseas. Her most recent are *Mickey's Little Book of Letters* (novel/audiobook) and *The Mother Workshops* (poetry and prose).

Aileen La Tourette is a twice-transplanted American who took root first in London, then Liverpool, almost a bigger move than across the Atlantic. (And a great one.) She teaches Imaginative Writing at Liverpool John Moores at BA, MA and PhD levels, and has recently published a collection of poems, *Touching Base* (Headland Publications), a follow-up to first collection, *Downward Mobility* (Headland, 2003). She has written two previous novels (Virago) and sundry radio drama. In 2007 she is looking forward to publishing a book of short stories *Oral History* (Headland), a novel *Late Connections* (Ilura Press) and a poetry reading tour in Cardiff and New York with Cath Nichols and Clare Potter.

Nigel McLoughlin BA (Lond.) MA, PhD (Lancs.) FHEA, FRSA is Field Chair in Creative Writing at the University of Gloucestershire and Course Leader for their MA in Creative and Critical Writing. His collections of poetry are: *At The Water's Clearing* (Flambard/Blackmountain Press, 2001), *Songs For No Voices* (Lagan Press, 2004), *Blood* (bluechrome, 2005) and *Dissonances* (bluechrome, 2007). He was a co-editor of *Breaking the Skin* (Blackmountain Press, 2002), an anthology of new Irish writing in two volumes. He is currently researching ways of integrating practice-led research with the pedagogy of Creative Writing and is working on a collection of prose poems.

Rob Mimpriss's early artistic endeavours were crushed by one Miss Lemon, primary school teacher, who published critical disdain of his straw houses. Undeterred, he turned his genius to literature, producing, in quick succession, 'The Gohst Holliday' and 'The Horrabel Bird' (unpublished mss, private collection). Hard years followed while he established himself as a writer, eating very little because he was so poor, and watching strange lights in the sky. Recognition came in 2005, when Bwthyn (Caernarfon) published his *Reasoning: Twenty Stories*, and Portsmouth University awarded him a PhD. He has recently finished *Valiant*, a second collection, and also publishes criticism.

Nessa O'Mahony lives in Dublin. She edits the journal *Arts Research Digest* and is Associate Editor of the literary journal *Orbis*. She is in the final stages of a PhD in Creative and Critical Writing at the University of Wales, Bangor. She is a tutor with Oscail, the Dublin City University distance learning programme, and teaches creative writing for the Women's Education Research and Research Centre at UCD. Her second poetry collection, *Trapping a Ghost,* was published by bluechrome publishing in 2005. Her third collection, a verse novel, is forthcoming. She was awarded an Irish Arts Council literature bursary in 2004.

Stephanie Vanderslice's essays on the teaching of Creative Writing have been included in books and journals such as *New Writing: The International Journal for the Practice and Theory of Creative Writing* (Multilingual Matters); *Profession* (Modern Language Association); *Teaching Creative Writing* (Continuum); and *The Creative Writing Handbook* (Edinburgh University Press). Her fiction and creative nonfiction has appeared in *Writing On-the-Edge*, *Other Mothering* and many others. Her collection, *Can It Really Be Taught?: Resisting Lore in the Teaching of Creative Writing*, co-edited with Dr Kelly Ritter, was recently published by Heinemann-Boynton Cook. She is Associate Professor of Writing at the University of Central Arkansas.

Jen Webb is Associate Professor and Director of Communication Research at the University of Canberra, and teaches creative writing and cultural theory. Her recent publications include *Reading the Visual* (Sage, UK, and Allen & Unwin, Sydney, 2004) and the collection of short fiction, *Ways of Getting By* (Ginninderra Press, Canberra, 2006). Her new book *Understanding Representation* (Sage, UK) is due out in early 2008. She is currently chief investigator on two projects supported by the Australian Research Council – Urban Imaginaries, and Art and Human Rights – and a third, supported by the Carrick Institute, to improve the delivery of Creative Writing higher degrees.

Jake Adam York is the author of *The Architecture of Address: The Monument and Public Speech in American Poetry* (Routledge, 2005) and *Murder Ballads* (Elixir, 2005), which won the Elixir Prize for Poetry. His second book of poems, *A Murmuration of Starlings,* will be published by Southern Illinois University Press in 2008. Raised in Alabama and educated at Auburn and Cornell Universities, he now lives in Denver, Colorado, working as Associate Professor of English at the University of Colorado at Denver and Health Sciences Center and editing *Copper Nickel* with his students.

Introduction

GRAEME HARPER AND JERI KROLL

1.

The chapters in this collection range across all three areas of its subtitle – Practice, Research and Pedagogy – testifying to the integrated nature of Creative Writing as a university discipline. The writers were given the option of concentrating on any one or more of the areas. Some chose to highlight practice, some research, some pedagogy; most, ultimately, combined two or more of these in their chapters, emphasising the connection between them. This cross-fertilisation is notable and worthy of celebration.

In addition, because of the relative newness of doctoral study in Creative Writing – even in the USA where it is well preceded by study at Bachelors and Master level – one writer in each of this book's three primary geographic locations was asked to concentrate on the nature of practice and research at doctoral level. In postgraduate study, issues emerge where students and supervisors develop notions, not only of writerly practice, but of how to undertake practice-led research in Creative Writing. The base question here is: what constitutes a research question in Creative Writing? More broadly, what various institutions, worldwide, understand as higher degree study is reflected in the types of degrees they award and what benchmarks they set in place. What kind of creative work might be produced for each? Internationally, too little has been exchanged about the variety of doctoral programs, methodologies and theories in this significant and still-expanding area, and encouraging some writers in this collection to consider it directly was seen to be important to the field.

This book, of course, concentrates on Creative Writing undertaken in English; though, naturally, this is in the manner of a case study, not in a manner of suggesting Creative Writing in universities is occurring only in English-speaking countries – far from it. In fact, throughout Europe, Asia and Africa, Creative Writing in and around universities is undertaken in a variety of languages, currently with various levels of local development. This is likewise the case *within* the UK, USA and Australia. Another book on Creative Writing in one or more languages other than English would be an extremely useful project.

Questions raised in various ways in the chapters of *Creative Writing Studies: Practice, Research and Pedagogy* include: what place should critical or theoretical discourse have in the discipline? How should critical understanding of Creative Writing be nurtured? How do we develop the best teaching methods at undergraduate and postgraduate levels? How do we develop practice-led research? How do we proceed as creative writers who are also teachers and/or students?

Because this collection offers a cross-section of Creative Writing activity in Higher Education, and a variety of approaches from a number of geographic locations, the instruction to the reader might well be to 'read between the lines' as well as to read the lines. Here are chapters by creative writers given a free rein to explore their field of interest, and they all have experience as creative practitioners, as critics or theorists, and as university teachers.

Those of us involved in Creative Writing in the university today are watching the discipline further invent itself, monitoring our own contribution to its construction and reflecting on how these processes affect our creative work, our research and our pedagogies. Creative writers in academia today are not deadlocked, but frequently encourage multiple meanings, as they reflect the shifting reality of their own artistic and professional lives.

2.

In **Chapter 1** of *Creative Writing Studies: Practice, Research and Pedagogy,* the Editors explore how Creative Writing has evolved most recently as a discipline, and consider the site of knowledge that it represents. We look at where it sits in the contemporary university, and make some observations about its current, and future, role in academe. **Chapter 2**, 'The Novel and the Academic Novel', finds novelist and PhD supervisor Nigel Krauth considering how the creation of a novel for 'new-breed, non-traditional doctorates' affects both the process and the product. On the one hand, writers obtain support and encouragement; on the other, they might feel constrained because these benefits, flowing from a bureaucratic structure, can impact on the novelist's freedom to create. In **Chapter 3**, Jake Adam York, focusing on new media teaching techniques, suggests ways in which the university Creative Writing classroom might be a place for pedagogic investigation of the nature of particular genre. In York's case it is the role of sound in the writing of poetry that forms the basis of this investigation and, ultimately, of his innovative teaching practices.

In **Chapter 4** Nessa O'Mahony, an Irish poet who has undertaken both a Creative Writing Masters degree and a Creative Writing Doctorate in the UK, considers the practical dimensions of the empirical research needed to construct a work of Creative Writing. She also considers the broader range of aesthetic, personal and career issues that form a backdrop to such study. As a useful counterpoint to Nessa O'Mahony's chapter Inez Baranay, already a novelist before entering the academy to undertake a doctorate, considers in **Chapter 5**, 'Six Texts Prefigure a Seventh', the concept that the creation of texts never occurs in a vacuum by interrogating her own imaginative universe. Writing her PhD encouraged Baranay to re-read her previous published work, which led to insights that suggest the reflexivity of writers in the academy involves not only self-critique, but memoir (recollections of each book's composition) and an analysis of the development of form and practice. Baranay represents the new breed of published writer who enters the academic fold seeking not only the resources of a university but structured self-knowledge.

The nature of knowledge, forming a bridge, also forms the subject for Stephanie Vanderslice in **Chapter 6**, 'Sleeping with Proust vs. Tinkering Under the Bonnet'. She traces the relatively recent history of formal Creative Writing teaching in the USA and UK and notes the need for something that draws together invention and technique, a new metaphor that might resolve a long-held pedagogic tension. Investigation of elements of this tension is also evident in **Chapter 7**, 'Workshopping the Workshop and Teaching the Unteachable', where Kevin Brophy confronts one of the most pressing difficulties facing anyone involved in Creative Writing in Higher Education: how to mediate the connection between emotion, ideas and art. In so doing, he analyses workshop dynamics, a place 'which foregrounds skill, learning, decision-making, the application of critical intelligence,' but also, as 'a live event,' allows spontaneity and excitement.

In **Chapters 8** and **Chapter 9,** respectively, Nigel McLoughlin and Nat Hardy reveal two alternate approaches to teaching Creative Writing in the university. In simple terms, the differences could be broken down into one pedagogical approach based on structured learning and one based on unstructured learning. But such a simplification hides some key elements of their discussions. In his chapter, 'Creating an Integrated Model for Teaching Creative Writing: One Approach', Nigel McLoughlin investigates 'the various ways in which research and scholarly activity, creative and critical processes and practices and pedagogical theories and methodologies interact within the discipline of Creative Writing,' while Nat Hardy's 'Gonzo-Formalism' seeks to enhance technique and interpretive understanding. In many ways, the similarities of view present in these two chapters are more important than the differences.

In **Chapter 10**, 'Acting, Interacting, and Acting Up: Teaching Collaborate Creative Practice,' Jen Webb analyses how her students work together on cross-media projects as a vehicle for investigating collaborative practice. In addition, in that reflexive circle that seems to result from so many teaching practices in the creative arts, she finds her own understanding of the possibilities open to her altered by her students' experiences. Allusion to self-understanding and collaboration is similarly found in Aileen La Tourette's **Chapter 11**, 'The Writer as Teacher, Teacher as Writer'. In this chapter she discusses mentors, craft and the needs of creative writers, while also alerting us to the social context of many experiences in the university Creative Writing classroom.

In **Chapter 12**, Rob Mimpriss focuses on a key issue in his own Creative Writing research, relating specifically to the creation of short stories and, in a somewhat different fashion to Aileen La Tourette, refers to notions of something that could indeed be called writerly mentoring (in this case, the influential role one author's work can have on another). His discussion of the nature of the short story, and the apologetic discourse he finds connected to the writing of it, is thought-provoking, especially given some mainstream publishers expressing a preference for the novel in the 21st century. Finally, in **Chapter 13**, Greg Fraser considers a number of theoretical positions and their possibilities for Creative Writing practice and discusses how models of what he calls 'critical consciousness' relate to a general writerly curiosity about the world. He suggests that 'creative writers (poets especially, perhaps) tend to be unsatisfied with pre-established grids. They tend to want to let language itself bring about reconceptualisations and expansions of reality.'

Creative Writing Studies: Practice, Research and Pedagogy addresses the lack of international publications concerned with the discipline of Creative Writing at university level, offering a platform to a range of individual voices. The creative writers in this book explore those issues they believe most significant, yet these explorations are decidedly interconnected, charting the progress of how far the discipline of Creative Writing has come in the USA, the UK and Australia to date. In effect, they have engaged, either explicitly or implicitly, with who they are as creative writers, teachers and researchers and what permutations these identities have undergone within the academy.

Chapter 1

Creative Writing in the University

GRAEME HARPER AND JERI KROLL

1.

A triumvirate of practice, research and pedagogy defines Creative Writing as a subject in universities around the world. Writing is first and foremost a studio art, like its siblings – music, drama, dance, visual arts, and so on. The teaching of the arts and attendant critical understanding about how to communicate the intricacies of specific disciplines followed on the heels of their introduction into the academy at all levels. Although the Master of Fine Arts (MFA) in the US is still, to some extent, thought of as primarily a practice-based (studio) degree, Masters and Doctoral study, generally, moved the discipline on to another plane because here the concept of Creative Writing as research began to be interrogated most vigorously. The movement of ideas between practice, research and pedagogy has now come full circle. Definitions of research and about the production of the type and forms of knowledge Creative Writing generates have begun to filter down to affect how Creative Writing is taught at undergraduate level in many institutions.

Witness the number of books published in recent years about the discipline. Likewise, research-led debates that in earlier times found their way occasionally into *The Writer's Chronicle*, the long-established organ of the Association of Writers and Writing Programs (AWP), and slightly more so perhaps into *Writing in Education*, the publication of the UK's National Association of Writers in Education (NAWE), are now able to be carried on regularly in independent specialist journals such as *New Writing: The International Journal for the Practice and Theory of Creative Writing*. Newer organisations have also developed their own international journals with tertiary education focuses, such as *TEXT*: the Journal of the Australian Association of Writing Programs (AAWP, founded 1996), published biannually. Concomitantly, the research interests expressed in publications by NAWE, whose brief covers all levels of education from primary to tertiary, and in AWP publications as well, have increased.

The teaching of arts practice, and the attendant critical understanding of it, has long been a part of academe – in fact, since the birth of Higher Education. Yet, the formalising of education in The Arts – in Creative Writing in this specific case – has often led to questions about the nature of the intersection between practice, research into practice and the critical knowledge connected with it, and teaching. Constant movement of ideas between these three aspects – Creative Writing practice, university research and university teaching – is now more common in institutions worldwide, but it is not yet firmly established generally. Much work still needs to be done on the relationship between Creative Writing as a practice-led activity, critical understanding drawn from investigating that practice, and modes of teaching Creative Writing at university level. In other words, the principles, methodologies and theories underpinning the discipline are still emerging in a variety of cultural and institutional contexts.

Definitions of, and about, the production, types and forms of knowledge developed and used in Creative Writing have only just begun to filter down to the way Creative Writing is taught. With a strong international network now in place, new discipline-based knowledge can travel widely. That said, different arenas – international as well as within national borders – have seen alternative emphases at various times, and one of the most exciting elements of the now international sense of Creative Writing in universities is the scope and strength of debate.

2.

Prior to writing this chapter, we generated a number of questions. These were mostly concerned with what we might achieve in such a chapter in a book that would also present contributions about Creative Writing as a university discipline from the perspective of three geographical locations. Here are some of those questions that helped to demarcate what we believe are critical areas of investigation in the development of that site of knowledge called 'Creative Writing'.

What do we perceive as the subject content of Creative Writing in universities? What is its *specific* subject matter and what is related to it, but perhaps not core to its interests? Who chooses to study it, and what are their expectations? What indeed are the results of this studying? Where within the university is Creative Writing activity most often taking place? What sort of activities does it cover? How is it defined in light of other subjects in the university? How is it valued, and by whom? How do we conceive of research in Creative Writing, and what is the relationship between creative practice and critical understanding that is integral to that research? What is knowledge of, and about, Creative Writing, and to what ends is it used? How does what occurs within universities relate to Creative Writing activities beyond universities? The list could go on.

Readers should note the inclusion of the word 'studying' in the paragraph above, as well as the word 'within'. The reasons to use these two words are themselves twofold. Firstly, this is a chapter concerned with Creative Writing as it is studied in and around universities. Needless to say, it is not necessary to *study* Creative Writing in order to undertake some Creative Writing. Now and then, the question has been raised as to whether Creative Writing even benefits from being studied within universities at all. We'd be the last people to answer that question without bias. So, bias in hand, we might simply rephrase the question: 'Does any field of knowledge not benefit from being studied within a university?' There's little doubt that Creative Writing in and around universities is impacted upon by the nature of the university environment, and that the discipline, in turn, impacts upon that environment. There is a myriad of ways that writers (and their students) are affected by this interpenetration and how, as a result, the discipline as well as the general practice of Creative Writing is advanced. Secondly, how Creative Writing is studied most often involves two elements: the act of writing creatively, and the act of critically considering that act and its results. In both cases, the 'studying' raises questions about how to marshal ideas and actions, how to employ discoveries, how to communicate information and how to evaluate understanding. In this sense also 'within' seems an appropriate addition to use in our discussions, and gives some indication of our focus and purpose.

3.

Let us explore the three areas of connected interest – practice, research and pedagogy – a bit more to illuminate the ideas being suggested here.

Creative Writing 'practice' is an all-encompassing term, and perhaps is the first that needs to be unpacked in order to reveal some elements of Creative Writing's nature. Practice, in this case, means the practice of writing creatively; but this can, of course, entail a great many practices, some simple acts of inscription, some acts of recording, some acts of invention, interpretation or distillation, some acts of revisiting, rewriting or editing, and so on. And yet, in talking of practice there is some indication that we are not talking, as the *primary focal point*, about the finished artifacts that result from that practice. This is important. Creative Writing can refer to an action, or set of actions, *and* a consideration of both action and artefact. However, the focus in the subject of Creative Writing on action and process differentiates it from the critical study of 'Literature', 'Theatre', 'Film/Media,' for example, all of which *can* involve analytical acts regarding pieces of Creative Writing but are subjects largely undertaken without creative practice involved.

Thus practice here means an approach to a subject based on knowledge acquired through the act of creating. This knowledge is not superficial. It results from sustained and serious examination of the art of writerly practice and might include not only contemporary theoretical or critical models but the writers' own past works as well as predecessors and traditions. In some incarnations, practice as research functions as the formal autobiography of an individual's craft, taking into account the significant influences and methods. Even the relationship between a doctoral student and supervisor can be understood in this manner.

This knowledge, while intersecting with that acquired by the post-creation act of criticism, is fundamentally different in attitude because its purpose is primarily to inform the practitioner (and, by extension, other practitioners), and therefore give her or him better access to ideas and approaches that might enhance their own practice. Artists outside of an institutional context might do this sporadically or systematically, but they are not necessarily interested in disseminating their findings (contributing to a body of knowledge as a primary purpose, for example). Within the academy, writers function in the private sphere of their own practice, but also in the institutional sphere as teachers and in a more public sphere as authors. These identities interpenetrate and reflect back upon practice.

Some of the resulting knowledge could perhaps be called 'applied knowledge'; however, such a term in Higher Education has tended to fall foul of a perceived intellectual hierarchy, with the 'applied' second in importance, and what might be called 'blue skies' knowledge situated in first place. What we are talking about here, to be clear, is higher learning attained through creative practice. It is in no sense second in importance to critical analysis detached from practice (what some might call 'intellectual' activity), and it is in no sense less capable of investigating the nature of the world, the individual or the culture. Practice here is taken to be an active engagement with knowledge producing creative results that embody levels of understanding and modes of communication. Perhaps here Creative Writing and other art forms have much to contribute to each other; however, in some cases Creative Writing has been excluded from relevant debates about practice as research. What Australia-based Paul Carter (2004: 177) deems 'the "balkanisation" of creative arts' has had negative consequences in some arenas, because this phenomenon has prevented the arts 'entering into dialogue with one another' and, thus, building on each discipline's insights. Nevertheless, Creative Writing scholars, as the ensuing chapters demonstrate, have not only been keen to explore resources both within and outside academe but have been innovative in their application.

The developing concept of practice situates itself well in the current history of Creative Writing in places of higher learning. The growth of the subject in universities over the past 10 to 15 years, and the slower but still considerable growth for the 40 or so years before this, has meant that Creative Writing practice is now undertaken in the university by individuals with a range of backgrounds and expectations. Universities were once far more elitist places; mass higher education has introduced notions of 'access for all', which naturally has opened up the number of possible individual 'life plans' that might exist in any one university.

So, for example, on the one hand most university students of Creative Writing – whether students in the sense of actual members of the university student body, or 'students of the field' in the more general sense of those Creative Writing proponents in academe – consider some element of recognised publication or performance of Creative Writing testimony to achievement in the subject. Practice therefore might be said to embody an 'industry' or 'consumption' ideal connected with 'making a living'. On the other hand, this is one of the most debated areas of Creative Writing study, and there would be any number of those connected with Creative Writing in universities who would question whether the market is a defining component of practice and whether the considerations of the market for finished pieces of Creative Writing should be the motivation behind undertaking them – or indeed for benchmarking creative work. In higher degrees, in particular, 'publishable' as an evaluative term has been questioned, and in many cases discarded, in recent years. Part of the reason for this is the desire to develop courses where there are a variety of recognised 'successful outcomes' (i.e. from publication or performance, to simply a far greater understanding of the nature of excellent creative writing).

It is interesting to note that in the past decade or two, particularly with the evolution of doctoral degrees in Creative Writing, authors with established reputations in the market have returned to universities, or in some cases turned up for the first time, to undertake higher degree study. Something similar was seen, prior to the birth of the Creative Writing doctorate, at Masters level. This is undoubtedly connected with the idea of achieving formal qualifications that bolster the chances of a writer obtaining university employment. But it would be cynical to believe this is where the interest stops. There is much evidence, albeit often anecdotal, that supports the idea that writers with considerable market profiles have returned to universities to investigate and develop their practice within an environment that actively encourages knowledge acquisition and the application of that knowledge.

Practice, therefore, can be viewed as a mode of investigation, and a mode informed by individual and cultural circumstance. Also, as an act of acquisition and exchange, it is informed by critical understanding of a specific kind related to creative achievement, but not always to notions of 'the market'. Writers in the university, conscious of their practice and context, are in a position even at a base level to theorise, along with their colleagues in other disciplines, about what they do if, as Terry Eagleton (2003: 2) suggests, 'theory means a reasonably systematic reflection on our guiding assumptions'. In fact, Eagleton asserts, this activity is still 'indispensible' even though the age of high theory is past. The connection between this point of view and the idea of Creative Writing 'Research' is perhaps already plain.

In order to pursue new knowledge universities have long been the home of a great deal of research activity. Some of this has been practice-led, and such research has been fully recognised within institutions, and by governments funding research. To take a broad example, the Sciences are supported by a range of practice-led activities informed by theoretical positions, and hold a place within modern universities based on being well regarded as a mode of engagement with the world. Many universities have devoted vast portions of their estate to such scientific practice and defended the importance of doing so with regard to the future of humankind. Alternatively, the Humanities and Social Sciences – subjects such as History or Theology, Literature or Philosophy, Sociology or Politics – have not seen practice as focal, but have instead highlighted the importance of critical modeling, theoretical positioning and comparative study. In this respect, universities have often devoted a great deal of their time, effort and budgets to such things as ensuring strong library collections, launching high-level conferences and seminars and appointing recognised critics and theoreticians.

When we come to the Creative Arts, the situation is not so clear. Creative Writing, as a creative art with little 'site identity,' is perhaps worse off than most. By 'site identity' we mean the subject's material location in universities. That is, while Music, Theatre, the Fine Arts, Film-making and so on have a need for – and therefore an identity connected with – physical locations in the university, Creative Writing has long been undertaken in relatively low-impact, low-profile locations. This lack of a site identity has been the result, in part, of the myriad of departments or schools in which it has often been housed (e.g. Creative Writing, English, Creative Industries, Theatre, Literary Studies, Media and Film, Communications and Cultural

Studies). Demanding little university estate, creative writers have pursued their practice-led research, informed by critical awareness, in between the edifices established for other Arts, Natural Sciences, Humanities and Social Sciences. In order to facilitate that research, university administrators have not often seen the need to create studios or spaces to store equipment or, indeed, to dedicate a portion of the university's information services grid to the discipline. In other words, the act of pursuing new knowledge of, and about, Creative Writing has gone on without change in most institutions' immediate physical surroundings, and yet the discipline has impacted upon the life of academe to an amazing extent. In the simplest terms, just consider the number of students it attracts, and their involvement in the life of the university.

Needless to say this relative invisibility, yet considerable impact, raises questions about the kinds of activities that might be considered research in, and about, Creative Writing. It raises questions about how institutions, and indeed governments, assess the quality of that research – and therefore determine whether it is of value and should be financially supported. And, as contemporary universities are places of compartmentalisation and what might perhaps be awkwardly called 'departmentalisation', it also raises questions about the ways in which Creative Writing research differentiates itself from other research, and in what way it can be incorporated neatly into a pattern of university management. This dilemma has been exacerbated by the number of departments in which Creative Writing has been taught.

Fortunately, or unfortunately, Creative Writing is an eclectic activity, drawing on knowledge from a vast range of fields. While some elements of the subject have relatively clear connections with other university subjects (for example, the background that the study of literature might provide for poetry and prose writers, or the potential models the study of film might provide for screenwriters), key elements of the subject are unique to it. The combination of willing, often enthusiastic, relations with other subjects, and a determination to use knowledge acquired in a specific creative way, continues to make Creative Writing a difficult prospect for university administrations and research funding bodies. Though this fact is increasingly addressed by the Creative Writing research community worldwide, there is still some way to go before Creative Writing research is properly understood by university administrations and those organisations that fund university research – which leads to the final component of this book's subtitle: Pedagogy.

It is perhaps too obvious to relate here the general principles of university financial management: that is, if a subject can support itself through research income then its engagement with teaching can be carried forward with that as a backdrop. If, however, a subject is not heavily funded for its research, then it is teaching income that must support it. Creative Writing, currently bound up in the evolution of an understanding that has not yet reached all corners of university research funding, has mostly supported itself in Higher Education through the considerable interest of students. More often than not this has meant that creative writers in the academy have been keenly engaged with pedagogic innovation and often have been well-versed in ideas about the encouragement, support and development of learners. Not unsurprisingly, given the increased student interest and the extent of development needed to ground Creative Writing as a research subject, those involved in teaching Creative Writing in universities have also shown a particular interest in the career trajectory and employability of their graduates, linked to the question 'Why teach Creative Writing in universities?'

One relevant observation might be that the majority of graduates of university Creative Writing courses do not become full-time creative writers earning their income primarily from the act of writing. Does this mean that those teaching the subject at university level are failing to deliver? Or is it the case that Creative Writing, much like its cognate cousins in the Arts and Humanities, is a subject that provides knowledge of a kind that can be used in a variety of fields, and therefore the relatively small number of opportunities to become a full-time, well-paid creative writer is not a determinant of the subject's success or failure? Equally, has it not always been the case that most creative writers are also actively engaged in other pursuits, often for financial reasons, and that Creative Writing is a subject that involves encouraging a high degree of adaptability? We could say it is primarily a subject whose bedrock is creativity and communication.

A second observation might be that, with the growth of the communication industries, fed by new technologies and underpinned in the Western world by increased leisure time, opportunities for creative writers in the media-related sector, or more broadly in the Creative Industries, have never been greater. Creative Writing graduates thus have acquired knowledge important to economies increasingly interested in the promotion and economic potential of creative endeavour

Whatever the possible answers to the question 'Why teach Creative Writing in universities?', there's little doubt that those teaching it have made a considerable personal investment in pedagogic exploration. 'Tools of the trade' such as the Creative Writing workshop, the creative portfolio, and the responsive critical essay have long been staples of Creative Writing

Higher Education, but their deployment has often been accompanied by critical investigation of such teaching strategies. The push to do so has come from many directions, driven not only by pedagogical interest but by the need to develop individual practice and also, on occasion, to generate publishing opportunities focused on Creative Writing teaching. In this latter instance, writers in academia have been able to bolster their scholarly publication record. In the contemporary university, therefore, the role of teaching as a method of testing ideas and practices as well as of developing new research directions has been strong.

Practice, research and pedagogy – the three areas we have introduced here, and which will be explored in the following chapters – demonstrate how Creative Writing has developed and continues to develop in the contemporary university. Although such terms are treated separately, for convenience, they in fact interpenetrate, as we have argued. The linguistic play of contributors' titles highlights those interconnections for readers, and also points to the contradictions that can yield new forms of knowledge. Titles are allusive, paradoxical, ironic and multi-layered, suggesting that attempts at imposing a rigid taxonomy on creative writers only invites subversion. In the academy writers-teachers-researchers study practice, play at teaching, teach about playing with language and new technologies, welcoming the imaginative and critical insights that emerge. Some of the writing produced by teachers and their students will remain within the university, some will be disseminated among other academics and some will reach a wider public through a variety of media in the form of books, films, plays, websites and so on. These different forms of discourse for different audiences demonstrate how Creative Writing as a university discipline often resists 'departmentalisation' as it moves into new territory in an effort to define itself in the 21st century.

References

Carter, P. (2004) *Material Thinking*. Melbourne: Melbourne University Press.
Eagleton, T. (2003) *After Theory*. New York: Basic Books.

Chapter 2

The Novel and the Academic Novel

NIGEL KRAUTH

Preamble

I supervise Creative Writing PhDs – those new-breed, non-traditional doctorates that worry university administrations, attract scorn from some older writers and academics, and bring in more candidates than we can handle. I supervise three times more PhDs (18) than my university's recommended load (only 6) because: (1) I like watching new work come to fruition; (2) I crave discussion with other writers over bottles of wine; and (3) I am, like most academics I know, a workaholic. I am also a novelist, so mainly I supervise novel-writing PhD candidates.

The writing of a novel for a Creative Writing PhD involves administrators, supervisors, coursework, critical exegeses, high-pressured examinations, and dressing up in colorful garb (for graduation) once the work is accepted by its critics/readership. Writing creatively in the academic context is different from normal creative writing.

This new beast, the academic novel, has some quirky features. You don't just write it, you enrol in it. You don't just live in a garret to produce it, you attend classes/workshops/progress meetings. You don't have a private, lingering, developing affair with it, you have a supervisor or a supervisory panel who butt in on the intimacy of your writing it. You don't simply send the manuscript off to a publisher once it's completed, you fill out official forms and submit it in triplicate. Importantly also, you don't write it for yourself and (hopefully) the thousands of others who will read it, you write it for your supervisors initially, and then, your examiners. The academic novel – following its rapid spread across English-speaking campuses during the 1990s – represents a significant evolutionary leap for the novel species.

What is all the university bother doing to the novel and its writing process? How is the novel faring in its new academic environment? I suspect the novel feels as if it has been sent to an orphanage, or a zoo – a well-meaning place, but not real family, not its natural homeland. I suspect the novel feels disoriented, but grudgingly pleased that someone is looking to its upkeep. I suspect the novel that simply wanted to go to bed with you as its gentle author, now finds itself under the glare of spotlights where process and product, technique and innovation, tricks and slick moves are anatomised, highlighted, teased apart, zoomed in upon, like some sort of pornographic display or anatomical teaching model.

In this chapter I seek to feel out what is happening to the writing of novels in the academic context of the Creative Writing PhD.

Some Facts about Fiction in the Academy

An increasing number of universities in the US, UK and Australia offer PhDs in Creative Writing (Harper, 2003, 2005; Krauth, 2001; Ritter, 2001; *AWP*, 2006: 40). The trend in the US is towards examination of three elements: 'research/theory/studio' (*AWP*, 2006: 6–7). This structure is an extension of the Literature PhD (research/theory), which involves coursework and dissertation. It contrasts with, while it veers back towards, the traditional MFA model, which is studio-only. In the UK and Australia, where the concept of the studio-based MFA does not have a significant history, the Creative Writing PhD has grown out of the Literature PhD as a sort of creative rebellion against a theory/research-only regime. Nevertheless, while it normally involves no coursework or studio/workshop at all, it places significant importance on the theory/research exegesis (up to 50% of the weighting can be required).

When I Google 'Creative Writing PhD+novel' I get more than 4 million responses. (This is not the number of university PhD courses in the world, but it might well be the number of prospective applicants!) My main aim in Googling is to examine the terms in which universities advertise the nature of the experience of undertaking a Creative Writing PhD that produces an academic novel. Many sites describe the coursework aspect of enrolment in detail, but the exegetical and creative components are typically elaborated upon less. Of course, it's hard to describe a new contribution to knowledge before it is written (Bolt, 2004) but I get the feeling that the description of the academic novel in university website promotions is almost no description at all:

- 'an extended work ... ranged in length from 95-550 pages, with an average length of about 165 pages' (University of Houston, 2006);
- 'an original literary text of exceptional quality written specifically for the degree ... [it] should show coherence and originality and attain publishable standard' (University of Lancaster, 2006);
- 'a book-length work in its genre' (University of Adelaide, 2005).

Usually the accompanying description of the critical essay/scholarly thesis/reflective study/exegesis is somewhat more specific than that provided for the creative component – if only because an accompanying critical component for a PhD is a new concept and is variously interpreted by different universities as their new creative PhDs come on stream. But in all of this, it seems that the academic novel's nature is somehow a given – something invariable and enduring – and that its production is not seen as a special outcome of the academic process. 'A novel is a novel,' this promotional material indicates. 'It doesn't matter where, how or why you write it – it will come out the same.'

In this respect, the website announcing the experience of writing an academic novel at the University of Newcastle Upon Tyne is pleasantly refreshing because it investigates the idea that such a novel is written in different circumstances – especially in its 'hybrid' and 'carefully balanced' relationship with the exegetical study:

> Your PhD will be a type of dialogue between two discourses. One, the creative, must be at liberty to pursue its own agendas and methodologies without circumscription. It is not obliged to 'answer' to literary theory, but it may well be profoundly shaped by it. The other, the academic, must be as responsible to its own disciplines, but it should also acknowledge the unique nature of its endeavour. (University of Newcastle Upon Tyne, 2005)

In this open dialogue between two forms there is the possibility of:

> ... the creation of a truly hybrid form, in which the strengths of each discipline contribute to a unique whole. In this instance, instead of the thesis being derived from the creative component, a poem or story or chapter or scene may arise directly from research and may indeed drive the academic writing on, so that an intertwined structure is created, observing the same proportions, but exploring the established relationship between text and criticism in a new and dynamic manner. (University of Newcastle Upon Tyne, 2005)

In pointing to the dynamic between the creative and academic components – and the way these running mates represent the discourses of very different practices, industries and cultures – the University of Newcastle Upon Tyne website reflects discussions between many supervisors and Creative Writing PhD candidates to date. In asking questions as simple and profound as: Which should I start writing first?, Should I write them simultaneously or keep them separated? and Which component will the examiners look at most closely? students indicate the difficulty of seeing through the dynamic to discover a set of practices to deal with it. Even established novelists who set out on a creative PhD are disoriented to begin with.

Research articles and symposia in the area have so far concentrated most strongly on the range of possibilities of the exegetical component (see, for example, Bourke & Neilsen, 2004; Brady, 2004; Fletcher & Mann, 2004; Krauth, 2002; Kroll, 2004) with far less attention given to how the creative component is faring in the academic context. Freiman (2003) examined the conditions for creativity in the academy and noted 'obvious differences between the creative writing done in the academy and the public reception of creative writing'. Arnold (2005) usefully attempted to place the creative product in an 'energising' relationship with the exegesis, and in doing so pointed out the problems of building an academic novel around a 'research question' (Milech & Schilo, 2004). All in all, there has been almost nothing about the actual academic novel. Abandoned to look after itself in its confusing new environment, the novel has been taking form – and new forms – diligently and unobtrusively, in spite of being yoked to exegeses, fattened on institutionalised workshopping, and offered up to sacrifice on the altar of academic examination.

The Academic Novel is Not Like a Normal Novel. *However* ...

(1) The academic novel is written before, after or alongside an exegesis. *However*, the research done for the writing of a normal novel can be similar to that for a contextualising or commentating exegesis. For example, detailed investigations of historical sources, and wide reading in related genres, are likely to be involved in both kinds of project. The writing of novels has always involved research.

(2) The academic novel is not written solely for commercial, cultural, literary, personal, political, professional or social reasons. (Have I covered all the reasons why normal novels are written?) The academic novel is also written for an *educational* reason – indeed, a *research into new knowledge* reason. *However*, good novels are always investigative, always educational, for the writer as for the reader. I don't believe many novelists – including the most successful or the most form-ularistic – can avoid learning more about writing and the world by taking on a new project. The writing of a novel is always an entry into new territories of understanding.

(3) The academic novel has the potential to be more experimental than the normal novel. *However*, experimentation in literature (as a form of disobedience) occurs for reasons associated with revolution, e.g.

intellectual, social, digital revolution, and the associated break-up of traditions. Being nurtured in a constricted environment (like a hothouse fruit or a lab-produced foetus), the academic novel might promise leaps forward in experimentation. But the production of a popular new revolutionary novel form will have to overcome the fact that universities have become alarmingly conservative in the 21st century, as have English-language readerships.

(4) For the academic novel, the question is not how publishable it is, but how examinable it is. *However,* traditional ways forward for a manuscript also involve examination. MSS sent to publishers are examined by readers and editors; MSS sent to literary awards are examined by judges. These examiners' criteria are usually stringent. Only the entirely self-published novel might avoid the hostile eye of examination ... that is, until after publication when the ineluctable eye of critics and book-buyers will examine it word by word.

(5) Although the academic novel is required to be 'of publishable quality', it is written initially for a series of very small readerships – the principal supervisor, the associate supervisor, the supervisory panel, the confirmation process assessors, the pre-submission examining board, and so on – each of them gatekeepers set in place before the final examiners (in a way, the 'ultimate' readership) are reached. *However,* the question of focusing on a readership is complex for any novelist. If publishers' readers or other readerships (general or specialist) were predictable, there would be few unsuccessful novelists. Pleasing academic examiners may not be more difficult than pleasing the world.

(6) For the academic novelist there is always a personal editor nearby – looking over the writer's shoulder – i.e. the supervisor. This is both useful and threatening. The supervisor/editor has to be two-faced – a mentor (representing the writer's creative interests) and an administrator (representing the university's interests). *However,* there are instances (I'm told) where the supervisor is less than hovering ever-near. I have (believe it or not) heard of cases where PhD students are left largely to their own devices in writing their academic novels. But a case similar to the supervisor being at hand from the beginning also occurs when a novel is commissioned by a publisher. In that case (admittedly not the norm) the publisher's editor looks over the writer's shoulder as mentor. Similarly in government-funded programs or private arrangements where emerging novelists are mentored by established writers, a master–apprentice situation pertains. The writing of the academic novel is not unlike some forms of mentored, almost normal novel-writing.

(7)   The supervisor as editor does not have her/his sights set on commercial and critical success, as publishers' editors do; the supervisor is oriented towards an audience of two or three (the examiners) and usually knows, or will know, who those will be. Usually the supervisor recommends the readership. *However*, while not just looking at current markets, possible trends, global marketability, film and translation rights, etc., the supervisor can view the longer term with a more literary or cultural sensibility. 'Literary' and 'cultural' are words now dropped from most publishers' lexicons. The serious literary novel may find its new home in academia. But does that mean it will get published?

(8)   The deadlines and pressures imposed upon the academic novel are significant. From the stresses of candidature student-novelists fall ill, contract high blood pressure, have nervous breakdowns, increase their intake of drugs and alcohol, and sometimes give up altogether. *However*, for normal novelists, it's exactly the same.

In spite of the *howevers* in the items above, the academic novel is indeed written in spaces very different from those that normally define the dynamics of the writing process.

The Academic Novel in the Three Domains of Writing Process

Normally, the domains of writing process are:

- *the first domain*: the intimate space in the novelist's head where the project is conceived, managed and monitored;
- *the second domain*: the private space of the desk where the physical aspects of the writing process are mainly undertaken; and
- *the third domain*: the public space that is the domain of the readership towards which the writing process is projected. (Krauth, 2006: 193)

Taking these in reverse order, it might be thought that the foremost of the domain differences for the academic novelist occurs in the public space – in the readership, and the vision of a readership, that the student holds in mind while writing. Personally (I did not write a creative PhD) I can't imagine writing a novel for a faceless academic assessment panel, even if when writing novels I have normally only the vague concept of a mass of faceless readers out there waiting. The difference is, I think, in the expectation of the reaction of the readership. The mass of faceless readers I envision are both keen and critical regarding the insights I can give them, but they also long to be entertained and delighted. I know there are bastards and ignoramuses among them, but there are also people who think as I do, who value others' considered perceptions, who want to see the world afresh, so I feel positively about my readership, while also feeling trepiditious. As a novelist writing for a general audience, I feel I can spread out, be broadly human in my perceptions and critique, appeal to the common denominator as much as to a variety of specialisms. The vision of the ogre-examiner/ pass-fail panel doesn't fit my novelist's all-embracing vision of readership at all. I tend to think that if three readers don't like my work, there are 50 others who will. For the academic novelist, those three unsatisfied readers might be the examiners.

Novelists (along with all arts practitioners) need ego. Probably, big ego. I write towards my mass of faceless readers with an egotistical confidence built on the fact that I haven't yet been rejected by my readership often enough for me to decide to give up, convinced I have nothing to say. I have built this viewpoint on the basis of my reception in the public domain. But academia is not the same sort of broad domain. It is a significantly closed space: its readership is restricted; in its intimate space students do not easily feel egotistical. Academia subjects individuals to learning, bows them to authority, assesses and ranks them and, in the case of the PhD, forces them to submit to a pass–fail (with perhaps messy, protracted negotiation) examination outcome. The equivalent in the real world would be that if the influential literary critic of just one influential newspaper gave me a bad review, my novel would be a failure. (And then, how successfully would I engage in messy negotiation in the 'Letters to the Editor' column?) Thankfully, however, outside academia there are other reviewers, there is word of mouth, there is multiplicity of readership, there is an expansiveness of possible responses.

As supervisor-novelist, I consider the readership of the academic novel is not general humanity, but a shrivelled slice of humanity. As supervisor-novelist, I tend to mentor towards the examiner-readership, the panel of critics who can kill this novel in the water (along with, and sometimes because of, its accompanying critical component). And even though I know that some novelists – i.e. those with rare publishers who still care about literary subcultures rather than global sales – can afford to write for select groups these days, I am convinced that the pressure on the academic novel to be 'publishable' is at odds with the fact that it gets 'published', initially, to just two or three examiner-readers.

In the intensely egotistical matter of novel writing, novelists care about the readership only as much as their egos allow them ... but academic examiners also have egos. Examiners apply their egotisms according to their understanding of their administrative and discipline obligations. In this dramatic context – ego of creative artist versus ego of academic examiner – the novel gets cauterised.

Regarding the second domain – the private space of the desk where the physical aspects of the writing process are mainly undertaken – in the case of the academic novel there occurs an appropriation. In comparison with the normal novelist's writing space – traditionally (and metaphorically) the garret, the view out the window to the panorama or roof-top next door, the cluttered desk-top, the occasional forays into the real world to hunt down details for the narrative (and the contemporary equivalent where all of this is done on the Internet on the desk itself) – there is for the academic novelist a different environment. The garret transforms to a campus workplace. The window view morphs to a prospect of the compelling postgraduate office reception counter (where the final submission is due). The escape into the World Wide Web transcribes into the official university web page, and the free-wheeling writerly research trips into the landscape and society become turgid official excursions on behalf of an institutional study plan. The novelist can't just go out and have a chat – s/he is too often circum-scribed by the university ethics committee's demands that interviews and surveys be officially approved beforehand. This is not the normal process-space for a novelist; what is lost in the appropriation is a sense of freedom of process. For novelists to critique the culture authentically, they must feel free to range where they will. The academic novel is not a product of free-ranging.

Finally, the domain most important to novel-writing is the intimate space in the novelist's head where the project is conceived, managed and monitored. In the head-space domain, the student does a double-take to handle the different requirements of the academic novel. Students have to pretend they are writing a novel while they are writing an academic novel. One of my students, Dr Inez Baranay, a highly-regarded Australian novelist who wrote her seventh book *Neem Dreams* for her PhD (Baranay, 2003a, 2003b, 2005) says: 'A novel that wants to be written will accept any means to bring that about'. But also she confirms: 'I was challenged to fit in – *just* – to the "academic" requirements in my writing while managing to write creatively and independently' (Baranay, 2006; italics in the original). Baranay says she wrote 'the most complex, difficult, ambitious novel I have ever written or ever hope to write' while being aware that the same process would involve, 'for inexperienced novelists ... the likelihood of a possibly unconscious lack of real artistic freedom ...' (Baranay, 2006). Summing up the academic novelist's situation she writes: 'I don't think a "real" writer ever asks what they "should" do' (Baranay, 2006). But the academic situa-tion for the novel is fraught with 'shoulds'.

Some New Forms ... and a Conclusion

I'm delighted by the fact that in supervising creative PhDs I have had the opportunity:

- to watch as a novel unfolded, revealing Anne Hathaway as the real writer of Shakespeare's canon while its chapters were alternately interleaved with an exegesis about male-dominated discourse in the academy (Loveless, 2005);
- to witness a heavily philosophical submission about the nature of the writing process – presented as a series of mirror-image chapters where creative product becomes indistinguishable from dissertation (academic novel *as* academic thesis) – overcoming a barrage of university opposition and winning through to graduation (Wise, 2001);
- to see a novel and exegesis about Los Angeles and its clone, the City of the Gold Coast (Australia), examined by Edward W. Soja and Michael Wilding and come up trumps (Breen, 2005);
- to examine Gareth Beal's wonderful PhD submission where he outlines completion of Chandler's unfinished novel *Poodle Springs* using Harold Bloom and Roland Barthes as guides for the writing process (Beal, 2004).

These creative PhD projects were audacious, revolutionary and convincing because they took on not just their specific projects, but also the project of freedom to create exceptionally in the academic context. I think there is a compelling sense in which the novelist must feel free – free to observe, to describe, to comment, to criticise and to build new structures. This freedom is at the heart of the role of the novelist/creative writer in the culture. Research that is sponsored by multinational corporations is never unbiased; research undertaken by government bodies is likewise never free of censorship. The lone novelist – 'freelance' in the truest sense of the word – is a mighty force only because of her/his unbounded power of individual critique. Novelists (as with other unfettered practitioners in the arts) are important to the culture precisely because (and only if) they are unregulated, unpredictable and unstoppable. Can academia handle this?

It is this aspect – the uncontrollability of the novelist – that I find most at risk in the academic context. There is no usefulness to society and the advance of human culture in a novelist who is restricted to prescribed ways of thinking and saying. Fully great novel projects – those that change the perceptions of societies – come out of left field, do not obey orders or procedures, defy authority, and ... best of all ... get published.

I hate to think of a future where novels are produced only by university courses and are subject to constricting enrolment, supervision and examination requirements. But I do contemplate a future where the novel finds a fertile field for experimentation and literary development on campuses worldwide. The Latin word 'campus' means 'field'. Originally the campus was an open space for animals to graze and for armies to fight. Nothing much has changed: knowledge is nurtured on campuses today and schools of thought fight it out there. On campus now the novel can be nurtured by grazing under the gaze of its protectors, or defeated by conflict with academic requirements. Unfortunately, the university campus is not currently *left* field.

The academy is not the real world. In taking in and accommodating the novel, the university needs to realise that it is minding, for a time, a wild animal, one that will always seek to be free.

References

Arnold, J. (2005) The PhD in creative writing accompanied by an exegesis. *Journal of University Teaching and Learning Practice* 2 (1). On WWW at http://jutlp.uow.edu.au/2005_v02_i01/arnold003.html. Accessed 20.3.06.

AWP (2006) *AWP Director's Handbook*, Association of Writers & Writing Programs. Fairfax, VA: George Mason University. On WWW at http://www.awpwriter.org/. Accessed 21.6.06.

Baranay, I. (2003a) Four Square Moon: An Exegesis / Neem Dreams: A Novel. PhD submission, Griffith University.

Baranay, I. (2003b) *Neem Dreams*. Delhi: Rupa & Co.

Baranay, I. (2005) Sun square moon: Writings on yoga and writing. Online at http://www.inezbaranay.com/books/sun_square_moon.htm. Accessed 21.6.06.

Baranay, I. (2006) Private email correspondence in reply to a survey. 28 March.

Beal, G. (2004) The creation myth: An approach to creative writing. P/S: Poststructuralism and Raymond Chandler's Poodle Springs. PhD submission, Macquarie University, Sydney.

Bolt, B. (2004) The exegesis and the shock of the new. *TEXT* Special Issue 3 (April). On WWW at http://www.gu.edu.au/school/art/text/speciss/issue3/bolt.htm. Accessed 20.3.06.

Bourke, N. and Neilson, P. (2004) The problem of the exegesis in Creative Writing higher degrees. *TEXT* Special Issue 3 (April). On WWW at http://www.gu.edu.au/school/art/text/speciss/issue3/bourke.htm. Accessed 20.3.06.

Brady, T. (2004) Exegesis: The debate in *TEXT*. *TEXT* Special Issue 3 (April). Online at www.griffith.edu.au/school/art/text/speciss/issue3/exegesis.htm. Accessed 20.3.06.

Breen, S. (2005) Future frontier/Ante up. PhD submission. Griffith University. .

Fletcher, J. and Mann, A. (2004) Illuminating the exegesis. *TEXT* Special Issue 3 (April). Online at www.griffith.edu.au/school/art/text/speciss/issue3/content. htm. Accessed 20.3.06.

Freiman, M. (2003) 'Dangerous dreaming: Myths of creativity'. *TEXT* 7, 2 (October). On WWW at http://www.gu.edu.au/school/art/text/oct98/freiman.htm. Accessed 14.3.06.

Harper, G. (2003) What is a postgraduate degree in Creative Writing? *Online Newsletter, The Higher Education Academy English Subject Centre* 5 (April). On WWW at http://www.english.ltsn.ac.uk/explore/publications/newsletters/newsissue5/harper.htm. Accessed 14.3.06.

Harper, G. (2005) The Creative Writing doctorate: Creative trial or academic error? *New Writing: The International Journal for the Practice and Theory of Creative Writing* 2 (2): 79–84.

Krauth, N. (2001) The Creative Writing doctorate in Australia: An initial survey. *TEXT* 5, 1 (April). On WWW at http://www.gu.edu.au/school/art/text/april01/krauth.htm. Accessed 14.3.06.

Krauth, N. (2002) The preface as exegesis. *TEXT* 6, 1 (April). On WWW at http://www.gu.edu.au/school/art/text/april02/krauth.htm. Accessed 14.3.06.

Krauth, N (2006) The domains of the writing process. In N. Krauth and T. Brady (eds) *Creative Writing: Theory Beyond Practice* (pp. 187–196). Brisbane: Post Pressed.

Kroll, Jeri (2004) The exegesis and the gentle reader/writer. *TEXT* Special Issue 3 (April). Online at www.griffith.edu.au/school/art/text/speciss/issue3/kroll.htm. Accessed 20.3.06.

Loveless, M. (2005) Mrs Shakespeare: Muse, mother, matriarch, madonna, whore, writer, woman, wife: Recovering a lost life. PhD submission. Griffith University..

Milech, B. and Schilo, A. (2004) Exit Jesus: Relating the exegesis and the creative/production components of a research thesis. *TEXT* Special Issue 3 (April). Online at www.griffith.edu.au/school/art/text/speciss/issue3/milechschilo.htm. Accessed 20.3.06.

Ritter, K. (2001) Professional writers / writing professionals: revamping teacher training in Creative Writing PhD Programs. *College English* 64 (2), 205–27.

University of Adelaide (2005) PhD in Creative Writing. School of Humanities. On WWW at http://www.arts.adelaide.edu.au/humanities/english/creative/phd.html. Accessed 20.3.06.

University of Houston (2006) PhD in Literature and Creative Writing. Creative Writing Program at the University of Houston. On WWW at http://www.class.uh.edu/cwp/cwp_coursework/phd.pdf. Accessed 14.5.06.

University of Lancaster (2006) MPhil/PhD Programme. Department of English and Creative Writing. On WWW at http://www.lancs.ac.uk/depts/english/crew/phd_crew.htm. Accessed 20.3.06.

University of Newcastle Upon Tyne (2005) Postgraduate Research Supervision in Creative Writing. School of English Literature, Language and Linguistics Postgraduate Study. Online at http://www.ncl.ac.uk/elll/postgrad/research_degrees/creatsup.htm. Accessed 20.3.06.

Wise, P. (2001) The turns of engagement: A thesis/novel on the circumstances of writing. PhD submission, Griffith University.

Let Stones Speak: New Media Remediation in the Poetry Writing Classroom

JAKE ADAM YORK

The documentary *Rivers and Tides* (Ridelsheimer, 2000) dedicates almost 13 minutes to British sculptor Andy Goldsworthy constructing a cone out of shale on a beach in Nova Scotia (from 19:00–31:00 minutes). As he begins, Goldsworthy announces he has seven hours to complete the form. He complains that he hasn't enough time, that time is coming up behind him. But as he complains he's working, chipping stones with other stones, stacking stone on stone. As we come to see, he's shaping something suggestive of a pine cone standing vertically on its blunt end.

After a few moments, the top layer of stone begins to shift. Goldsworthy explains, 'The stone is speaking.' He continues, 'I've never had one do this before, and I think it possibly is either the sand that's settling or the weakness of the stone or even a combination of the two' (20:57–21:31). The cone wants to fall apart, to come away from its center. Goldsworthy changes his plan: he will begin tapering the form, finishing it, in response to the tendencies of the sand and the stone. Quickly, however, the cairn splits away from its center.

He begins again. This time, the diameter is greater, but soon this cone, too, falls apart. He tells the camera: 'That's the fourth, the fourth collapse, and the tide is coming in.' He looks at his watch, then says 'I think it would be better to wait.' He continues, offering the terms of both his frustration and of the poetic that will enable him, perhaps require him, to try once more: 'The moment when something collapses, it is intensely disappointing, and this is the fourth time it's fallen, and each time I got to know the stone a little bit more, and it got higher each time, so it grew in proportion to my under-standing of the stone ... I obviously don't understand it well enough. Yet' (24:52–26:02).

I show this segment more and more often, because it expresses and visu-alizes two ideas I find increasingly difficult to communicate to my Creative

21

Writing students: first, dissolution, difficulty, and frustration are natural parts of the creative process; and, second, that dissolution, difficulty, and frustration arise as part of our struggle to understand and work the raw material of our writing, language. The first of these two ideas is difficult to communicate convincingly because the students' fear – of a loss of control or the possibility that they might not be talented – is stronger than any comfort I can offer by example. The second of these is difficult to communicate, not because the expressions are weak, but because the very premise – that words are materials with resistant properties apart from their meanings rather than transparent or merely instrumental operators – is strange, so strange the students seem as though their entire world must be changed before they can begin to appreciate this.

That the concept of linguistic materiality, or lexical materiality, is strange is an index of changes in our disciplines and in our curricula, particularly with respect to the relationship between literature and writing and even to the relationship between different kinds of writing. Though the current state of English in American higher education is a matter of debate (see Mayers, 2005), in my own experience and in the experience of colleagues at dozens of American universities I have observed over the past decade a gradual separation of composition from literary studies, not just as an academic or research discipline but as a teaching program as well. Literature, as such, is increasingly immaterial to composition training. While a short story or poem may appear as reading in a composition course, the purpose of composition – to sharpen students' argumentative skills – seems more and more to exclude analytic techniques specific to particular disciplines, English or otherwise. At the same time, second-year literature surveys, which were once imagined as opportunities to teach not just books but literature, to educate students in the literary and thereby in language, now use or approximate the Great Books model and teach books as ideas, as themes, as plots, and more rarely as material language.

These changes may indeed be appropriate in the service of a more broadly applicable core curriculum – or not; I don't mean to argue these points at all. However we feel about such trends, teachers of Creative Writing must recognize them, as these changes mean that each semester's students are less familiar with language, *per se*, and increasingly ill-equipped to enter a discussion of *poetics*, a consideration of the material and the arrangements of language that create, enforce, undermine, or interact with meaning. And insofar as our disciplines require of our students some knowledge of poetics, we must adjust our teaching practices accordingly.

This is especially true in the poetry-writing classroom. There is much to teach about creative process that can be taught without the benefit of poetics. But much of what distinguishes poems from stories, fables, short-shorts, and blog entries and much of what makes the process of writing poems potentially distinctive from the process of writing stories or essays is rooted in poetics, the direct confrontation with and embrace of language's material – that is, its sonic and its graphic, not just its semantic – dimension.

But in 14 weeks – or 10 – how can I teach both that relationship with language that is fundamentally important, a first principle, and lead the students through enough writing, feedback, and revision to satisfy their expectations of the course as a moment in which to write? How can I quickly prime my students to attend to language as material so they may also learn those techniques that are especially peculiar to poetic composition and thereby be prepared to continue improving, indefinitely, as writers, not just within the feedback-workshop?

In this chapter, I mean to propose one way of addressing the underlying problem, a lack of familiarity with the material dimensions of language. I mean to propose one new pathway into the compositional work that can make students better poets and thereby better writers, writers more attuned to all the properties of language. My proposal involves equipment that is easily found on almost any college campus in the United States. My proposal exploits one sense that seems extremely well developed in our young students, the visual sense, in the service of awakening and refining the other senses and returning them to the service of writing. It requires a minor investment of the instructor's time in preparation that can be amply rewarded by a refinement in students' attention to language that can make subsequent teaching much easier. The proposal is more suggestive than exhausting, as the pedagogy I imagine is emergent rather than fully extant: in the following pages, I describe a process I have developed over the last several years and have only recently begun to implement on a sizeable scale.

I mean to take my students, for approximately five hours (though we could take up to nine), into a computer lab designed for audio and video editing, teach them the rudiments of one of the editing programs, then give them a series of short assignments, each of which is followed by a return to our regular classroom for work that, though framed and informed by new media methods, is more traditionally focused on written language. The goal is to change students' relationships to language, to make language into a material to be used in writing, into a material on which they can found their writing to greater effect and which they can trust for greater ease.

*****

First, I want students to experience and consider word sounds more directly and more completely. I want them to have a phenomenological experience of words, so I have to remove them from their 'normal' ways of thinking about words. The students arrive, in a sense, tricked and trapped by the way words look. Words are graphically discrete, and they may appear to function discretely: each has its meaning and its shape, and the trick to making a sentence can seem, primarily, to be getting the meanings in the right order and making sure they have spaces between them. Students know to look for mis-spelled words and misplaced commas. But beyond that, the investigation is usually narrative or expressive: does this sentence, do these sentences, say what I want to say? Do they tell the story clearly? If students are to perform the broad consideration of a poem more effectively, they need to enter sentences more deeply, to consider them more minutely. They need to move beyond a reliance on the graphic discontinuities – the spaces between words that mask more serious disturbances that compromise a draft. They need to read into and across those spaces if they are to think more directly and particularly about the patterns of rhythm, of sound, of syntax and the like that connect discrete words into something larger that has a definite shape not limited to a semantic order, namely a poem.

I want to use new media software to encourage students to place their own senses, all of them, in the service of reading and in the service of writing. I want to use this software to place their bodies back into writing. As Stewart Garrett writes in his *Reading Voices*, the body must be resituated at the center of reading experience anyway:

> That this locus of reading should be insisted upon, to any theoretical profit, as the place of the body is, however, a relatively late development ... The very fact that these somatic implications of reading should have come so slowly to the surface in the course of research devoted to the play between phonic and graphic articulations should serve to demonstrate, for a start, how far the body, the reader's sensorium, has traditionally been kept from the field of literary concern. (Garrett, 1990: 2)

I want to reinscribe the body into the process. But first I must bring the students' senses into play through the widest entry, their eyes.

The graphic environment of a non-linear editor – such as *ProTools, FinalCut, Avid, Adobe Premiere, Adobe Audition,* or Bias's *Peak* and *Deck* – allows us to show the students, to make them *see*, quite literally, the ways in which words are, and can be, connected to one another. In the audio editor (Bias *Peak, ProTools,* or *Adobe Audition,* though you can also use the audio functions without the video in *Premiere* or *FinalCut*) sonic information is translated into graphic information. We can see sounds represented as waves. These waveforms can surprise us, as they show that the sounds of words may begin before we expected they would and continue on long after we'd expected them to end. They show us that speech is not, like printing, a series of discrete packets: it is instead a continuous stream of sound with peaks and valleys and silences of various degrees.

This, of course, is no new revelation, except to my students – most of them anyway – who just haven't thought much about it. To make them think about it, I take them to the media lab, where I ask each student to begin by recording his or her own voice reading a paragraph. I then ask the student to look at the waveform of the recording. The student can see, with the editor's timeline set to a scale that will show the entire passage, that there are peaks and valleys, graphically heavier and lighter areas that seem roughly to correspond with words or syllable stresses (Figure 3.1).

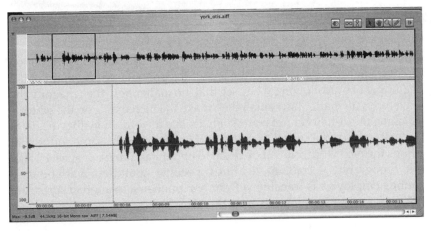

Figure 3.1

But once the student zooms in on the timeline to observe a passage more closely, at greater magnification (Figure 3.2), he or she will see that the valleys, which one might have assumed to be dead spaces between words, are not flatlines, even though they may appear to be.

Instead, the sonic information continues and the recording is never completely silent: words bleed or fade into one another, and the more closely you look or listen, the more sound you can hear, or see (Figure 3.3).

Because of this, it is difficult or impossible to separate completely the sounds of one word from another if the words are uttered in a sentence. So that the students will see this, I ask them to take the recording and begin to segment it into single words. I tell them to take care to play each segment

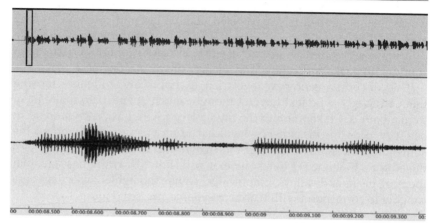

Figure 3.2

after they've made a cut to see if they've got the entire word, and they often discover they also have part of the end of the previous word or part of the beginning of the following. They see that, no matter how they magnify the waveform, no matter how small they make the increments on the editor's timeline, they often cannot completely isolate a word. Now they begin to understand that the sound that may end one word is the same sound that begins the next word. Now they begin to understand that our speech – like our typography – contains ligatures, peculiar sounds or variations of sounds employed as transitions from one phoneme to another: these are the gray zones that can never fully be demarked.[1]

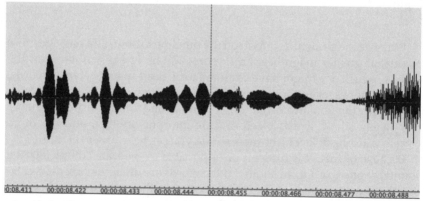

Figure 3.3

This demonstration has laid the groundwork for the realization that the management of a poem's sound texture is a matter of attention beyond an ear to assonantal or consonantal pattern or metrical pulse or rhythm: we must consider how the sounds of words – all the sounds – interface with one another. But two further exercises must be undertaken if the student is to understand the implications of these observations for the production or refinement of new texts.

Once the students have played at separating words and have confronted the difficulty of making isolating cuts, I tell them they are now to make a new phonotext of clipped words, a text in which the only real concern should be how the sounds will join one another. They may quickly become frustrated, as the rough cuts they've made create a series of hiccups, rough passage between their words, so that the easy joining of word to word cannot be accomplished. Though some students are interested in the rough rhythm, most want the smoother joinery of fluent English.

There are several workarounds for the hiccup. The first is to cut the wave a bit before and bit after the passage they want to use and then to use volume, which also may be controlled by means of a line drawn over the waveform, to fade into and out of the word, effectively masking below the threshold of hearing the bits that belong to words fore and aft and avoiding the hiccup. As they build a more seamless phonotext, they learn how words are married, sound to sound, or divorced. They begin to learn what combinations of sound produce smooth transition and which produce rough movement. The second workaround is for the student, having gotten close, to re-record the words in a new order. Once this is done, the student can compare the original sound-collage with the new recording and hear the way sentence-rhythm, the auditory signal of grammared writing, can be imposed on any language, regardless of sense. But even this may be imperfect, and the only solution will be to record even more material in a search for the perfect ligature between two passages, a ligature that can be imagined by isolating the sounds that need partners and considering all the words that would begin and end with those sounds.

As I've noted, the goal of this work is not, ultimately, a smooth phonotext, so we return to our traditional classroom to write words on paper.

*****

Back at our desks, I show the students how to perform these new exercises without the computer equipment and using only printed texts. I can offer them a variation of Tristan Tzara's (1981) cut-up poetic, handing each a spread of newspaper and inviting them to cut out words they like for any reason. Once they've cut a deskfull, I can invite them to arrange the words, not randomly as Tzara recommended, but according to the way the sounds of the words interface with one another, the goal being a smooth, fluent-sounding text. They may want to cut additional words from their news-paper, but I encourage them to keep working with what they have, to keep working the sounds they have until their words marry one another with ease, and to return to the newspaper only as a last resort. The goal of this exercise is to encourage the internalization of the new sound work, to ask the students to learn to attend to the sounds without the machine and without the playback, to be able to think through the sounds.

Again, this is preparatory. The test of this skill comes in a return to a poem they've written but have not yet finished. Their next assignment is to find a draft of a poem that they intend to improve and then to isolate either a moment when the poem shifts from good material they want to keep to material they want to eradicate or a moment they want to preserve though it's imperfect. The students are to take these moments, then, and subject them to the tests of their ears, listening to the passages, word by word, to see if the sounds of each word lead on to the sounds of the next. If there is some discontinuity, I tell the students, they should trust their ears to supply the next sound and the next and so forth until they can easily reconnect with the next word of the original text. They are to type their new drafts and bring them to the workshop, where we look at the original version and the version that has been edited by listening through the gap.

Of course, when we read these new versions, there is often an obvious difference between the passages that were written with some narrative intent and the new aleatoric passages, a difference that must be smoothed or accommodated. What's important here, however, is not a perfect fix in the short term, but a new opening into the poem that often provides, through its new sounds, a hint towards solving the difficulty with the poem or a new direction that will radically reform the poem into something more satisfying to the student writer.

*****

I can show the benefits of this approach in my own writing, by looking at any number of poems. I like, however, to turn to a poem I worked over for more than four years, a poem only recently published, entitled 'Aubade' (York, 2006). I have over 200 pages of drafts and worksheets for this poem, a folder I use to show my students my own version of Goldsworthy's return to the shale cone on the Nova Scotia beach. But for this exercise what's most salient is a look at four beginnings that mark important shifts in my work on the poem. The first draft is from March 1997. It begins:

For the boy
The night is full of winds and heard-
things that maze and build
in the river warrens ...

I ask my students, with their newly-tuned ears, to read through this passage and settle on the moment when the sound-texture seems most clearly disrupted. Invariably, they stop at the turn between the end of the second and the beginning of the third line. If we were to use phonological charts, we might say that the shift from the hard stop of the 'd' at the end of 'heard' to the fricative 'th' at the beginning of 'things' requires a serious readjustment of the mouth's musculature. This results in the most serious pause and also a comparatively awkward moment in the experience of the poem, since most of the other word-transitions are relatively simple and smooth. But all that the students need to note here is that this is the difficult moment in the poem.

I then show the students the next significant draft, completed more than 18 months later, in November 1998. It begins thus:

Tucked, he hears night wind
under doors, curl the sheets
like the river's whisper as warren bums
sound the dark.

I ask them first what's been cut, most conspicuously, and indeed it is the troublesome phrase, 'heard-things.' Now that catch-all noun has been translated into both a verb and a number of particular sounds. The students recognize this particulation as a good example of turning to show rather than tell. Their recognition of this turn allows me to suggest that a recognition of the sonic disruption of the text might have signaled a deeper, more serious discontinuity: in this case, the hardest sound-transition witnesses the moment in the poem when evidence is suppressed.

So, listening has helped me move from one iteration of the poem's beginning to another. But is the new version free of trouble? This time, the students actually find more troubled moments in the draft than before, most of these at the turn from line to line, but some within lines as well. Many feel that the staccato, spondaic 'he hears night wind' is a bit too clustered, that the turn from aspirated 'h' to vowel and back to the aspirated 'h' is tough repetition and that the movement from the hard stop of the 't' to the liquid 'w' is again a difficult shift in so short a space.' Others don't like the way the sibilant closing 'sheets' has to be stopped hard in order to make the liquid 'l' at the opening of the third line.

We turn then to the third draft, executed in late 2000. It begins like this:

Night kissed, tucked in,
he drifts in the cricket's *listen*,
the county's noise,
every sound that clears ...

Is this better, I ask them? Usually, they hear that the first two lines, especially, have improved immensely. Here, the sounds at the ends of words allow for easier entries into the sounds of those that follow, and syntactic pauses have been used to create transition moments between sounds that might have butted more roughly – the hard stop at the end of 'kissed' and again at the beginning of 'tucked' for example.

Here, though, the students are also starting to notice how different the sentence is, not just in terms of its sonic texture but, perhaps more intriguingly, in terms of its semantic or narrative import. Now, 'night' is not a condition of 'things' nor the site or time of the 'wind": it is now a condition of the 'he,' and it helps, being subordinated to the kiss, to age this pronoun-character. Furthermore, he isn't finding night full or even hearing any longer. Instead, he 'drifts' in the sound, the 'crickets' *listen*,' the new verb clarifying his posture a bit but, more importantly, signaling in the interface of verb-sound and object-sound the true nature of this drift as a tending of one thing toward another through sound.

As I've noted above, the initial intention was to get students to recognize that a rough moment in a poem's sound contour may signal a deeper problem – a narrative or semantic problem that may be difficult to meet head on. I note that I wrote this draft shortly after I began editing sound to create aleatoric collages and as well to produce audio-texts of my own poems.

But also I wanted students to see that trusting the sound above all else can create new opportunities to solve not only the difficulties of the poem's sound but also to solve the narrative difficulties. So, we turn to the final draft, in which this very attention to sound helped me solve all kinds of narrative problems. In each of these drafts, I had worked to situate the boy, but I also wanted to get the poem out of the bed and out of the room. In earlier drafts, the opening imagination was chased with long catalogues. In the final draft, I was able to trust the sounds to get me out of the room. So it begins like this:

Night kissed, tucked in,
he drifts in the crickets' *listen*,

but the meteors burn
too fast to hear. Curtains

ghost, then fall to breath.
The river quoting wind.

In the first two lines, the short 'i' sound is worked quite extensively, almost to the point of abuse, so the poem, in moving out of this room, also has to move out of this sound space. The window is provided by the main character, who is to perform the action. The long 'e' in 'he' suggests the long 'e' in 'meteor,' while 'burn' can counterpoint 'tucked' as it distorts the same vowel toward a different consonant and lightly consonates with 'in' and 'listen' above by reprising the nasal 'n.' 'Burn' clearly suggests 'Curtains,' 'fast' suggests 'ghost,' and the entire first stanza requires 'river' and 'wind' with their short 'i' sounds to round the opening movement. By working through the sounds, I have managed to shape the first six lines in ways that maintain the original ideas – the boy listening, the presence of the river, an outward trajectory.

*****

The effects of such listening may not be as wide-ranging in every case, but every student sees that listening through a poem suggests avenues that might not open if all we're asking is *How else can I say the same thing?* The sound, the very material of the language, must be allowed to form the work and to change what's said, at least provisionally, so at last we arrive at a text where the material dimension and the semantic dimension interact and inform one another in some way. That, I claim, is what makes a durable text, in poetry anyway.

This sequence, even if it merely opens another approach to revision or reconsideration (re-audition? call back?) of a poem, is worthwhile. But something more can be made of this. Certainly, in my own development, something else began to change in my approach to composition at the same time I began relying on the sonic character of the words to guide my work. I started to think of the composition of the poem as a much less linear process, much less simply expressive. Instead, I began to imagine the poem coalescing out of separate phrases, each of which had its own internal coherence, that needed to be connected: my writing became a two-stage process of first generating strong and accurate phrases and then of finding ways to make those phrases work together, which meant being willing to re-order the entire poem to let the material qualities of the language support anything else, any argument or narrative.

My students may begin to see something of this as they observe the shifting order of elements in the opening lines of 'Aubade,' but I need again to return to the media lab to make this point clearest.

This time, I will give them a longer recording, perhaps of me reading a story from the Sunday Business section of *The New York Times,* something that will run for about five minutes or so. This time I will ask them not to cut away single words but phrases instead. This segmenting work is much easier than cutting words away from one another, because the pauses between phrases in a sentence are much more pronounced: often there is some true or near-true silence in the recording and the phrases can be easily separated from the surrounding recording (Figure 3.4).

Once the phrases are separated, we want to place them in tracks and begin editing them in a multitrack interface. This means we will line them up to succeed one another and draw in the volume curves so the transitions will be as smooth as possible, so phrases will arise out of dead silence rather than recorded silence, which is never really quiet (Figure 3.5).

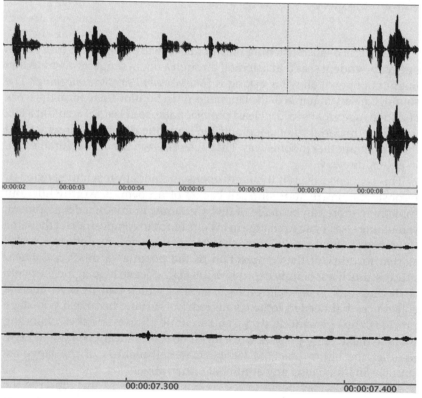

Figure 3.4

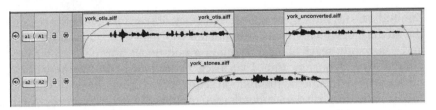

Figure 3.5

This work is no different from the assembly of words into phonotext that was one of the first assignments I gave the students to complete in the media lab. The software tools are the same, and the experience of the wave-forms is similar. The students are even using volume, as they did before. The material is, however, slightly different, as is the framework in which they're allowed to consider it. Now, instead of working solely with words, they're working with phrases, so the semantic dimension of each word cannot be entirely ignored: the words exist in the context of phrases. I no longer ask them to make the sonic interface of the words or phrases their primary concern. I now allow them to consider both the way joining might sound and what joining might mean. Now they are building a poem by attending both to sound and to meaning, searching for the proper join between the elements they've chosen to preserve and centralize. To complete their work, they may have to record a few new phrases or liga-tures here and there, but for the most part, a poem can be made.

The goal of this exercise is not to champion collage as a genre or even to suggest that the found poem, whether graphic or auditory, should hold some special place, though I am not at all disappointed to see students playing with found poems afterward. The goal of this exercise is to give the students a visual model for phrase-based writing that eases our discussion of revision. They can now imagine revision as a process that begins by cutting away material and continues by re-arranging what's left and then developing new connections between the salvage. Their own poems become the raw material from which new poems may arise.

*****

I have found this interface, bringing the student before the machine, much less difficult than the other ways of solving the same pedagogical problems. Each term, I have at least one student, for example, whose Romantic idea of the poem as an expression of his or her *self*, means that it has to come out of him or her as a spontaneous utterance, in a linear form that can't be reconsidered or redressed. I can argue against the wisdom of the student's mythology or against its history, or I can take the entire class to the media lab, which seems like a sanctioned truancy, for a new adventure and essentially teach the same thing: a non-linear approach to writing poems.[2] And at the same time, I can teach the students skills they may use in other classes – the media production sequences in our College of Arts and Media or our English department's own multimedia writing courses – or in their personal lives, as more and more of them edit home videos and make their own music on their home computers.

I might, I am sure, have taught the same techniques through paper collage or even sculpting. I might have taken them to the beach and asked them to wrestle, like Andy Goldsworthy, until the stones begin to speak and teach them how to arrange them, how to dispose them, how to shape them. I do show them once again the segment from *Rivers and Tides* (Ridelsheimer, 2000) and then I read them some version of the Orpheus legend. I like Mark Strand's short treatment, 'Orpheus Alone,' in which the ancient poet wanders:

> the hills
> Outside of town, where he stayed until he had shaken
> The image of love and put in its place the world
> As he wished it would be, urging its shape and measure
> Into speech of such newness that the world was swayed,
> And trees suddenly appeared in the bare place
> Where he spoke and lifted their limbs and swept
> The tender grass with the gowns of their shade,
> And stones, weightless for once, came and set themselves there,
> And small animals lay in the miraculous fields of grain
> And aisles of corn, and slept. The voice of light
> Had come forth from the body of fire, and each thing
> Rose from its depths and shone as it never had. (Strand, 1990)

If we want such power, I say, it is natural. It is the original fantasy of poetic effect. If we are able to speak the stones into place, we will be over-joyed. Until then, though, we must lift each stone, know its weight and balance, its shape. Only then can we stack stone on stone to make a home or even a simple poem.

Notes

1. Again, the observation isn't new. Linguists have been using sound-graphing equipment for decades in attempts to understand the nature of a syllable or of a certain vocal sound, and such investigations have had direct if limited effects on prosody. Now, however, many – and maybe most – schools have the technology

and the equipment to enable students to make these observations on their own. The software and the equipment are so cheap, most students could configure their own home computers for less than $50.

2. Psychologists at University College London have just published a study suggesting that novelty eases the learning process. According to a report on *Science Daily*: 'A region in the midbrain ... which is responsible for regulating our motivation and reward-processing responds better to novelty than to the familiar. This system also regulates levels of dopamine, a neurotransmitter in the brain and could aid in learning' (*Science Daily*, 2006: 3).

References

Mayers, T. (2005) *(Re)Writing Craft: Composition, Creative Writing, and the Future of English Studies*. Pittsburgh: University of Pittsburgh Press.

Science Daily (2006) Novelty aids learning. 4 August. On WWW at http://www.sciencedaily.com/releases/2006/08/060804084518.htm. Accessed 27.6.07.

Ridelsheimer, T. (2000) *Rivers and Tides: Andy Goldsworthy Working With Time*. Mediopolis Films.

Stewart, G. (1990) *Reading Voices: Literature and the Phonotext*. Berkeley: University of California Press.

Strand, M. (1990) Orpheus alone. In J. Graham (ed.) *Best American Poetry 1990*. New York: Scribner's.

Tzara, T. (1981) *Seven Dada Manifestoes and Lampisteries*. Calder Publications.

York, J.A. (2006) Aubade. *H_NGM_N*, #5. August. On WWW at http://www.h-ngm-n.com/h_ngm_n-5/Jake-Adam-York.html. Accessed 27.6.07.

Chapter 4

That Was the Answer: Now What Was the Question? The PhD in Creative and Critical Writing: A Case Study

NESSA O'MAHONY

In this chapter, I seek to set out the experience of undertaking a doctorate in Creative and Critical Writing and to explore the range of issues that can arise over the course of three years of full-time study for the degree. It is important to point out that, at time of writing, I have not quite completed the PhD so can only describe what is still a work in progress. As a result, many of the questions posed, both about the PhD project itself and indeed the entire process of undertaking the project, have not yet found definitive answers. But by focusing on the process, rather than the product, I hope to provide some insight into the various pressures and challenges that a typical Creative Writing doctoral candidate might be expected to face, and to give an impression of the typical relationship that exists between that candidate and the university in which he or she is studying.

Preparing the Ground? The MA in Creative Writing

I decided to undertake the PhD in Creative and Critical Writing on completion of a Masters in Creative Writing in 2003. I was one of the few students in my year group to make the decision to go further with my study. In fact, in my experience, the majority of MA students in Creative Writing do not go on to do doctorates. There are a number of reasons for this. Many writers choose to do the MA because they want to take time out of their professional lives to work on a creative project and believe that a university course will provide them with a good structure in which to work. They are not necessarily looking for a career in academia, although some hope that the Masters qualification will help them obtain teaching jobs elsewhere, for example writers' residencies or schools-based schemes. There are also clear financial reasons why few writers go on to undertake doctorates in the UK; a full-time PhD costs over £9000 in fees alone, not to mention subsistence, a cost prohibitive to most full-time writers. Academic funding doesn't always offer a solution. Few UK universities are in the financial position to offer bursaries to Creative Writing doctoral candidates. And, to date, Creative Writing doctoral candidates have been less than successful in their attempts to attract Research Council funding. Why this should be the case is an interesting question. It has been argued that creative writers have made less persuasive cases for research funding because they have been less skilful at framing the research questions than, for example, candidates from the field of English literature. If this is the case, it begs the question about the comparative grounding that creative writers and literature postgraduate students receive in learning how to frame research questions in the first place. To explore this point further, I would like to spend a little time contrasting the experiences of doing a Masters and a PhD in Creative Writing.

I completed my Masters in Creative Writing at the University of East Anglia (UEA) in 2003. When I attended UEA, the MA in Creative Writing was run along the workshop model. Poetry students attended one weekly two-hour poetry workshop, submitting work and learning how to give constructive and meaningful feedback to others. There was little if no theoretical context to the workshops; each student was expected to know something about poetics and/or critical theory before coming on the course. In hindsight, I would argue that it is wrong for universities to assume that all students have this level of knowledge. Only three of the eight in my year group had actually studied theory and poetics as part of an undergraduate degree in English and Creative Writing in the recent past. The rest of us were mature students, not all from English literature backgrounds, coming back to study after many years and whose memory of theory, critical or otherwise, was buried in the distant past. We had somehow expected that studying poetry at postgraduate level would reacquaint us with that theory, and teach us about new ones, as well as provide us with a more profound understanding of the craft through a thorough grounding in poetics. We were to be disappointed.

In the UEA workshops, we learned about each other's writing and learned more about our own writing within the context of a mutually supportive environment. To some extent, these workshops were little different from the writers' groups that many of us had attended in our previous careers as writers. Perhaps we all now took the task of workshopping a little more seriously, because there was a postgraduate degree at stake. But in other ways, the type of feedback we exchanged and the sorts of support we gave each other was modelled on previous, non-academic, experiences. Admittedly we now had regular access to an established writer who led our workshops and commented on our work. We were able to form a relationship with this mentor who was in a position to watch our work develop over the course of the year and who could give us the benefit of his own experience while helping us to find our own way as writers. But the only time that we were encouraged to place our work in a wider context was during the preparation of our dissertation, which was to be a themed collection of 24 poems accompanied by a short introductory essay. There was no requirement to include an overtly critical framework in this introduction; rather it was intended to provide a synopsis and to explain our aesthetic intentions.

It is fair to say that, over the course of the Masters, there was little attempt to get students to consider their work in the context of contemporary writing or to consider a theoretical basis for their work. In the end, the Masters was about practice, not theory. There was little by way of preparation for the more theoretical approach that would be required of students who wanted to take the next step up the academic ladder and undertake a doctorate. Small surprise, therefore, that few aspiring doctoral candidates were in a position to frame a research question sufficiently convincing to attract Research Council funding. Their postgraduate experience to date had not taught them the necessary skills to frame such a question, nor to see their work in such a theoretical light.

Beginning the PhD Process

In my case, I began to investigate the possibilities of undertaking a PhD in Creative Writing without any real sense that a doctorate would require me to think about my writing in a much more theoretical way. In fact, my motivation was entirely practice-led; I felt that I had gained considerable benefit from spending the MA year concentrating on my writing and wanted to investigate the possibility of taking further time out in order to complete a longer body of work than the MA had allowed. At that point, I had no specific research question in mind; rather I was motivated by a desire to continue working within an academic environment and to further enhance my craft through contact with other writers. I also wanted to gain experience of teaching at university level and hoped that the qualification would ultimately lead to a job somewhere within the academic sector. My perhaps cursory reading of the sometimes scanty course literature about doctorates published on various university websites did little to disabuse me of the misapprehension that a desire to write a longer work over a longer time frame, within an academic community of writers, was sufficient motivation for undertaking a PhD in Creative Writing.

Although I did not yet know my research question, I did have a concept of what my creative project might be. In 2002, I had edited a book of contemporary accounts of women's lives in 19th century Ireland (Ó Cléirigh, 2003). During that process, it had struck me that many of the voices contained in these accounts, particularly those describing the experience of emigration, were interesting and dynamic in their own rights; I became intrigued at the notion of attempting to bring them back to life through some form of creative recreation. I began to wonder if a collection of poems based on documentary evidence such as letters and journals might form the basis for a PhD in Creative Writing. In my doctorate applications, I thus included the broad outline of an idea that focused on the type of work I would be interested in producing. I had completed a short verse narrative during the Masters at UEA, and this experience had convinced me that I would like to experiment in producing a verse novel. In my application, I stressed that this would be a piece of action research; I wished to use the actual writing of the verse novel to explore the form. I had only a vague idea of the content or subject matter at this point; I trusted that the universities I applied to would give me the time and space to research my idea and bring it to fruition. The choice of universities where one could do a PhD in Creative Writing was more limited than it had been for the Masters programme. At the time of my application, only 20 universities in the UK (and none in the Republic of Ireland) ran Creative Writing doctoral programmes (compared with 70 offering MA programmes). My choice was further narrowed by my understandable desire to find a poet as supervisor whose work I responded to and whom I felt might share some understanding of the aesthetic perspective from which I was coming. In the end, I applied to only two universities, and was accepted by one, the University of Wales, Bangor.

Once accepted, I got to work on defining the nature of my research and to find a subject matter on which to write the verse novel. The shape of my first year's work was guided by the structures put in place by the parent department. When I started at my university, the Creative Writing department was a subdivision of a larger English Department[1] and Creative Writing students were expected to join with other first year postgraduate students in departmental research seminars specially designed for postgraduates. These seminars included introductions to literary theory as well as a history of publishing and printing. Although the seminars provided a useful overview, they had not been specifically tailored to the needs of Creative Writing students, and on more than one occasion I felt that we lacked a specific dimension that would make discussion of critical theory relevant to the practice of creative writing. And, given that the academics running the seminars tended to be from a literature rather than a Creative

Writing background, it seemed difficult to bridge that gap between their theory and my practice. I am aware that few universities have the resources to create entirely self-standing Creative Writing departments, and that there will probably always be some degree of tension between the academic and creative wings of those departments that attempt to splice English and Creative Writing. And yet, depending on the balance of power between those two wings, there is a danger that the tension created will not always be entirely healthy for the students, who may feel they have to develop dual personalities in order to satisfy the conflicting demands of creativity and criticism.

During those first few months at the university I also looked around, with little success, to my surprise, for the community of writers I was expecting to find, based on my previous experience. Inevitably, given that UWB had a much smaller Creative Writing programme than UEA, there were far fewer writers on the ground at that time. But though there were a few doctoral students, I gradually discovered that the nature of doctoral study meant a great deal of seclusion and very little peer-group workshopping. Writers worked on their own, formed relationships with their supervisors, but rarely came together to share work. I had begun to teach Creative Writing at undergraduate level, so had some access to the workshopping process, though obviously not for my own work. I did find, however, that workshopping creative work with undergraduate students had some benefits for my own process; helping other students grapple with issues of plot and characterisation was very helpful when it came to ironing out problems in my own manuscript.

So during this period, I had occasional meetings with my supervisor, but the main focus of my work was to read as widely as possible the relevant literature (in other words, to undertake the classic doctoral literature review) and to plan the shape and structure of my creative project. In my case, the literature review was two-part. I needed to read as many verse novels as possible in order to get a sense of practice in the area, both contemporary and historic. But, because I had chosen a theme that included a historical strand, I also needed to research texts in Irish history to identify a period or a source material that would provide me with a framework for the narrative. Thus the first year of the doctorate involved a lot of reading, a good deal of note-taking, but little or no creative work. This became a source of increasing frustration as it seemed to completely contradict my preconception that doing a doctorate in Creative Writing would actually involve writing creatively. But I could not get the creative project under way until I had found my source material and further defined my research question.

Researching the Source Material

Having earlier decided that I wanted to use some aspect of the 19th century Irish emigration experience as the subject for my narrative, the first task in finding a suitable source for the story was to consult a range of material drawn from Irish archives housed by the National Library, Trinity College Dublin and the National Archives. I was looking for documents with the scope necessary to generate a long narrative, and trawled through diaries, manuscripts, official reports and contemporary correspondence. My search ended when I discovered the Butler archive, housed in the National Library in Dublin.

The Butler archive[2] is a collection of 22 letters and assorted fragments of notes and letters that were written principally by Margaret Butler, an Irish Catholic from Kilkenny who emigrated with her family to Australia in 1854, to her relatives who remained in Ireland. The letters date between 1841 and 1917, but the vast majority refer to the period post-emigration when the family was settling into Australian life. The archive was deposited by Irish relatives of the Butler family with the National Library of Ireland in the late 1990s and has thus far been unsorted and unpublished, although the letters have been transcribed.

Reading through the transcriptions, it struck me that the letters were bursting with narrative energy. They painted a clear and vibrant picture of a middle class, prosperous family leaving Ireland because they wished to make a new life in a new country, not because they were forced out of their old one, and who made a highly successful transition in Australia. They were thus very far from the stereotypical image of transported convicts or evicted tenants that we have come to associate with stories of Irish emigration to the Southern Hemisphere. It seems to me that the Butler archive, which demonstrated very different experiences and preoccupations from those of evicted tenants or failed rebels, offered the potential for inspiring a creative work that would offer an original take on the emigrant experience.

So, I had found the source material on which to base my verse novel. But my initial reading of the letters raised interesting questions about the creative decisions and directions to be taken with the project and, in beginning my Creative Writing project proper, I had to find answers to those questions. The most obvious issue was the existence of large hiatuses in the narrative flow of the letters. In many cases there were gaps of seven and ten years in the correspondence; one could assume that other letters were sent and received in the interim, but these had not survived. So, in order to achieve a coherent narrative, it would be necessary to fictionalise quite substantial parts of the Butler story. I would have to use historical research to fill in the blanks.

Alongside my historical reading, I was also researching the literary genre I had chosen for my creative work. Reading the work of others who had faced creative issues similar to my own would help me make decisions about the shape and form of my own work. I discovered that other verse novelists had adopted myriad formal approaches to their work. By reading as widely as I could, I hoped to find a model that I could adapt for my own creative purposes.

Shaping the First Draft

As I began work on the first draft, a number of issues quickly came to the fore. It was clear that the issue of voice was crucial to the success of the project. In order to engage readers with the narrative, I needed to have believable and sympathetic narrator or narrators. I had to decide whether to centre the story through the eyes of an individual narrator, and the main correspondent, Margaret Butler, seemed to offer the most obvious model for this. But the other choice was to allow other narrators to take their share of the story. I experimented with various narrative techniques to discover which worked best in the particular context.

Another early consideration was whether to weave a modern narrative or commentary through the historical narrative. In the early stages of planning this project, I envisaged a two-strand approach in which my own experiences, or rather those of the poet narrator, were counter-pointed with the historical action. Over time I broadened this approach, settling on a four-strand approach to narrative that included a modern narrator, a historic narrator, and imagined historic voices that were intended to act as a commentary on the two main narrative threads.

The ultimate question that I hoped the writing of the verse novel would answer would be the added value of taking such an approach in the first place. In the belief that every work of art finds its appropriate medium and it is a measure of its success if the reader or viewer, upon experiencing it, cannot imagine any other medium in which it might appear, I wanted to explore whether the use of the verse novel form, itself a hybrid of other forms, could be justified as the only appropriate form for the subject under consideration. This research question would prove to be a difficult one to answer, but was the one that I sensed would be fundamental to the entire process.

Completing the First Draft

I spent the second year of the doctorate drafting and redrafting the verse novel, in the expectation that, once the creative work was completed, I would be in a better position to write the critical response (a 20,000 word essay placing my work in a critical and theoretical context), which was also a requirement of the PhD in Creative and Critical Writing. This was, of course, my own personal view of the process. I had come to realise that each student was taking his/her own very individual approach to getting the balance between creative and critical work. Some were working concurrently on the creative project and the critical work. Others appeared to be reading theory and then beginning a creative work that would explore ideas that had been raised by that reading. But to my mind, the only approach that would work for me was to write the creative project first and, once a complete draft was been finalised, return to and re-read other examples of the genre in the belief that I would have a greater understanding of both my own and other writers' processes as a result. Over the course of the year, I had a number of meetings with my supervisor, in preparation for which I submitted excerpts from the verse novel and after which I responded by further refining the draft. Once I had completed a full first draft, I found that I had made a series of strategic and creative choices that had led me to diverge considerably from my original idea of what the narrative might contain. It might be useful at this stage to consider that process in greater depth.

Identifying the Characters

Having identified the Butler letters as ones that contained a strong, coherent voice and narrative, I had begun to work on a novel outline that would allow me to explore through a creative treatment of those letters the themes of emigration, home and identity. But although the 22 extant letters were a rich source, there were so many gaps in the narrative that it appeared to require significant degrees of fictionalisation in order to create a coherent story. This became clear when I began to work on the outline and realised that, in order to create a satisfying fiction, I would need to choose a main theme and then create a narrative to explore that theme. It soon became evident that I would have to consider writing additional letters to fill in the gaps left by the existing archive. It seemed to me that I had two main choices. I could either leave the letters as they were, gaps and all, and create an interweaving narrative based around one of the characters mentioned in the letters, or else I could add additional letters to follow up on the leads generated by the original letters in order to propel the story I wanted to tell or, in fact, to create an entirely new story. Further historical research was required to supplement the information contained in the Butler letters to help fill in such gaps but luckily there was no shortage of historical accounts of emigration and journeys to Australia to which I could refer.

At this point, issues arose about what form the poems would take, particularly as I had opted for a parallel and interweaving modern narrative, featuring a 21st century narrator who would discover the letters and respond to them in ways that would clarify the doubts and issues she was having in her own life. I felt this modern strand was needed on two grounds. Firstly, and pragmatically, I was a writer settling into a new land-scape and environment and wanted to respond to that new environment creatively. Therefore, such an approach would allow me to incorporate those responses into the overall narrative in a reasonably harmonious way. Secondly, I believed that the interweaving of a modern and historic narrative would help to illuminate the themes I wanted to deal with. I believed that there was much to be explored in contrasting the modern and historic experiences through the medium of the verse novel. But it soon became evident that, in order to achieve this contrast between past and present, there needed to be a clear contrast in form between the modern and historic narratives. Having decided that the modern narrator was to be a brusque, slightly jaded character who saw herself, somewhat delusionally, as a hard-nosed survivor, it seemed appropriate to come up with a rather tight stanza form that would remain consistent throughout the narrative. In this I was influenced by my earlier reading of verse novels by Australian poet Dorothy Porter (1997), whose structure of terse couplets for her narrative, *The Monkey's Mask*, seemed to provide a suitable model.

However, for reasons of clarity, the historical narrative strand needed to contrast with the modern style, both in tone and appearance. I spent a good deal of time experimenting with loose versified versions of the letters before deciding that a prose form would suit their informative narrative a great deal better than any verse form could. Furthermore, if I was going to 'manufacture' Butler letters to fill the narrative gaps left by the real letters, the more authentic-looking they were the better. So I chose a two-strand approach with a tightly formed three-line stanza for the modern narrative and prose paragraphs for the letters. But still the narrative seemed to lack the necessary contrast between a strong modern and a strong historic voice.

If I have already described Margaret Butler as possessing a strong and vivid narrative voice, why then did I feel it necessary to augment her narrative by creating an entirely new voice and character? In the letters, a combination of lengthy hiatuses and a sense that there was only so much that Margaret Butler would allow herself to tell her relations back home, seemed to detract from the strong sense of an inner life that I wanted to portray in the verse novel. I needed a 19th century protagonist whose journey of self discovery would match that of the 21st century protagonist. However, as my reading of studies on emigrant writing had shown, the conventions of 19th century emigrant correspondence (in which the writers restricted themselves to superficial accounts of their lives and expressed themselves in similar styles and with similar expressions) would not provide the type of emotional and psychological detail I needed for my novel. Thus the question for me was whether to create an inner life for Margaret through the development of a story line told through her letters, and find some way of overcoming her natural decorum as a correspondent in order to tell that story, or else to find some other way of casting light on her experience. Feedback from my supervisor at this stage suggested that I might seek to introduce a more introspective voice for Margaret, an issue I resolved in the second draft of the novel.

In my historical research of the period, I came across references to a group of Irish 'orphans', as they were called at the time, who were brought over to Australia on an assisted emigration scheme in 1849–50. These girls, many of whom still had parents back home in Ireland but all of whom resided in poorhouses and state asylums, were brought out to help address the shortage of females, both as domestic servants and potential wives, that afflicted the new colony at the time. It struck me that I could create an excellent counterfoil for Margaret Butler by imagining an entirely new character, a young woman who came over with the Thomas Arbuthnot orphans and who, unlike Margaret, positively embraced the new experience and new country because it rescued her from a life of poverty and cruelty in Ireland. This character, whom I christened Lizzie, would be provided with her own narrative and her own voice which would be threaded around the two other narratives. This narration would act as a commentary on the events mentioned in the Butler letters but could provide far more detail about the emotional and psychological context for those events.

Framing the Critical Context

I completed the first full draft of the creative element towards the end of the second full-year of the PhD and began work, in earnest, on the critical response while I waited for feedback from my supervisor about the verse novel. Having completed the draft, I felt that the most crucial aspect for the critical response piece was to focus on ways in which other writers had used the verse novel form to explore a variety of themes. I hoped that by focusing on the process of other writers, I might help to elucidate the creative challenges that had faced me in my own work. I therefore decided to undertake a historical survey of the development of the verse novel genre, beginning with the early verse narratives of the romantic poets and concluding with the most recent proponents of the genre. By reading new writers, and re-reading the work of other verse novelists whose work I had first become acquainted with during the literature review phase of my project, I began to have a better understanding both of their own process as writers, and also of my own. For example, to my surprise, I found that my writing and my concerns had a great deal in common with Elizabeth Barrett Browning, a writer whose work I was not previously familiar with and whose verse novel, *Aurora Leigh*, proved to be an engrossing and surprisingly modern exploration of the challenges facing women writers. Although her diction was Victorian, Barrett Browning's voice had an immediacy and modernity I recognised in other women writers. It had not occurred to me before beginning my critical survey that in taking on the verse novel, I might be following in the footsteps of generations of other women writers who had used the form to claim back territory in some shape or form. Barrett Browning asserted the right of poets to take on contemporary themes in general, and of women to write poetry in particular. More than a century later, writers such as Bernadine Evaristo and Derek Walcott (1990) would use the form to explore postcolonial issues of gender and race. These writers regarded themselves as in some degree or other marginalised, either by their nationality, their race, or their gender. One of the questions I would be required to answer about my own work was whether I too was coming from a perspective that was marginalised. Thus through my wider reading, I began to see how I could place my own work in a wider context. The task as I saw it for the remainder of the doctorate was to formulate a complete or coherent thesis to describe that place.

It may yet prove problematic that I have steered away from theory or criticism and focused on a historical basis for the critical response to my creative work. And yet it is my firm belief that each writer, undertaking a PhD, must adopt the work approach best suited to his or her own personality as a writer. Being a writer who focuses on the practical response to things rather than on framing a theoretical framework, I prefer to concentrate on the concrete issues surrounding practice rather than seeking to theorise my writing. I believe that the unique quality of the PhD in Creative Writing is that it gives writers the opportunity not only to write, but also to find ways of elucidating the process of writing by referring not only to their own work but to the work of other writers who have gone before them. In undertaking the PhD, I genuinely believe that I learned a great deal more about my own process, and about the themes and concerns that are of greatest importance to me. My desire is that the final project will give others an insight into the mind of a writer, and the way that individual writer works.

Notes

1. Since then, Creative Writing has become part of a collaboration between the new National Institute for Excellence in the Creative Industries™and the School of English.
2. Butler Archive, Access Number 4205, National Library of Ireland, Dublin.

References

Barrett Browning, E. (1994) Aurora Leigh. In K. Hill (ed.) *The Works of Elizabeth Barrett Browning*. Ware: The Wordsworth Library.

Ó Cléirigh, N. (2003) *Hardship and High Living: Irish Women's Lives 1808–1923*. Dublin: Portobello Press.

Porter, D. (1997) *The Monkey's Mask*. London: Serpent's Tail.

Walcott, D. (1990) *Omeros*. London: Faber.

Chapter 5
Six Texts Prefigure a Seventh

INEZ BARANAY

Introduction

My doctoral dissertation was an interrogation of the writing of my fifth novel and seventh book, *Neem Dreams* (Baranay, 2003), a novel set in India. *Neem Dreams'* four main characters are Pandora, an Australian feminist scientist, Andy, an English lawyer, Jade, an Australian buying products for a New York store and Meenakshi, an Indian running a women's development project. They meet as a result of their separate quests related to the uses of neem, India's 'miracle tree', used since pre-history for medicine, agriculture and household purposes and, in the 1990s, also at the centre of an intellectual property dispute.

In part an examination of the relationship of yoga practice to writing practice, in part an examination of representations of India by non-Indian writers, and in part an examination of issues in writing fiction, my work led me to re-read my six previously published books: *Between Careers* (1989a), *The Saddest Pleasure* (1989b), *Pagan* (1990), *The Edge of Bali* (1992), *Rascal Rain* (1994) and *Sheila Power* (1997). I examined in turn questions raised by this re-reading: in terms of memoir (how the re-reading stimulated memories of each book's composition), of stages (how a writer develops a body of work through stages that might be seen as analogous to the stages of yoga practice)[1] and finally of the way a writer's earlier work might be read as prefiguring her latest. In this case the six texts revealed concerns that were re-visited or developed in *Neem Dreams*.

The effect of this was to find that it was impossible to ever assign a definitive interpretation to these texts.

> The act of writing is an act of production whose result, writing, continues to produce, independent of its 'author'. Through unlimited readings and rewritings, it defers meaning. In this infinite deferral of meaning, it undermines notions of representation and truth which hold that there is some original presence, some source of truth that can be restored to the text. (Cixous & Clément, 1986: 168)

My books were written and thereafter even their own author's own readings would produce a different set of meanings each time.

Between Careers: Feminism and Sex

Between Careers (Baranay, 1989a) is set in Sydney in the 1970s and explores the double life of a well-educated young woman called Vita, who takes a job as a call girl using the name Violet. In one scene, Violet is in a car with three co-workers on their way to a job and crawling through the streets of Kings Cross, with its

> crowds of tourists, touters, bikies and the odd local pushing through with a shopping bag. Susie stared at the streetwalkers: big-breasted flaunters strutting their stuff, transsexuals posing in doorways, and drug addicts curled up inside their scanty rags, heavy-eyed, nodding.
> 'How could they?' Susie said, all prim outrage. 'Standing out there on the street like that for anyone to see.'
> Not like us princesses, us chauffeur-driven dolls who keep off the streets and can even say no, within reason.
> 'They're just prostitutes,' Fay muttered.
> 'So are we,' said Violet.
> Susie and Faye were shocked ...
> 'They did this study,' Amber said, all seriousness, 'in three American cities, looking at five levels of prostitution, and they found the girls on the street would say that money was the only possible reward and they would see it as a matter of survival, not so much choice. Then when you go ...' (Baranay, 1989a: 67–8)

This scene was included in early treatments and drafts during the years various film producers were trying to develop an adaptation of the still-unpublished novel, and, in the Australian way, going to government funding agencies to pay for it. It was singled out for particular derision in a derisory recommendation against funding by a man who claimed he was 'staggered' to find that the Women's Film Fund had funded a first draft. From his more-feminist-than-you stance, this assessor claimed both that this conversation could not possibly have been had by the girls in the car, and that other scenes were unrealistic and male-oriented pornography. Feminism, then as now, is often a matter of 'What I am and they're not' or 'What they are and I'm not'. The fruitless submissions for further development funds were abandoned. (The film adaptation you want to see is one that gets the *tone* right. That wasn't going to happen.) Later it became clear to me that the staggered man had read the objectionable scenes as filmed from the man's point of view, whereas I and my co-developers had not. We had imagined them as from the woman's point of view. Which would have made a film as cruel, then, as the novel is, and reading it today I find it cruel. Frank Moorhouse,[2] having provided the publishers with a cover line that did not make it to the cover, described *Between Careers* as 'Pain wit style cruelty – Australia's Jean Rhys' and I especially liked the word cruelty. I liked the idea of being taken for cruel, not quite sure I had it in me. Now I am an older woman reading a young woman's pitiless descriptions of men she judges as lacking her kind of style and wit, her own studied detachment; heartless in the way of the young.

Cruel it is, *and* the novel is as feminist as anything. The very question of what 'feminist' can include is explicitly raised by Vita (in those days feminism was used only in the singular).

Vita reports that 'It's not the feminist thing to do' is one of the reasons people give her in their objections to her new line of work. Her reply: 'But it's winning the war between the sexes.' She argues:

> What about how you're treated in a straight office job, always being scrutinised for proof of incompetence, irrationality and willingness to fuck? (Baranay, 1989a: 52)

Feminism needed plurality. Not that plurality is the end of any 'What's feminist and what's not' arguments. But these days it's more commonly argued that occupations like housewife or prostitute should not exclude women from feminist ranks, as long as we are assured of the exercise of 'choice'.

There was another paradox, along with the paradox of sex being the form of sublimation rather than what was being sublimated. The paradox of the fury, disgust, the 'How dare they!' indignation directed at middle-class women who took up prostitution as a choice, when for other women it was degrading and inescapable. These were arguments Vita takes some account of and which I pondered a great deal. I could only come back to a correlation as old as the oldest profession and think, What about marriage? You don't say no woman should get married because for some women marriage is degrading and inescapable.

And who is going to say which jobs under patriarchy are more or less the feminist thing to do? There was greatest condemnation for a choice that felt like a demonstration of greatest freedom, that was the paradox.

In the early 70s I loved and believed in and felt part of Women's Liberation, all the liberations. By the end of that mythical decade I was saying I was a gay man in a woman's body. This seemed to me a fresh and unique conviction, though I have seen it reproduced many times since. Madonna says it. Camille Paglia says it. Anne Rice says it. Characters in Edmund White novels say it. Someone in Mark Doty's memoir says it (Doty, 1996: 97). There's a woman in a short story I've just read on the Internet who is 'really' a gay man (Greenman, 2001). The world is full of women who are 'really' gay men.

I recognise my own attraction to the gay world of the time in this passage from Keith Fleming's memoir of life in the 70s as the teenaged ward of his uncle Edmund White:

> I realised how theatrical my uncle was; how he and his friends had evolved a manner that could be very much like being onstage, with every sentence a potential 'line' and every facial expression a clear, even exaggerated register of what was being felt ...

> Ed and Keith would agree that they no longer had any patience for heart-to-heart talks, which were pointless as well as exhausting; they'd then go on to declare, in the spirit of Oscar Wilde, that everything of interest could be found on the surface of things and that deeper probing almost guaranteed a tedious conversation. (Fleming, 1999: 167, 170)

Then, as now, *gay* and *feminist* did not necessarily occupy the same space, though they might rub shoulders on a dance floor. Now, plurality and multiplicity and diversity describe all our worlds, gay and feminist overlap only part of their territories, and no dance floor is all-inclusive.

The puzzling plurality of possible feminisms is implicitly posited when Vita and her old friend Liz, another unlikely sex worker, a qualified doctor, discuss their new milieu and the madam and co-workers at their escort agency:

> '[S]he really impressed me, so tough, no bullshit. Yet this business is meant to be so – what would they say ...'

> 'The worst exploitation of women ... I can tell you I've never felt less exploited in a job...They're so strong and independent, without education or the women's movement ...' (Baranay, 1989a: 41)

But this is not the end of the story. And certainty, in this writer's world, is never to be trusted, always to be destabilised. The story continues, and certainties wobble.

The 'safe' sex of the 70s only meant that any STDs were cured almost as easily as you might take an aspirin for a headache. Condoms were rarely used. Violet's packet of condoms 'never gets opened because the odd strange man who wants to use them brings his own' (Baranay, 1989a: 17) – a line that was added in later drafts of the novel, for readers who no longer could take for granted sex without them. Between the writing of the first draft and the publication of the novel 10 years passed, AIDS had appeared and our world altered extremely. Between the first two parts of the novel and its Coda, the alteration has begun and the characters have noticed.

Safety, perhaps, was always an illusion – the denial of sex's darkness, its chthonic power, its infinite complexity not always successfully excluded even in zones where the agreement is: simple fun no strings.

The advent of AIDS inevitably skewed the discourse on sexuality towards the dark revelations and mysteries of AIDS. These days I spend time with young adults who were born while I was writing this novel and for whom, therefore, AIDS has been a fact of life all their lives. And still, more than ever even, differently than ever perhaps, sex is not only commodified in increasing ways and via new media and new technologies, it is still represented as the thing we most desire, as the thing that power tries to repress while we the people defy oppression to find our truer selves in its liberating joys. And that might still be the actually oppressive belief.

By the time I wrote *Neem Dreams*, it was impossible to create a well-peopled realistic novel that did not include gay characters. Or contemporary characters that had not been touched by feminism and by AIDS. Or to write a novel worth reading that had neither. The characters in *Neem Dreams* in the mid-1990s have long lived with AIDS and also with the ever-developing discourse on feminism. Their writer has too.

It's as if taking on the issues around feminism and sex in my first novel was preparation for writing *Neem Dreams*.

Andy and Pandora establish a connection of sympathy and compatibility, not least because each understands the other has recently lost someone close, to an AIDS death – Andy his lover, Pandora her brother. Andy himself is in India in an uncertain quest for a better cure for HIV; he is positive. All he has to say is 'I'm positive' for Jade and Pandora immediately to know what he means:

> You look the person in the eye, you nod slowly and thoughtfully, you take it in, you wonder what to say, you are reminded of so much sadness, you send your thoughts to the ailing, and to the departed, you bring yourself back, be here now, look him in the eye.
> Jade and Pandora for a moment with no difference between them. (Baranay, 2003: 192)

While in the real world contentions about feminism and post-feminism seem in some places to rage and in some to expire in tedium and irrelevance, in *Neem Dreams* Meenakshi's women-based development project and Jade's independence and careerism, as well as Pandora's ecofeminist credentials, belong to a world where feminism is an established premise. *Between Careers* prefigured an abiding concern with these issues.

The Saddest Pleasure: Fractured Time, Pattern and Composition

The Saddest Pleasure (Baranay, 1989b) is a collection of short prose in three parts: travel diaries, short stories and a novella.

There are surprises here for me as the present reader, who has forgotten how the novella 'Pearl of the Orient' had been plotted. Reading, exclaiming 'Oh no' and 'Oh good' to the writing and 'Oh!' to the revelations ('Oh' Bruce knows the amah, 'Oh' Christine has already met Paul). And, at the end, Bruce's explanation of earlier events surprises me, I do not remember until then. Was it I who wrote that? All the cells in my body have been renewed twice over since then.

Now I remember I had first begun to write 'Pearl of the Orient' as a play – I so wanted to write a play, I still want to write a play – but it wasn't going to make a play. So Part 1 is 'Act 1', the set being Melissa's living room in Penang in 1965, with 'its red-tiled floors, whirring ceiling fans, cane sofas ... a terrace that looked out to the sea' (Baranay, 1989b: 107), and 'Act 2' is set in Pearl's nightclub.

> [The] songs were new, then; they were songs of new arousals and aches and angers, they throbbed with newness and a promise of renewal ... the turning mirror-ball scattered its reflections of the string of blinking coloured lights. (Baranay, 1989b: 124)

It turned out I was writing not a play but prose and Part 3 of 'Pearl of the Orient' circles the 10 years since the events of the first two parts, which take place over less than 24 hours. This singular shape oddly works, I find today; it is not the peculiar structure that makes me go 'Oh no'.

As *Between Careers* already indicated, as the overall structure of *The Saddest Pleasure* and the pattern of this novella 'Pearl of the Orient' demonstrate, this writer will persist in the refusal of a prescribed scheme and will concern herself with the creation of arrangements specific to each piece of writing.

> [T]he composition (the architectural organisation of a work) should not be seen as some preexistent matrix, loaned to an author for him to fill out with his invention; the composition should itself be an invention, an invention that engages all the author's originality. (Kundera, 1995: 172)

Kundera's 'composition' is what we usually call 'structure' and what E.M. Forster in *Aspects of the Novel* (1927) called 'pattern and rhythm', saying, 'For this new aspect there appears to be no literary word' (Forster, 1955: 149). Forster identifies a choice writers make: whether or not to shape their material to:

> the rigid pattern: hour-glass or grand chain or converging lines of the cathedral or diverging lines of the Catherine wheel, or bed of Procrustes – whatever image you like as long as it implies unity (Forster, 1955: 163)

Forster concludes that his own prejudices are with the view that as this cannot be combined with:

> the immense richness of material which life provides ... life should be given the preference and must not be whittled or distended for a pattern's sake ... [T]he disadvantage of a rigid pattern [is] it may externalise the atmosphere, spring naturally from the plot, but it shuts the doors on life and leaves the novelist doing exercises, generally in the drawing room. (Forster, 1955: 163)

I'm with Forster on eschewing the demand for a rigid pattern or imposed structure while maintaining an internal, meaningful structure – what he calls rhythm. I don't know if I ever made explicit these ideas when I began to write, but they seem always to have been there. In 'Pearl of the Orient' the composition uses the method of focus on several characters; although it is largely Melissa's story, Chris and Paul and Bruce are also focalised. The present reader might find that this pre-figures or predicts the method of *Neem Dreams*.

Chronology is fractured in *Neem Dreams*. The novel contains one main thread, a story taking place over a few days, in which its characters meet in the south of India. Woven through this story are several sections that recount episodes from the pasts of the four main characters, both the very recent past of the few days before the main story, and the more distant past. In Pandora's case, episodes from childhood form a couple of these sections. This method emerged out of the writing, rather than being a given of the novel's composition. It is a risky method; a story usually requires a dominant forward movement. But it is in his chapter on 'Quickness' that Calvino remarks:

> Implicit in my tribute to lightness was my respect for weight, and so this apologia for quickness does not presume to deny the pleasures of lingering. (Calvino, 1996: 46)

Faith in the pleasure of lingering with characters in order to revisit with them some of the past moments that have brought them to, and remain part of, the present; faith in the pleasure of lingering so as to see characters in other contexts and return with deeper understanding to the context of the main story: this faith was required as this odd structure emerged. If *Neem Dreams* is going to work, the reader must be content to circle and weave rather than maintain a steady trot down a path with a single direction, however much more elegant that option might have been.

Reading *The Saddest Pleasure* now, I'm saying 'Oh No' where I want to delete. If, as seems possible, writers are of two kinds, the taker-outer and the putter-inner, I'm a taker-outer, and I already was then. But reading this today, I still want to slash. And I wouldn't use the word race today as it has been used here: 'Spices and the sweat of several races, the scent of incense in the temples' (Baranay, 1989b: 107). Though Ajit, political radical in Part 2, resort hotel owner in Part 3, uses the word deliberately, mischievously in pre-Malaysia Malaya:

> 'You free in here!' said Pearl. 'Anything you want.'
> 'In here. Out there, better change your race,' said Ajit. (Baranay, 1989b: 130)

As Melissa steadily keeps drinking in Pearl's a few hours after she finds out her husband was killed in Vietnam, she:

> watched time and space swirl about in the smoke, turning the lights, blurring perception and existence, dissolving her certainties, leaving her in the shadow between memory and experience, between living and telling, obscuring the outlines of the imaginary and the actual ... And that was before she tried the *ganja* on the beach. (Baranay, 1989b: 131)

On her way to the beach, she exchanges a few words with the soldier who did not want to leave the war in Vietnam, longs to return there. And his monologue, following her exit, begins to fracture the realism in which this piece has been located.

I had heard of a theory in Physics that intrigued me, someone uneducated in Science. I applied this idea to the characters in 'Pearl':

> They were all particles of the universe that went on affecting each other at vast distances once they had collided, invisibly connected into infinity. (Baranay, 1989b: 148)

Shifts in perspective and fractured chronology are also employed, and acknowledged, in *Neem Dreams* especially in a key sentence:

> Time proceeded at no orderly pace in India, thought Andy, it stretched and compressed and turned on itself in spirals and fractals. (Baranay, 2003: 185)

In Part 3 of 'Pearl', the section about Chris in the hotel room (Baranay, 1989b: 146–148) can be read as Melissa's dream. Earlier that night, Paul, meeting Melissa 10 years after the night at Pearl's, mentions that Chris has also been back to Penang; and Melissa might imagine, or know, that Chris had stayed in the same room of the new resort hotel that had been built on the site of the former Pearl's. A soldier who might be the soldier from that long-ago night appears.

There was silence until the soldier spoke. No, he didn't speak. He did speak. (Baranay, 1989b: 147)

He continues to speak as the version of the soldier we know from the obsession with the war in Vietnam – my obsession and, briefly, the culture's obsession. When I began to write 'Pearl' it was 1985, 10 years after 'Act 3' took place, 10 years after:

Marcus was celebrating the liberation of Ho Chi Minh City, while Teng's family mourned the death of certain hopes with the fall of Saigon. (Baranay, 1989b: 138)

'Pearl of the Orient' reflects a preoccupation of the cultural moment, of the *zeitgeist*. Many years later, so does *Neem Dreams*, with its own preoccupations with globalisation and intellectual property, as well as with contemporary forms of feminism, the aftermath of AIDS and travel in a postmodern age.

Pagan: Plurality, Spirituality

Pagan (Baranay, 1990) is set in Sydney and based on a real-life scandal in 1956 linking a famous conductor with a notorious bohemian artist.

In 1950s Australia, feminism, let alone 'women's liberation', was not a common phrase. The two main female characters in *Pagan*, Nora and Eveleen, however, have never seen themselves as the 'magazine housewife' promoted as the ideal of womankind.

Nora is an ambitious young music student, a devotee of the great conductor, Eduard von Kronen, and Eveleen is a so-called 'witch', a pagan and occultist. Their worlds intersect in Sydney's bohemian area of Kings Cross, where the novel is set. The character of Eveleen can be read as prefiguring the 'women's spirituality movement' that later Pandora, in *Neem Dreams*, explicitly takes as her 'tradition'. Eveleen, isolated in the Australia of the 1940s and 50s, was hungry for the new works on wicca. She had read Margaret Murray's *The Witch Cult in Western Europe*, published in 1921, which claimed to reveal the ancient religion of Western Europe:

A joyous religion, Eveleen! A women's religion! A religion of ancient feminine knowledge and celebration. Now you know who you are ... Now when they came and asked you, 'Yes!' you told them, proudly. 'Yes, I am a witch.' (Baranay, 1990: 103–104)

Part of her involvement with the conductor was for his access, on his travels abroad, to new works – Gerald Gardner's 1954 *Witchcraft Today* was a major new source of esoteric knowledge – and the paraphernalia for rituals.

In the early 1980s new books by New Age women elaborated Murray's claim. The publishing of books on women's spirituality and wicca continues. I bought books on witchcraft in feminist bookshops, and popular exponents of contemporary wicca, such as Starhawk, began to be sold in mainstream bookshops. As I was researching *Pagan*, I became involved in the idea that the political and social discourses of feminism were expanding to a feminism of the spirit, deconstructing patriarchal religions and the patriarchal colonising of our souls.

Although I was doing this research for *Pagan*, it became part of the background to my understanding of the world of *Neem Dreams*, as Pandora's background includes an immersion in a type of New Age feminism concerned with these developments.

Eveleen in the 1940s and 50s had no peers and few resources and a taste for the left-hand path. This is part of her tragedy. In the words of a witch I spoke with in the late 1980s:

Aleister Crowley? ... If she was following his stuff that explains a lot. He was a great magician but he really got off the track ... Evvi trusted the demons too much ... she invoked demons, not only the Deities. That's dangerous stuff ... We believe in working in groups. For psychic power and psychic protection. She was very much on her own ... she got a chaotic, undisciplined power. (Baranay, 1990: 126–7)

Writing *Pagan*, set in the mid-1950s, can be seen as preparation or background for the context of ecofeminism in the mid-1990s. Pandora is typical of the adherent Mies and Shiva are speaking of here:

Ecofeminists in the USA seemingly put greater emphasis on the 'spiritual' than do those in Europe. [Australia, in this as in many matters, is more like the USA than Europe – IB] ... The critique of the 'spiritual' stand within the ecofeminist movement is voiced mainly by men and women from the left. Many women ... do not easily accept spiritual ecofeminism, because it is obvious that capitalism can also co-opt the 'spiritual' feminists' critique of 'materialism'.

This, indeed, is already happening. The New Age and esoteric movements have created a new market for esoterica, meditation, yoga, magic, alternative health practices, most of which are fragments taken out of the contexts of oriental, particularly Chinese and Indian, cultures. Now after the material resources of the colonies have been looted, their spiritual and cultural resources are being transformed into commodities for the world market ... It is a kind of luxury spirituality ... the idealist icing on top of the material cake of the West's standard of living. (Mies & Shiva, 1993: 18–19)

By the 1990s, feminism had reached into every aspect of religious and spiritual life; even the most conservative of churches was challenged over the ordination and participation of women. Women took up the celebration of full moons and solstices, bought books of spells and the belief in goddess-centred religions of a bygone day became widespread. All of this was becoming so commonplace that it could be satirised in, for example, Francine Prose's 1995 novel *Hunters and Gatherers*, in which a group of contemporary women become devotees of Isis Moonwagon, an academic New Age priestess, and worship the goddess with her in the upmarket beaches of New York's Fire Island and the Arizona desert:

Oh, don't you wish we could just revert to that pre-agricultural stage, when the most essential knowledge was the names of plants, which herbs cured which diseases, natural uppers and downers, and you never doubted the usefulness of each little thing you did! Every woman a doctor without the trauma of medical school! Imagine if we could time-travel back to the matriarchal era when women ran the world and everyone lived in peace! (Prose, 1995: 20–21)

And now ...

belief in ancient matriarchy is popular among middlebrow feminists ... matriarchy is part of the general feminist atmosphere rather than a tenet of a specific school. (Osborne, 2000)

In turn, this widespread belief in a remote past dominated by matriarchy, goddess worship and ecological balance, shattered by some kind of patriarchal revolution, bringing male rule, war and sexism, is being challenged by books (such as Cynthia Eller's *Living in the Lap of the Goddess: The Feminist Spirituality Movement in America*, discussed in Osborne, 2000) which point out its historical and factual inaccuracies, essentialism and ideology

Pandora (*Neem Dreams*) comes of age in a time when the women's spirituality movement is at its height and she embraces one of its offshoots, ecofeminism. She is a character whose background contains awareness of the kinds of precursors represented by the character of Eveleen in *Pagan*. As the author of both of them, I feel that my time in Eveleen's world turned out to be preparation for writing Pandora's.

The Edge of Bali: Dreams

The Edge of Bali (Baranay, 1992) is a novel structured as three novellas, each with a tourist in Bali as the central character: 20-year-old Nelson, 40-year-old Marla and 30-year-old Tyler.

> The truest stuff you knew, it was impossible to say it properly, like telling your dreams. (Baranay, 1992: 16)

These are the thoughts of Nelson, a lost 20-year-old girl pondering the limits of verbal communication in Bali.

Although I don't recall any plan or theory guiding me, I find mention of dreams in each of the sections of *The Edge of Bali*. It is in the *practice* of writing character that I discover that attention to my own dream life has convinced me that to know characters well, know them from the inside, is to know their dreams, dream their dreams:

> She woke into a dream and woke into a dream and woke into a dream. Dream after dream opened, doors in a long long corridor, opening, opening. She was on a bed in Bali and woke to find herself on a bed in Bali and woke to find herself on a bed in Bali, in a dream ... (Baranay, 1992: 145)

Marla's dreams are prophetic. First she dreams of the lover she soon will meet, then, rather more uncannily, of the unusual scene where they first kiss:

> A large black rock, a jagged black spire, rises out of the sea, lashed by waves. It is a solitary cliff. The waters swirl and darken around it. It is a formal composition, a large dark carving of rock.
> She wakes from this dream ... (Baranay, 1992: 154)

And even Tyler, less caught up in the world of imagination, art and mystery than Marla, even Tyler, who travels to Bali to search for his missing friend, must have a dream life:

> Up to the day he had left Sydney, Tyler had dreams about Neil. He dreamt that Neil returned, bent with the weight of treasures, from imperative, magical voyages; he dreamt that Neil just showed up, in a normal way; he dreamt that Neil had been there all along and they just hadn't noticed. (Baranay, 1992: 221)

Reading this novel brings back the sense of magic, the particular atmosphere, of the Bali I experienced and the fictive Bali I created. It is not only the descriptions of the places and events on that island but the evocation of its stimulus to the imaginative life.

My own dreams were vivid and fantastic there, and that was a kind of experience I found widely reported. A place will be experienced and remembered partly through the dreams one has there and the dreams it creates. Bali was the first place I travelled to as an independent adult; this as well as the peculiar enchantments of its highly-refined culture and the fascination Bali famously held for artists and anthropologists of the modernist era, contributed to the hold Bali took on my imagination. The concern for dreams might have been initiated here with the realisation that the conscious, rational mind, crudely identified with the West, was insufficient to appreciate the Balinese values of the invisible world, the practice of magic, and the divine inspiration needed by artists.

I have written elsewhere about how important dreams are to my writing. *The Edge of Bali* is the first of my novels to incorporate my own dreams and the dreams of my characters, and these were not always separate. By the time I came to write *Neem Dreams*, as its title indicates, the dream life had become an explicit concern.[3] This concern is prefigured in *The Edge of Bali*.

Rascal Rain: Writing the Other

Rascal Rain (1994) is my first non-fiction book, an account of a year spent in Papua New Guinea, where I had gone as a volunteer to work in women's development.

> Uh-oh, hang on a minute, she checks herself, am I allowed to think of Jolly as *sweet*? Sweet, that word meaning a gentle, attractive demeanour, you can't call just anyone sweet, sinister meanings are attributed to adjectives applied to identifiable Others. Let's decide, she decides again, that there are sweet people in all the locations of the world and that I mean the same thing by it wherever I am, though that's not the end of it according to the professional perversities of certain pundits, critics keen to crow over forbidden perceptions, and whatever you might say about Others is forbidden. Never mind.
>
> 'The tea's really good,' she said. (Baranay, 2003: 56)

The author who wrote this is clearly pre-empting a certain reader response.

Pandora, who has published her PhD on working with women in development in the Pacific, is, just as clearly, no stranger to rote criticisms in the age not of orientalism but of *Orientalism*, the age of post-coloniality.

I am trying not to say 'political correctness', aware that it's a term whose meaning must be determined by its context and is most commonly used to deride or ridicule legitimate concerns about language and justice.

But there does exist a fashion in thought that gives a superior position to sentiments that deride Western culture and Enlightenment values and those that, however uncritically, valorise non-Western cultural practices and beliefs. Linked with this is a belief that every non-Western person represents the Other in some absolute way. And that every Western person represents The West and its imperialism, its imperialist crimes.

This is what a friend of mine refers to in an email from Port Moresby, apropos his own research into education in Pakistan:

i was fascinated by ur comments on india; westernisation, greeting cards, cities; this is my thesis essentially. i have come out in my new rewrite and stated that i theorise through modernity and not post modernity. i love this connection i have been reading about which equates posty with fundamentalist islamic movements and that posty is a child of the 80's neoliberal economic agenda. that in allowing the 'local' in third worlds countries u allow the hegemonic power bases that control the situation now to hold sway: papa doc is good because its local. cant complain and if u do then u the academic are charged with 'orientalism' that is the critique of 'other culture' which is a form of eurocentrism. fuck that: when women are burned by kerosene by husbands who can divorce them because they are too scarred without even telling the wife of the divorce u KNOW there are Enlightenment ideals from europe which have mitigated against such barbarisms and if they are western then jolly good. same with gays. so same with equal rights in schools ... and i take this line about how my small middle class group in Pakistan who want modernity (civil rights) are on the track to getting equitable education if they can institute such changes; which they cant because they live under fundamentalism which is 'local' which is supported by postmodernism ...

so type in 'fundamental sex'. (personal email, 12.03.01)

In the hasty shorthand of personal correspondence based on many conversations, shared experiences and common assumptions, my friend is conjuring years of our consideration of our interactions in the developing world.

He happens to be one of the real-life originals for the only composite character in *Rascal Rain*, Jack. He and 'I'/the narrator puzzle over the philosophical bases for our work in Papua New Guinea:

Nothing's too clear in this game called Development, with its many denominations. We are The West and we are working outside of The West (as if we could, we're always in The West that enfolds us). We are on the side of Development (education, health, women) rather than Exploitation (mines, logging). We believe in Development that responds to the desires of the people or does it always respond to needs that we define? We create? It's our knowledge, our way of life, that of the West, apparently, that is desired, what we are there to offer. Do we tell people they shouldn't think life in the West is what they see on TV and videos? ... Theory tells us it's as if the only model were evolution, as if the direction and pattern of change were immutable, and privileged knowledge of it claimed by those further advanced along its course. History is denied those who have development done to them, even while we postmods are told that we know first and last not to judge the Other on our own terms. What it looks like is, power is retained by the West, even at a time when the ecological crisis forces considerations of the limits to growth. The West's answer is, 'So let them limit their growth, we're here to tell you we know they should'. Development can be seen as a new imperialism, and if it were?

Jack and I, with Lucifer bounding along nearby, get as far as we can along these lines. We go for vigorous walks ... (Baranay, 1994: 241–2)

Still, *Rascal Rain* was reviewed and critiqued as if it were not full of such passages, but a defense of imperialist projects and attitudes. A typical reviewer scolded that to describe a Melanesian man as 'sweet' was a patronising put-down. I admit my vocabulary of description of gentle, good-natured men was limited, but I also described an Irish-Australian priest and a Dutch horticulturist as sweet which, unremarked, must have been all right. When a literary journal piece slammed my book along with Alice Walker's *Warrior Marks* in terms that seemed to me to sacrifice any sensible critical points in its tone of triumphant fault-finding, and in its suggestions that are untenable to a writer's integrity, let alone practicable (e.g. I should have asked permission before writing these people into my narrative), I decided all that should not remain on the record unchallenged and published a reply:

It seems that the only permissible representation is none at all, or one couched in terms so carefully correct that a non-academic writer is forbidden the territory. (Baranay, 1998: 53)

Writing *Rascal Rain* only emphasised that writing about identifiable Others was fraught territory.[4] But *Neem Dreams* was always going to have an Indian character, even though the contemporary writer is aware of identity politics that claim exclusive representation of certain experiences. It's not only that; even to look around an Other culture, you look, as the above passage pointed out, from 'the West that enfolds [you]'. To the *pomo*-correct critic, this means you can't create a pure, exempt position, without complicity with The West. Oh, the wicked West. Today, terms such as *culture cult* and *designer tribalism* (Sandall, 2001: *passim*) are employed to identify the piousness and forbidding of the worst of such fashions in post-modern attitude, but in turn, regrettably, are also employed to eliminate valid deconstructions of representation.

The passage from *Neem Dreams* I quoted above ('Uh-oh ... am I allowed to think of Jolly as *sweet*?') is my nod to this problem. To write *Neem Dreams* was, in effect, an answer to, or defiance of, the objections made to my *Rascal Rain* and to the foreseeable objections to the very project of writing a novel set in India with Indian characters. Although part of the material of *Rascal Rain* was an engagement with the problem of representation and position, that could not prevent a kind of criticism, stupid and useless as it might seem to me, that smugly scolds a writer for being a Westerner writing of non-Western people. It seemed that there was no solution to the problem of acknowledging this problem and yet not compromising the artistic or aesthetic sense of the work. I had bitten off more than I could chew. I consoled myself with the thought that Italo Calvino would understand:

> Overambitious projects may be objectionable in many fields, but not in literature. Literature remains alive only if we set ourselves immeasurable goals, far beyond all hope of achievement. (Calvino, 1996: 112)

In Calvino's terms, I set myself immeasureable goals in both *Rascal Rain* and *Neem Dreams*, and find that it is this very fact that provides their value.

Sheila Power: New Directions

Sheila Power (Baranay, 1997) is a satirical novel set in 1990s Sydney and Venice. It seems as different as could be from *Rascal Rain*. For one thing, I completed *Sheila* quite satisfied. Unlike either *Rascal Rain* that preceded it or *Neem Dreams* that follows it, *Sheila Power* is marked by qualities of lightness, melodrama, meta-fiction. *Sheila*'s characters are based on characters and types rather than on people, its story on storylines rather than life, its tone on a shared joke rather than a common conundrum of practical philosophy. I thought of it as 'camp', as defined by Susan Sontag:

> A sensibility (as distinct from an idea) ... It is not a natural mode of sensibility ... Indeed, the essence of Camp is its love of the unnatural: of artifice and exaggeration. (Sontag, 1983: 105)

While *Neem Dreams* has an element of the fantastic in its fractured chronology and attention to dreams, and in its implication that its ending/s can be taken as dreamt rather than 'real', it is more firmly based in the experienced world and actual people than *Sheila Power* was.

While I might find in *Sheila Power* indications of future concerns in subject and theme, these concerns will become manifest in works after *Neem Dreams*. I hope to have that kind of fun again, for one thing. And yet, *Sheila Power* prefigures *Neem Dreams* in the writer's method of changing direction, immersing in a new world for a new work, departing from a known method of constructing a novel and a known kind of novel.

My next novel will be something quite different, but its seeds are undoubtedly already sown, not only in the above works, but in *Neem Dreams* also.

Conclusion

As John Fowles (1998: 382) says, The major influence on any mature writer is always his own past work. It is also true that new work influences the meaning of the past work.

If a writer examines her previous books taking into consideration her latest one, she finds new ways of reading them, new ways of understanding what the author who wrote them had achieved. And she can find in the earlier output a pre-figuring of the novel that followed.

A writer's work continues as long as the writer produces writing, and the production of each new major piece of writing effects changes upon the meaning of previous writings, for they become literary presages of the newest creation.

Readers and critics inevitably read a writer's work differently according to the extent that they know her other work. My study of my own texts shows that even their author can provide new insights when reading older texts in the light of the new.

Notes

1. Discussed in my *sun square moon: writings on yoga and writing* (Baranay, 2005).
2. A chapter of *Between Careers*, 'The Sex Part', had been published in Moorhouse's (1983) anthology *The State of the Art*.
3. More writings on the importance of dreams to writing can be found in my *sun square moon: writings on yoga and writing* (Baranay, 2005).
4. I have written further on this in an essay called 'It's the other who makes my portrait: Writing self, character and the other' (Baranay, 2004).

References

Baranay, I. (1989a) *Between Careers.* Sydney: Collins.

Baranay, I. (1989b) *The Saddest Pleasure.* Sydney: Collins.

Baranay, I. (1990) *Pagan.* Sydney: Collins Angus and Robertson.

Baranay, I. (1992) *The Edge of Bali.* Sydney: Collins Angus and Robertson.

Baranay, I. (1994) *Rascal Rain.* Sydney: Collins Angus and Robertson.

Baranay, I. (1997) *Sheila Power.* St Leonards: Allen and Unwin.

Baranay, I. (1998) Theory couldn't help me. *LiNQ* 25 (1), 52–56.

Baranay, I. (2003) *Neem Dreams.* Delhi: Rupa & Co.

Baranay, I. (2004) It's the other who makes my portrait: Writing self, character and the other. TEXT 8, 2 (October). On WWW at http://www.gu.edu.au/school/art/text/oct04/baranay.htm. Accessed 10.7.06.

Baranay, I. (2005) *sun square moon: writings on yoga and writing.* Brisbane: sun square moon.

Calvino, I. (1996) *Six Memos for the Next Millennium* (P. Creagh, trans.) London: Vintage.

Cixous, H. and Clément, C. (1986) *The Newly Born Woman* (B. Wing, trans.). Minneapolis: University of Minnesota Press (first published 1975).

Doty, M. (1996) *Heavens Coast.* London: Jonathan Cape.

Fleming, K. (1999) Uncle Ed. *Granta* 68, 161–174.

Forster, E.M. (1955) *Aspects of the Novel.* Harmondsworth: Penguin (first published 1927).

Fowles, J. (1998) *Wormholes: Essays and Occasional Writings.* London: Jonathan Cape.

Greenman, B. (2001) What 100 people, real and fake, believe about Dolores. *mcsweeny's.* Online at http://www.mcsweeneys.net/2001/10/27dolores.html. Accessed 11.11.01.

Kundera, M. (1995) *Testaments Betrayed.* London: Faber and Faber.

Mies, M. and Vandana, S. (1993) *Ecofeminism.* Melbourne: Spinifex Press.

Moorhouse, F. (ed.) (1983) *The State of the Art: The Mood of Contemporary Australia in Short Stories.* Ringwood, Victoria: Penguin.

Osborne, L. (2000) False goddesses. *salon.com.* On WWW at http://www.salon.com/books/features/2000/06/28/matriarchy. Accessed 2.07.00.

Prose, F. (1995) *Hunters and Gatherers.* New York: Farrar, Strauss and Giroux.

Sandall, R. (2001) *The Culture Cult: Designer Tribalism and Other Essays.* Boulder: Westview Press.

Sontag, S. (1983) Notes on camp. *A Susan Sontag Reader.* Harmondsworth: Penguin.

Chapter 6

Sleeping With Proust vs. Tinkering Under the Bonnet[1]: The Origins and Consequences of the American and British Approaches to Creative Writing in Higher Education

STEPHANIE VANDERSLICE

Let's begin with the obvious commonalities. In both the US and the UK, the discipline of Creative Writing has long struggled, in the face of patronization and marginalization, for a place at the table in Higher Education. The degree to which the discipline has conspired with itself to inscribe this outsider status differs from program to program and cultural context to cultural context. Still, it is fair to say, as Shirley Geok-lim Lin (2003: 154) does in 'The Strangeness of Creative Writing: An Institutional Query,' that 'Creative Writing is everywhere in English departments ... but hardly visible as a disciplinary component of the profession.' In countering the position of Creative Writing as 'third cousin to almost every other Higher Education discourse,' writer, teacher and Creative Writing advocate Graeme Harper (2007) argues that the 'primary epistemological ammunition ... for Creative Writing in the academy *must* be the declaration of a viable and systemic pedagogy.' A sensible analysis of the challenges to the discipline in the US and the UK, it is in the respective responses of both countries, as well as the histories and exingencies that shaped these responses, that key differences in the status of the field – in theory, practice and pedagogy, emerge.

The Origin of the Species

To better understand the histories and contexts that drive the current state of affairs, it is useful to compare the trajectories of the field in both countries. As most of us in this reading audience are well aware, Creative Writing in American Higher Education has been traced back, in a vast over-simplification of the work of D.G. Myers, Wendy Bishop and others, to courses in essay-writing at Harvard and in verse-making at the University of Iowa in the late 19th century. Iowa ran with the ball from there, allowing creative MA theses under Norman Foerster in the 1920s and 30s. This innovative practice lead to the founding of the Iowa Writer's Workshop, an MFA program that blossomed into a full-fledged American icon under poet Paul Engle. The first graduate program in Creative Writing, the workshop retains its luminary status today as incubator of some of America's top literary talent, Flannery O'Connor, Philip Roth, Jane Smiley, and Richard Bausch among them. Once this program began graduating writers who went on to accept university teaching positions, exponential growth, fueled by increased college enrollments and even the post-World War II GI Bill, soon followed as disciples fanned out across the country to form Creative Writing programs in the image of their alma mater. Thus, the Iowa 'Workshop Method' as a dominant form of Creative Writing pedagogy took hold. As of 2004, there existed 109 MFA programs and 42 PhD programs in Creative Writing in the US, a number that does not include the hundreds of undergraduate majors and concentrations as well as MA concentrations (AWP, 2004).

In the UK, although writers have found a place on campus almost since the university was established at Oxford, the formal trajectory has been traced back to two developments in the late 1960s. The first was the founding of the Arvon Foundation in 1968 as a 'year round program of residential writing courses taught by professional writers (Arvon Foundation, 2006). Then, two years later in 1970, Malcolm Bradbury and Angus Wilson established the MA degree in Creative Writing at the University of East Anglia. While the latter is often heralded as the first official Creative Writing program in British higher education, the subject had already taken root at polytechnic institutions and in adult education courses. After an incubation period, by the late 1980s/early 1990s both graduate and undergraduate Creative Writing courses, modules and programs began to dot the British university landscape in larger numbers. In fact, in her chapter 'Creative Writing: Structures and Trends,' Siobahn Holland (2003: 8) reports that '24 HE institutions [were] offering named undergraduate programs in Creative Writing in 2002–03, a number which increases if programs in Creative Arts or Creative Studies with writing elements are included'. At the same time, she notes, 'graduates can choose between 21 taught and 19 research-based postgraduate degrees in Creative Writing' (Holland, 2003: 8) while still more universities are developing Creative Writing courses.

As these courses spread across the UK, there was and continues to be a parallel rise in courses in Creative Writing offered by community centers and primary and secondary schools, courses that might trace their ancestry back to the Arvon Foundation. Moreover, Graeme Harper (2007) observes that there has been a gradual shift from a 'cultural context in which the few provided works of Creative Writing to the many, to one in which the many want to experience the learning of Creative Writing.'

Indeed, the promulgation of Creative Writing programs and the enormous popularity of Creative Writing courses both inside and outside academia indicate that similar trends prevail in the US. Moreover, organizations such as the Arvon Foundation and the National Association for Writers in Education in the UK, emerging in tandem with formal degree programs such as those of the University of East Anglia, and the comparative organizations in the US of the National Writing Project and the Teachers and Writers Collaborative growing apace with the rise in MFA programs suggest that in both the US and the UK a tension exists between the 'ideal of democratic participation, of entitlement to imaginative creativity,' and the 'Romantic ideal of the "Master Class"' (Cook, 2001: 299). However, in Higher Education itself, the landscapes of the field in both countries, and subsequently, their results, could hardly be more different.

Perhaps the overriding difference lies in the highly centralized nature of Higher Education in the UK, abetted by its compact geographic size in comparison with the US, a practicality that should not be ignored. It is this centralization that has resulted in Creative Writing programs that are held to the same standards as other academic programs in post-Dearing Report[2] British Higher Education, where outcomes assessment and the definition of specialized student learning outcomes remain a driving force. Further, according to Moira Monteith (1992: 13), this atmosphere has induced writing programs to approach the teaching of writing as a 'verbal,' or 'vocational art in the manner of film or music,' as a way 'out of the cul de sac'.

Another exingency operating in the British system is the length of the undergraduate degree. Students in the UK complete highly specialized three-year degrees while American students are free to loll about the curriculum for a minimum of four years, some taking much longer (another discussion, for another time). Within a significantly shorter time span and a subsequently more proscribed curriculum, Creative Writing in the UK cannot, according to Robert Miles (1992: 35), afford a reputation as a 'tasty' extra but as a part of a larger curricular paradigm, it must earn its 'curricular keep'.

One result of this attention to the curriculum in the UK has been a more formal division of undergraduate and graduate writing program pedagogy. Until recently the undergraduate writing course in the US has seemed something of an afterthought.[3] Conversely, Cook (2001: 301) acknowledges that in the UK the recognition of a distinction 'between an exercise-driven workshop and one that starts with the writer's own work ... ends itself to further distinctions about levels.' Indeed, Julia Bell (2001: 292) further allows that undergraduate workshops in the UK are 'more taught.'

Such attention to curriculum has also led Creative Writing programs in the UK to lay out and continually revisit the goals and aims of their courses and pedagogies with an eye towards providing practical opportunities for students to achieve learning objectives. As far back as the early 90s for example, George Marsh (1992) was able to divine and summarize the aims of Creative Writing programs in Great Britain in relatively focused terms:

(1) to train professional writers;
(2) to illuminate criticism by learning experientially about the construction of a text (Marsh, 1992, p. 48);
(3) to develop communication skills – a good command of language – valuable for many kinds of employment (p. 49);
(4) to do literary writing because it is intrinsically worthwhile (p. 50);
(5) to teach literary writing (p. 53);
(6) to develop the mind of the student or to develop imagination and creativity (p. 52);
(7) to prepare school teachers for teaching Creative Writing (p. 52).

The first aim is of particular interest in that it represents practice-based literary analysis and appreciation, another concrete value added to the Creative Writing course in the UK that does not exist to the same extent in the US – although D.G. Myers (1996) identifies it as an occasional factor in *The Elephants Teach: Creative Writing Since 1880*. In other words, Creative Writing is also seen in the British context as an acceptable way of teaching literature.

Current Climates

Lacking these exingencies, Creative Writing programs in the US operate under a far more decentralized umbrella, seldom, according to Shirley Geok-lim Lin (2003: 156), subject to 'the scrutiny of outsiders' or 'required to account for themselves'. In this way, moreover, US Creative Writing programs have been described by some as more thinly-veiled patrons of contemporary writers than anything else. Philip Roth's listing of the aims of the US Creative Writing program, when held up against Marsh's, is telling in this respect. Quoted in Tom Grimes's *The Workshop*, Roth asserts that the basic functions of courses like the writing workshop function to: (1) give young writers an audience, (2) give them a sense of community, and (3) an acceptable category – that of student (Grimes, 1999: 4–5).

In the absence of more specialized aims, then, varied circumstances rush in to fill the void. Chief among them is a firmly entrenched star system in American Creative Writing programs, a system that results in a pedagogy characterized by an anti-intellectual cult of personality. Such an environment privileges the testimony of the writer/teacher in the workshop over other more varied teaching techniques that might be more closely aligned with learning objectives. Indeed, defined learning objectives rarely exist. This pedagogy, one based in philosophizing and testifying about writing and the writing life at the expense of more practical issues of craft and professional development, alludes directly to the metaphors invoked in the title of this essay. In fact, the title itself is drawn from two very different accounts of a writing workshop, *Master Class: Scenes From a Fiction Workshop,* by Paul West (2004), and 'One Month's Work,' by David Craig (1992). *Master Class,* hailed on the cover as a 'pitch perfect' memoir of West's last writing class at the University of Pennsylvania, in which West imparts the writing wisdom he has learned over the decades. It is described as a perfect example of the cult of personality that the classroom can foster (West even boasts that by the end of the semester, his students can tell his stories *for* him) as the professor exhorts his students to read a particular page of Proust before succumbing to sleep each night until the words suffuse their dreams. David Craig's description of his workshop class, 'One Month's Work,' on the other hand, is distinguished by it's *lack* of abstraction and 'master-apprentice' emphasis, as, much like Cook's (2001: 302) ideal workshop: 'conversation amongst technicians to make an engine work better.'

Likewise, in the *Creative Writing Coursebook,* loosely based, according to editors Julia Bell and Paul Magrs, on the University of East Anglia perspective, aspiring writers 'won't hear talk about muses, flashes of inspiration or powerful overflow of emotion' (Bell & Magrs, 2001: 17). Such a declaration echoes what American writer and teacher Janet Burroway observed in England in the 'unpretentious, workaday attitudes or writers' during her time there in the 1960's. This 'workaday' craft/technique-based pedagogy may also hark back to early conceptions of the workshop, a term closely associated with nineteenth century Great Britain and describing the 'world of industrial or artisan labour' (Cook, 2001: 296).

Burroway goes on to lament that perhaps this 'unpretentious, workaday,' atmosphere has declined over the years, that the UK may be evincing an unnatural interest in the star system (hiring star writers who teach very little, just to attract attention to a program) that so many American writers openly disdain but seem powerless to overthrow – or are not interested in overthrowing. Although as an outside observer it is difficult to comment definitively on whether the star system in the UK has the kind of foothold it does in the US, it is easy to see that the UK *does* have the benefit of the American example as a cautionary tale. Caught in the stranglehold of a system that renders many Creative Writing programs ungainly cash cows that pursue high profile, semi-permanent, semi-available faculty, the current status quo degrades the quality of Creative Writing instruction in both undergraduate and graduate classrooms. These classrooms evince, according to American writer Rick Moody (2005: 12), diluted teaching and a general lack of long-term mentoring. What's more, such superficial systems are bound to perpetuate themselves, as graduate students have little recourse but to, as Kelly Ritter (2006: 8) observes 'imitate the teacher in the absence of viable alternatives.' Ethos in the creative writing classroom, Ritter notes, is not enacted as best practice but 'through the personal experiences and highly respected testimony of the successful author,' where to learn is to 'bask in the ethereal glow', aka to sleep with a volume of Proust and to hope one day just to be like said writer (Ritter, 2006: 8).

This is not to overlook the small but vocal number of US creative writers, the late Wendy Bishop, Hans Ostrum, Katherine Haake, Patrick Bizarro, Mary Ann Cain and Tim Mayers, to name a few, who have lobbied hard to promote reflective teaching in the creative writing classroom, to suggest alternatives to the traditional 'workshop' and to unpack its aims and intentions. Still, as Kelly Ritter and I have pointed out (Ritter & Vanderslice, 2005), the lack of attention of university Creative Writing programs to the pedagogy of the field continues to exist as a general condition in the US. This condition is perhaps best illustrated by an anecdote, one that is unfortunately not uncommon in the teaching of Creative Writing in the US today. Not long ago, a nationally-recognized author and faculty member at a well-known undergraduate Creative Writing program (where he'd also had a turn as director), came to visit our campus and work with our students. When I discussed with him some of the work I do promoting Creative Writing pedagogy, he admitted, rather ingenuously, that he had never heard of any 'alternative''s to the workshop and wondered if I might share some with him. That there might be an emerging field concerning the teaching of Creative Writing was a revelation to him – a teacher of Creative Writing.

A Forward Glance: Possible Solutions

So what to do? And what does the status of Creative Writing in the US have to do with that in the UK? First, creative writers who engage in 'craft criticism' – what Tim Mayers (2005: 36) describes as the kind of reflective writing about teaching and curricular issues that can revitalize the Creative

Writing classroom – must continue to call for 'a greater willingness on the part of those institutionally defined as creative writers to acknowledge the crucial role that institutions have played in shaping who they are and what they do' as opposed to regarding their institutional position as 'purely incidental to what and who they are' (Mayers, 2005: 60). Second, while American programs may not have to answer to the same centralized governing bodies as their British counterparts do, there are definitely national movements afoot (embodied in initiatives such as the National Commission on Writing) to improve writing in the population overall. They might consider preemptively hitching their stars to these movements, so to speak. Such an endeavor would merely involve articulating and promoting the ways in which Creative Writing courses *do* improve the communications and critical thinking[4] skills of their students, as well as the ways in which they can assist student's understanding and learning of literature. Such skills are unquestionable assets in any contemporary work-place.

Beyond this 'easy' solution, however, lies the indisputable fact that despite recent efforts, US practitioners still need to unite to declare the sort of 'systemic pedagogy,' Harper describes. In doing so, moreover, they need not reinvent the wheel; a cursory glance at the reflective teaching occurring – and being described in essays, books, and websites – in the UK and other English speaking countries will provide a healthy springboard for discussion and reflection.

Perhaps most evident, however, is that the teaching and learning of Creative Writing, like that of most disciplines, is not well served by black-and-white generalizations that Creative Writing can't be taught, that attempts to focus on teaching and reflect upon its institutions and practices only distract from the sacred process of composition. Rather, room exists at the table for both the Romantic concept of creative writing, involving, as Tim Mayers (2005: 66) describes them, an 'aesthetics of inspiration,' and for a Craftsman model driven by an 'aesthetics of work.' Surely, a 'declared' pedagogy invoking – and understanding – both aesthetics rather than dismissing one or the other will provide the strongest fabric for teaching and learning and for ensuring the sustainability of the discipline. Perhaps neither sleeping with Proust nor tinkering under the bonnet work to explain and undergird Creative Writing as a discipline then, as each meta-phor severs two intricately intertwined aspects of the process: invention and technique, neither of which can exist in isolation from the other. Perhaps the next step is identifying a new metaphor which unites them both.

Notes

1. Also known in the US as the hood.
2. A report commissioned by the Blair administration in 1997. Its conclusions called for increased attention to pedagogy at the university level as well as for enhancing and assessing student learning outcomes.
3. There are notable exceptions across the nation, but as a whole undergraduate writing curriculum in the US has suffered by receiving the hand-me-down of graduate workshop pedagogy, an ill-fitting garment at best.
4. For a succinct discussion of these connections, see Graeme Harper (2006) 'Responsive critical understanding: Towards a Creative Writing treatise.'

References

Arvon Foundation (2006) Online at http://www.arvonfoundation.org. Accessed 14.05.06.

AWP (2004) *The AWP Official Guide to Writing Programs*. Fairfax: Association of Writers and Writing Programs.

Bell, J. (2001) Introduction: Workshops. In J. Bell and P. Magrs (eds) *The Creative Writing Coursebook* (pp. 292–295). London: Macmillan.

Bell, J. and Magrs, P. (eds) (2001) *The Creative Writing Coursebook*. London: Macmillan.

Burroway, J. (1992) The American experience. In R. Miles and M. Monteith (eds) *Teaching Creative Writing: Theory and Practice* (pp. 59–65). Philadelphia: Open University Press.

Cook, J. (2001) A brief history of workshops. In J. Bell and P. Magrs (eds) *The Creative Writing Coursebook* (pp. 296–302). London: Macmillan.

Craig, D. (1992) One month's work. In R. Miles and M. Monteith (eds) *Teaching Creative Writing: Theory and Practice* (pp. 145–155). Philadelphia: Open University Press.

Grimes, T. (1999) *The Workshop: Seven Decades of the Iowa Writer's Workshop*. New York: Hyperion.

Harper, G. (2002) Creative writing in the university comes of age. National Association of Writers in Education. On WWW at http://www.nawe.co.uk/metadot/index.pl?id=30781&isa=DBRow&op=show&dbview_id=2487. Accessed 18.01.07.

Harper, G. (2006) Responsive critical understanding: Towards a Creative Writing treatise. *New Writing* 3 (1).

Holland, S. (2003) *Creative Writing: A Good Practice Guide*. London: English Subject Centre.

Lin, S. G-L. (2003) The strangeness of Creative Writing: An institutional query. *Pedagogy* 3, 151–69.

Marsh, G. (1992) 43%: A commentary on aims and assessments in the teaching of literary writing. In R. Miles and M. Monteith (eds) *Teaching Creative Writing: Theory and Practice* (pp. 45–58). Philadelphia: Open University Press.

Mayers, T. (2005) *(Re)Writing Craft: Composition, Creative Writing and the Future of English Studies*. Pittsburgh: University of Pittsburgh Press.

Miles, R. (1992) Creative Writing, contemporary theory and the English curriculum. In R. Miles and M. Monteith (eds) *Teaching Creative Writing: Theory and Practice* (pp. 34–44). Philadelphia: Open University Press.

Monteith, M. (1992) Creative Writing: A historical perspective. In R. Miles and M. Monteith (eds) *Teaching Creative Writing: Theory and Practice* (pp. 10–23). Philadelphia: Open University Press.

Moody, R. (2005) Writers and mentors. *The Atlantic Monthly* (August), 9–13.

Myers, D.G. (1996) *The Elephants Teach: Creative Writing Since 1880*. Englewood Cliffs: Prentice Hall.

Ritter, K. (2006) Ethos interrupted: Diffusing 'star' pedagogy in the Creative Writing classroom. Unpublished manuscript.

Ritter, K. and Vanderslice, S. (2005) Teaching lore: Creative Writers and the University. *Profession*, pp. 102–112.

West, P. (2001) *Master Class: Scenes From a Fiction Workshop*. New York: Harcourt.

Chapter 7

Workshopping the Workshop and Teaching the Unteachable

KEVIN BROPHY

A Poet doesn't make a poem, something in him naturally becomes a poem.
Basho

Poetry is everywhere; it just needs editing.
James Tate

In order to write a poem you must first invent the poet to write it.
Antonio Machado

You cannot be a poet unless you have first read a poem.
Anthony Hecht

Go home and write
a page tonight
and let that page come out of you –
then, it will be true.
Langston Hughes

Bring the balloon of the mind
... Into its narrow shed.
W.B. Yeats

The intellect is characterised by a natural inability to understand life.
Henri Bergson

Fergus's brain was a perpetual workshop of scheme and intrigue.
Sir Walter Scott

In 1929 Mary Cecil Allen, an Australian painter and art teacher living in New York, wrote a book called *Painters of the Modern Mind*. The preface opens with a question put to a hypothetical artist: 'Why do you paint?' The answer given is, 'Because things I see excite me and I want to reproduce this feeling'.

This seems simple. Nothing could be more direct or more simple than this, could it? The artist bursts into drawing just as a singer or a bird might burst into song. The beauty of the painter's answer is its acceptance of the primary place of emotion in the production of art. But we sense at once that there is something missing in this answer, or perhaps in our understanding of what the artist means. Is excitement really what art and literature are

75

about? The questioner in Allen's preface goes on to ask: 'Then if you reproduce visible nature on canvas, you will also reproduce your excitement?' The artist answers, 'No, because it is not an image but an idea that excites me. It is the idea I want to realise on my canvas. If I realise the image hoping that it will also realise my idea, it is a travesty because it is only raw material at the end and not an idea at all' (Allen, 1929).

This extension of the artist's answer complicates the picture. Excitement is central, yes, but the intellect apparently drives this excitement into existence. Allen's depiction of the modern artist reverses the lastingly influential stance of the imagists who held that accurate, unadorned depiction of particular material objects must be paramount in order to avoid the dreariness of most people's ideas. In the introduction to a 1930 anthology of imagist poetry, Ford Madox Ford (1930: xiii) asserted that 'poetic ideas are best expressed by the rendering of concrete objects'. In his later autobiography William Carlos Williams (1951: 390) famously remarked, 'for the poet there are no ideas but in things'. In the same passage, he remarks, 'it all depends on what you call profound', signalling that, like Mary Cecil Allen (1929), he considers ideas to be central to the production of art, but wanted to find those ideas through the medium of the particular, the local, the concrete. How complex is the relation between idea and feeling, feeling and idea, and how might the artist-writer manage it? These will be the concerns of this chapter.

Mary Cecil Allen's book was aimed at helping viewers understand how to look at the then relatively new art of surrealists, expressionists, futurists, precisionists, cubists and other progressives. She insisted that a painting must be more than an illustration, and more than raw material, if it is to be art. She pointed out that when Turner painted clouds and mists he was not intent on illustrating English weather conditions for us, and when Matisse drew a woman's body he was not defining the anatomy of an individual for us. These painters were investigating ideas that excited them as artists. Turner was intent on technical strategies for producing the moving effects of light in opaque oils on canvas, while Matisse was investigating the meaning of rhythm and beauty in each line he placed on a surface. In addition, they were both responding radically to a cultural history. Allen made the point that a naive viewing of art sees paintings as essentially sentimental, scientific, pornographic or moral illustrations. Such an approach to art leads to disappointment or outrage when art does not illustrate accurately enough or does not illustrate at all. The same goes for literature when readers seek in texts either merely the effects of realism or illustrations of whatever values they desire to see validated.

I might equally ask of myself, why do I write poetry? – and give the same answer that Allen's hypothetical artist gave: namely, I am excited by what I have experienced, and I want to reproduce this feeling in words. But can this be all that is going on? If I write a poem about something my child said or did, or a poem about the front doors in my street or a dog up the road, is it enough to transcribe what is said to me or describe what I see and hear as accurately as possible? Would that be enough? After all, I could argue, don't the spontaneous words of a first draft convey original excitement most directly – as something in me *naturally becomes a poem*?

Workshopping the Workshop

Denial of the naturalness of art or literature begins and justifies the process of the workshop; and the writing workshop in these times signals to students that they are part of a Creative Writing class. The workshop, by its nature as a deliberate and conscious training-ground for apprentices or a place of learning-through-experiment, denies the spontaneity of art for it foregrounds skill, learning, decision-making, the application of critical intelligence and theoretical frameworks, the presence of a demanding audience, the revisions and redrafting necessary to reach an intimate ideal or standard.

Yet the workshop itself is a live event, dominated by spontaneous responses, group dynamics, all the naturalness and excitement of live reactions to a piece of writing – alternately sentimental, political, personal, inspirational or dampening. It is possible that Allen was glossing over the almost insurmountable difficulty of bringing both excitement and ideas into play at once. It is, perhaps, rather in a *contest* between excitement and ideas, between intellect and emotion, that art can be produced. For this reason, I want to argue in this discussion that it becomes important always to be workshopping the workshop and aiming to teach the unteachable.

I will address some of the immediate problems I have encountered with both the workshop and the practice of creative writing in the light of Allen's assertion that excitement is connected with ideas when art is at its best, and in my consequent suggestion that this connection is best characterised as a contest or at least an uneasiness.

'Initiatory rites are always bloody', Stevie Smith (1972: 56) writes in her poem, 'Sunt Leones'. While initiating a new group of 24 students into a Creative Writing workshop at the beginning of a semester, one student asked if there would be restrictions on what they could write about. This question seemed to arise out of anxiety over what the rules of engagement or ritual might be, and possibly signalled students' anxiety over what the eventual devastation might be for individual writer-students if they took too many risks. At the end of the previous year I had received a note from a student who was unhappy with the mark she received for her creative work, which did take risks. She wrote that she was proud of the piece of writing for which she had received a mediocre mark. It was, she said, the style of writing she had developed at school and university and it had always been received favourably by her other teachers. She allowed that everyone's opinion could be different, but did not want to believe that assessed work ultimately came down to personal taste. She added that she had six different people read her story and each one had uncovered a different interpretation, a fact that did not trouble her but rather excited her to continue to write. The workshop, and with it the delivery of criticism, opinion and eventually grading, can be for some students a dismemberment of that excitement so crucial to the impulse to create. At the end of that note I was relieved to read the student's expression of determination to continue.

In his recent long meditation on university education, and taking his lead from Foucault, George Steiner (2003: 4) has proposed, 'Teaching could be regarded as an exercise, open or concealed, in power relations'. It would be no consolation to students to hear that teachers and lecturers do not feel powerful and do not revel in the responsibilities that might seem to students to be an exercise of power. Yes, it is sensible for students to pay close attention to the particular bent, the particular enthusiasms of a teacher. But even this strategy taken in anxiety and possibly disillusion need not be reduced to a cynical lesson in the exercise of power relations, for there can be learning in both submission to instruction and assertion of oneself against one's teacher. The clear answer to the student's question about whether there would be restrictions on what can be written must be that there are no restrictions. But of course there are always restrictions, as Freud discovered when he invited his patients to speak freely and without inhibition.

The above almost insoluble problem for the workshop can be a source of that uneasiness, that contest that can sharpen both excitement and ideas. The workshop, in this view, should be a flawed, unequal and difficult experience if it is to provoke and stimulate creativity of the kind Mary Cecil Allen described.

Aside from this question of power relations, there is the question of what kind of conversation is generated in a Creative Writing workshop. We are generally clumsy at talking about emotions in a public forum or an educational setting. With writing workshops, however, as already noted, descriptions of one's emotional involvement are often the first resort when expressing reactions to a new piece of writing.

Why is it that workshops so often fall into discussion of writing as illustration of experience or feeling? I was asked not what *kinds* of writing would be acceptable, but whether there were restrictions on what students could write *about*. There is no escaping feelings once writing becomes creative, but if we remain with feelings then practice is dissipated through a delta of ultimately isolated individual consciousnesses. Every writer, every student, becomes their own authority, their own universe. After asserting that there are no ideas but in things, and that 'the poet thinks with his poem', William Carlos Williams (1951: 390–1) does go to considerable length to describe the ideas that informed his long poem, *Paterson*. Like Allen, he acknowledged the importance of including ideas in any discussion of poetry, not just feelings.

The workshop, I argue, must be a strange and difficult process if it is to work. Each writer wants to know, and I am convinced needs to know, what the literate, interested, intelligent reader makes of his or her work. But at the same time the workshop is meant to function for students as a technical and intellectual training ground where they can experiment safely. The trick is to keep the conversation moving between the immediacy of excitement and the teasing out of those ideas that embed writing in an intellectual history. Moving too far to one side of this discussion will enervate the workshop. Keeping both elements present makes the workshop almost an unworkable occasion. For the teacher, the strangeness and difficulty must become the point, for as Donald Barthelme (1997: 15) has written, 'Art is not difficult because it wishes to be difficult, but because it wishes to be art'. Such uneasy workshops must aim to position students to bring the best out of themselves.

So far I have raised the problem of unequal power relations in a Creative Writing workshop and the importance of finding a way to retain excitement and spontaneity in discussions while also exploring, analytically and intellectually, the ideas relevant to a piece of work. Instead of discovering solutions to these challenges I am suggesting that they need to be fostered as ongoing contests, and managed as ongoing provocations to creativity.

A further risk is that for the student sometimes this strangeness and difficulty can produce a workshop experience so potent it becomes its own end. What do students learn from workshopping? Might it be that some (too many) learn no more than how to survive workshops? Breaking down the process of education we might say there are three steps to it:

(1) the student absorbs or creates information (sometimes called knowledge);

(2) the student performs this knowledge in a written assignment, exam, laboratory exercise, thesis, or actual performance;

(3) and finally the student receives feedback in the form of comment, grade, indication of success or failure.

The workshop ideally fits somewhere late in the second step and has a place in the early parts of the third step. One difficulty, though, with this three-step model is that it suggests a process where feedback occurs at the end of a semester, a subject, a year, a project. Over the time I have been teaching, when we receive student evaluations at the end of a subject, no matter how well students evaluate their Creative Writing lecturers for being well prepared, well organised, clear and interesting in communication, there is almost always an expressed desire for more feedback. Feedback might work best when it is frequent, focused on specific skills, and occurs at all three steps of the educational process, despite the suggested order of events in the above traditional model. This is difficult to manage across one semester in a classroom with 15 or 20 students who must first discover and absorb terminology, ideas, and models (e.g. through reading fiction, poetry or scripts and critical or theoretical commentary) then have time to produce work of a standard that can be workshopped fruitfully. At best a student might receive feedback twice in the course of a semester, which is, as students keep pointing out, not enough. Nevertheless the workshop dominates a Creative Writing semester's class time, so much so that what a student learns most effectively might be how to cope with the workshop as a ritual, as a contest, a conversation, a group event, a formula. By the end of a semester of Creative Writing it might be that a student has become more a skilled practitioner (or addict?) of the workshop than a committed writer. This is the danger of all teaching – that the lessons learned will be the unintended ones. The danger for students is the very usual one for anyone under stress, that of seeking a path of least effort. What can be lost sight of is the contest between excitement and ideas: that is, the writing itself that needs to happens outside the workshop.

Perhaps one strategy for keeping the focus on writing rather than on negotiating survival, expressing feelings, or achieving mastery of a workshop regime is to create more frequent feedback and vary the methods by which students receive it. Sometimes the workshopping might include the whole class, sometimes it could be broken into small groups from within the class, or done in pairs. Sometimes it is possible to set up an Internet forum where workshopping of another kind can be pursued among interested students. Sometimes groups of students form their own peer workshopping outside the subject, and this too can be encouraged by providing contact details and spaces where students can gather. Sometimes, instead of workshopping the actual texts students write, it is possible to invite them to talk with another student about their work without showing it. Another form of workshopping is the public reading, for simply reading one's work aloud in front of others can ignite in the writer a critical consciousness not otherwise easily produced. This variety might keep reminding students that the point is always the writing itself, not mastery of classroom procedures and power relations. One risk in such a varied approach is a loss of the kind of control that prevents the conversation veering too far to one side of the necessary tension between excitement and ideas. I have taken some cautious steps towards intensifying and varying the forms of feedback in Creative Writing workshops, with my own anxiety rising from the possibility that these varied forms of workshopping might not be moving students towards the kind of understandings I will be seeking evidence of when the marking happens. I am convinced, though, that more feedback leads to more writing.

Hopefully the writing outside the workshop becomes a habit and a compulsion tinting all thoughts and all experiences with its presence. Many students have the desire to do it but not the habit, not the compulsion, not the identification with themselves as writer. When the writing arrives at the workshop there can be no guarantee that the experience will be positive or even useful. It must be a risk. The teacher's job might most usefully be not to take too much of the risk out of the experience.

I am committed to the workshop because it does expose writing to audiences. It is possible to discover for oneself that one's writing does not yet excite or invite interest in readers. When a piece of writing has excited interest, puzzlement, and complex thinking, this too can often become clear. With workshopping there is the added excitement of encountering work whose potential one can sense, and when this happens it is as if everyone has become involved in a journey this work might take as it discovers its particular elusive shape and voice. The workshop must always take place as the natural consequence of the necessary and primary solitude of the writer writing.

I have been arguing that the workshop might be most successful when it mirrors that contest between ideas and excitement central to creativity. In doing this, the workshop might never settle into predictability; it must always be not only a risky experience but an unsatisfactory one – though hopefully one that participants will relish.

Teaching the Unteachable

The workshop cannot happen, as already stated, unless writing takes place first. In telling students there are no restrictions on their writing, I might be sending them helpless to the confounding blankness of the blank page (or screen). How does a poem get written? Does it arise naturally? Do we have to learn how to do it before we do it? How do I find a place somewhere between excitement and ideas? Is writing after all unteachable?

With these troubling questions in mind I want to show some poems and discuss them, one of mine included, each of them about sitting down to write a poem. These are more than meditations on the blank page, such a common starting point for writing, but given that blank page these poems suggest ways of tipping images out of the mind into a poem.

First, 'The Balloon of the Mind' by William Butler Yeats:

> Hands, do what you're bid:
> Bring the balloon of the mind
> That bellies and drags in the wind
> Into its narrow shed. (Yeats, 1956: 155)

This seems to be a call to himself, the poet, as he sits at his desk in front of his difficult blank page. What to do with the wild and shapeless, current-driven thoughts of the mind as it flies past the poet at his desk? There are three recourses suggested for the poet. One is to make his hands do the work, for it is the hands that produce writing, as much as it might be the mind. In other words, the body is involved in this process and in fact directs it. Secondly there is that narrow shed. How are we to understand the narrow shed? It is a shape that houses the shapeless, a place to rest the wind-blown, wind-torn fabric of the mind for a time; I understand the shed to be the poem or the idea of the poem, a place of narrowness as lines and rhythms shape it. A poem argues, or asserts, that form is necessary if the mind is ever to be in contact with others or even itself. The shed-poem is a place we can enter. The third recourse of the poet is imagery or trope. The hands understand how to reel in the mind. The mind is a wild balloon in the wind, and the task of these hands is to bring the balloon in to the narrow shed that will house it. Just as the poem begins with the body ('Hands'), its most abstract elements are made physical through this imagery.

Yeats's poem is not triumphal and is not simply about what is happening, for the reluctant hands here need to be commanded. The mind seems not only wild and loose but large and possibly terrifying. It is not certain that the hands will be able to confine it to the narrow shed, nor is it clear that the mind won't lose its power once it is confined. The poem might be one that calls on poetry to bring the wild mind back into shape or it might be a call of despair as the mind, again, refuses to be fitted to a mere shed. This possibility of double reading is part of the kind of thinking important to poetry. It is this doubleness that can generate the critical distance from an experience that shapes it as poetry.

The poem brings us to the shed as an endpoint. The shed is such a strangely unexpected place to find ourselves in at the end of this poem. What suggested this image to Yeats? It might have been as simple as looking out the window at his garden as he sat there with his blank page and wild mind. Similarly, it might have been drizzling outside the window when Dylan Thomas called the 'painful, voluntary work' (Fitzgibbon, 1965: 327) of writing 'my craft or sullen art ... / ... on these spindrift pages' (Thomas, 1988: 926). Looking out the window can be as important as looking into the blank page. Yeats's short, strangled cry of a poem works because it takes up what is to hand and works it.

More than two years ago I began a poem grown from the title 'Difficult'. In part it was a response to Wallace Stevens' (1988: 302) poem, 'The Plain Sense of Things', itself a difficult and opaque poem despite its title's promise of clarity. Wallace Stevens (1996: 784) reflected that his poem seemed to have nothing to do with anything in particular except poetry. In it, like Yeats, Stevens is writing into the idea of blankness: 'It is difficult even to choose the adjective/ For this blank cold, this sadness without cause'. My poem turned out to be a poem about writing a poem – a possible poem. It took up the image of the poem as a place one could enter.

It is difficult to choose the reader for this poem.
I have left its windows open
so you might as well climb inside
where you can be safe for now from weather,
and though your sudden presence feels intrusive
think of yourself as a museum visitor
to a reconstruction of a life now silenced.
The bed, I know, has not been made
but the silver cutlery on the formal dining table is meticulous.
You will not be roped out of any room
and you can be confident
the writer left before you and your party arrived.
The place is left as realistic as anything you might write yourself.
Dirty clothes (for instance) are piled into a predictable straw basket,
their odour not quite animal or human,
though the stiffening socks were plainly meant for feet.
It is difficult to choose a visitor who must arrive by chance.
Parents too are difficult to choose
though they're chosen all the same.
The plain truth is the bricks outside are wet with rain
and now you find yourself inside

the couch is sprinkled with the drops that just blew in with you
through the curtains of the open window.
Sounds of possums in the poem's ceiling must distract you,
a blackbird in the yard outside is startlingly alive,
the cat inside will stay asleep despite your tread,
and a green bin steaming with the evidence of wasteful life
in a corner of the kitchen is what you've come to expect from art.
The lived-in emptiness of every room
makes it difficult to choose a reader for this poem.
No meal has been prepared and no money has been left
in an envelope with your name on it.
The vases are all empty.
A man has written this you must suspect.
Blue sky outside presses down on us its single thought.
A green and oily ocean's creeping closer every century
and an ochre desert lies less than three thousand kilometres away.
It is difficult to know what is the greatest threat to this poem:
reader, silence, landscape, weather or its absent occupant. (Brophy,
2004: 12)

The poem that might be written has been the inspiration for many poems. When Alice Sebold, at a workshop at Syracuse University wanted to write of the experience of being raped, Tess Gallagher gave her the opening line: *If they caught you.* This gave Sebold a way to begin writing the poem that until then could not be written (Sebold, 1999: 106–107). This line took her wild, bellying, unformed thoughts and feelings into their necessary shed, a hypothetical one.

'Difficult' also has its connection to a poem by Billy Collins (1988), titled 'Introduction to Poetry'. In part, this goes as follows:

I ask them to take a poem
and hold it up to the light
like a color slide

or press an ear against its hive.

I say drop a mouse into a poem
and watch him probe his way out,

or walk inside the poem's room
and feel the walls for a light switch. (Collins, 1988: 58)

This poem does not just ask us to take up the poem we are reading now and treat it as imaginatively as possible, but as it progresses it asks us to consider what kinds of workshops we take our poems to, and what kind of education might surround them. Part of the cleverness of the poem is its play against its textbook title. One can imagine sitting, as a student, with such a textbook on one's desk, wondering how to begin a poem of one's own. Why not begin with what is here at hand.

From poem as shed, house, and darkened room we move to the poem as assignment, for I want to end with the following assignment-poem. This poem workshops the act of writing poetry. It is an initiation rite. The poet, Langston Hughes (1902–1967) was an Afro-American whose father wanted him to become an engineer. In the following poem he reflects on the experience of being asked to do some creative writing in an undergraduate university subject at Columbia University in the 1920s. Soon after this, he dropped out of university, though he returned to study in later life. The poem encapsulates many of the issues raised in this discussion. Interconnectedness of all people and all things is a pervasive idea throughout poetry. Culture and politics, history and power are there pressing in on the poem. Who is learning from whom? What is expected when a poem is itself *and* an assignment? Should the poem ignore its existence as an assignment? The question of whether a poem is the simple expression of an individual's thoughts or something else is addressed. It contests the aesthetic principle apparently offered by his teacher: that if the writing truly comes out of you, the writing will be true – one side of the contest we have been tracing in this discussion. Hughes's poem includes verbatim the words of the teacher, then obediently rambles through biographical details only to explode against the word 'you' (linked with 'true' in the teacher's dictum), playing it out across 'part of me' and 'part of you', including 'America' and the problem of black and white – always an issue when truth (as well as power) is at stake. Finally, against the teacher's rhyming of 'you' and 'true', the poem ends with 'free' and 'English B' – a rhyme that sets its two parts against each other as much as with each other. The poem is about writing complex poetry in plain language. It faces, squarely, the terror and the trouble of getting that balloon into its narrow shed. The poem is called 'Theme for English B', and following are lines extracted from it:

> The instructor said,
> *Go home and write*
> *a page tonight.*
> *and let that page come out of you –*
> *Then, it will be true.*
> I wonder if it's that simple?

I am twenty-two, colored, born in Winston-Salem.
I went to school there, then Durham, then here
to this college on the hill above Harlem.
...
It's not easy to know what is true for you or me
at twenty-two, my age.
...
So will my page be colored that I write?
Being me, it will not be white.
But it will be
a part of you, instructor.
You are white –
Yet a part of me, as I am a part of you.
That's American.
Sometimes perhaps you don't want to be a part of me.
Nor do I often want to be a part of you.
But we are, that's true!
As I learn from you,
I guess you learn from me –
although you're older – and white –
and somewhat more free.

This is my page for English B. (Hughes, 1994: 409–10)

Each of the above poems arises from the difficulty of beginning, or from the most unpromising starting point, but each of them finds an excitement of feeling and intellect to shape it. The excitement can be something that happens quietly in a room at a table, gazing out the window, a book open in front of you, an assignment there to be done.

Importantly, reading poems can be a source of the kind of excitement that creates new poetry. Poems I read excite me to want to write. In my experience, the writing of students gathers force and direction when it is driven into being not just from experience but from that strange mix of excitement and ideas found in others' poems – in the workshop, in anthologies, on CDs, at live readings or out there on the Web. In order to make clear what a poem is the teacher points to a poem, many poems. In order to understand what a poem could be a student sits in front of a poem and examines it. Pointing and gazing. These are perhaps all that are needed for poetry to generate excitement and ideas.

References

Allen, M.C. (1929) *Painters of the Modern Mind*. New York: Norton.

Barthelme, D. (1997) *Not-Knowing: The Essays and Interviews*. New York: Random House.

Brophy, K. (2004) Difficult. In P. Rose (ed.) *Australian Book Review* 261 (May), 12.

Collins, B. (1988) *The Apple that Astonished Paris*. Fayetteville: University of Arkansas Press.

Ford, F.M. (1930) *Those Were the Days. Imagist Anthology 1930*. London: Chatto and Windus.

Fitzgibbon, C. (1965) *The Life of Dylan Thomas*. Boston: Little, Brown.

Hughes, L. (1994) Theme for English B. In A. Rampersand (ed.) *The Collected Poems of Langston Hughes* (pp. 409–410). New York: Knopf.

Sebold, A. (1999) *Lucky*. New York: Picador.

Smith, S. (1972) Sunt Leones. In *Collected Poems* (p. 56). New York: New Directions.

Steiner, G. (2003) *Lessons of the Masters: The Charles Eliot Norton Lectures 2001–2002*. London: Harvard University Press.

Stevens, W. (1996) *Letters of Wallace Stevens* (H. Stevens, ed.). Berkeley: University of California Press (first published 1966).

Stevens, W. (1988) The Plain Sense of Things. In R. Ellmann and R. O'Clair (eds) *The Norton Anthology of Modern Poetry* (p. 302). New York: Norton.

Thomas, D. (1988) In My Craft or Sullen Art. In R. Ellmann and R. O'Clair (eds) *The Norton Anthology of Modern Poetry* (p. 926). New York: Norton.

Williams, W.C. (1951) *The Autobiography*. New York: Random House.

Yeats, W.B. (1956) The Balloon of The Mind. In R. Finneran (ed.) *The Poems: A New Edition* (p. 155). London: Macmillan.

Chapter 8

Creating an Integrated Model for Teaching Creative Writing: One Approach

NIGEL MCLOUGHLIN

The aim of this chapter is to examine the various ways in which research and scholarly activity, creative and critical processes and practices, and pedagogical theories and methodologies interact within the discipline of Creative Writing. Let me say at the outset that what follows is drawn from my own reflective consideration of my personal practices as a writer, critic and teacher. I see these roles as deeply interconnected within a system that integrates the practices and theories within each of the sub-disciplines in such a way that they inform and reinforce each other. There are areas of conflict certainly, but conflict is good. If used correctly these conflicts can allow us to bring to bear a number of separate viewpoints on a problem and get a more three-dimensional view of it. That is what this chapter attempts: to use the various viewpoints of teacher, writer and critic to walk around the discipline of Creative Writing and get an overview of how the relation-ships within the discipline operate. For me, research and scholarly activity in Creative Writing takes place in four directions: I have come to refer to these as the four 'ps': poesis, praxis, process and pedagogy. I intend to unpack the ideas surrounding each of these and how they impact on my work as a writer, critic and teacher. The ultimate purpose is to come up with a model that can be used to look at how I might teach writing, criticism and pedagogy at an advanced level using practice-led research to inform teaching and transferring the skills in each area to students in the most effi-cient and writerly manner possible.

When I sat down and examined what exactly I did, I realised that my functions as writer, critic and teacher could be represented as a series of concentric circles. At the centre I write. Everything stems from that. If I didn't write, I would not be interested in writerly criticism, because to write means one must also criticise in a writerly fashion. Writerly criticism is different from literary criticism. There is a difference of viewpoint. Literary criticism is concerned largely from the reader's viewpoint. What impact the text has on the reader, how different readers may read a text. While writerly criticism is concerned with that also, it is only part of the story, it is only ever a means to an end. A writer will examine a text critically in order to look closely at the effects it might have on the reader, and at different ways the text may be read, but the motivation is different. The writer may want to add an ambiguity or remove one; a writer may wish to engender a specific effect or set of effects on the reader. Either way, writerly critics are concerned with making the text 'better'. They tend to start from the premise that, this would work better if ... Each draft one writes, one acts as one's own critic with regard to whether the work satisfies or not and what changes might be made in order to make it satisfy. In effect one also becomes an editor. So that becomes my second circle: in effect that of the critic/editor.

Outside of that again there is another circle: I teach Creative Writing. For me the change between these two functions is part of an organic process. In criticising the work of others and making suggestions for textual changes while working with writer's groups and later within further and higher education, I began a journey towards teaching Creative Writing. At the outset I espoused the rather simplistic strategy of showing how certain pieces of writing might be, in my opinion, made better. This, of course, is not what teaching Creative Writing is about, making suggestions for improvement is only part of the process. Teaching creative writing, I soon realised, is about teaching the writer methodologies and practices that enable them to criticise and edit themselves. It is not just about saying: if you make these changes, it will be good. It is about enabling writers to learn from themselves. It quickly became apparent that exemplars of good and bad writing worked much better as a way of demonstrating, in practical terms, particularly fine writing or cliché and redundancy etc. in a less emotionally charged atmosphere. It enabled students to criticise and edit the writing of others and by extension their own writing, through using worked examples from other writers that pointed out certain features that students could recognise in their own work or try and adapt to their own uses. I still use the 'diagnostic workshop' to provide critique and advice on students' work, but now it is much more integrated into a mixed-methods approach rather than being the mainstay of my teaching.

Outside of that again, I teach students to criticise work, both their own work and the work of others. Teaching students to be critical requires balance between bringing out ideas they may have about how a text is working (or not working) and whether the text is good of its type. That means also teaching them that just because they don't 'like' a text, it does not mean that it is not working, or that there is nothing they can learn from it as a writer. In order to teach this, as great a variety of texts as possible are introduced and the students are asked to interrogate the text from several viewpoints: Does the text work? How does it work? Could it be improved and if so how? What are the constituencies out of which the text is written? What can the student learn from the text as a writer?

Finally, it occurs to me that I also teach the teaching of Creative Writing. Since most Creative Writing teachers learn to teach through watching their predecessors teach them, most pedagogical practices are passed on in a rather unstructured, piecemeal and almost osmotic or subliminal fashion. This is how I learned. I used the same methodologies my teachers used with me, and I learned to adapt them to different situations through experience and experiment. I learned or invented new methodologies from reading around the subject or through what I was experiencing in my own writing practices as I evolved as a writer. This atelier approach is changing. More and more modules are being offered in the teaching of Creative Writing, not least because more Creative Writing students intend to teach the subject when they graduate and are demanding modules dedicated to the pedagogy of their subject. The other reasons are, of course, that Creative Writing is such a growth area that we need teachers to teach on our undergraduate programmes, and we don't have time for them to 'learn by experience' because we need them now – so we need to invent courses and modules to fast-track the process. This may also be the reason why the literature on the pedagogy of writing is currently growing exponentially; after all we need materials in the form of theories and case studies to teach the courses!

On reflection, this presented a series of questions: What ties all of these things together? Is there an overarching approach that takes in all of the things that are taught? How is such an approach structured so that there is progression for the student? What processes act on them so that they come out at the other end of the programme as skilled writers, critics, editors and teachers? I began to examine what skills are needed: for the writer, there is the craft, obviously – the toolbox with which they make whatever it is that they make. Next there is the critical 'faculty' or, in the case of writers, perhaps critical 'faculties' is a more accurate term since there are different ways of criticising what we do. Obviously, there is also some form of practice-led research involved that takes what we discover through our previous writings, and our study and criticism of the writings of others and applies that knowledge to new work we produce either through the creative process or through the editing and rewriting process. Finally, there are the reflective elements where we examine what works best for us as writers, under what conditions we write best and how we trigger ourselves to write. This often involves the reflective consideration of a variety of stimuli. What we learn from this research and reflection is applied to our own processes and it influences our pedagogy. Certain stimuli are used as trigger exercises for students, and what one discovers through writing a poem is used as the basis of advice given to students. This led me to divide my research and my teaching methodologies broadly into four categories: poesis, praxis, process and pedagogy.

Poesis

I use 'poesis' in its platonic sense to refer to the skills necessary to enable the writer to 'make meaning' in the piece of writing. This is the craft element where the student looks at form and structure and 'gets the thing made'. This definition also contains the Socratic viewpoint of poesis as 'the imitation of imitation' since the words on the page describe the author's perceptions of reality, not reality itself. For a poet, poesis is inextricably linked to a 'toolbox' of forms and tropes that must be learned and understood. The key here is the 'understanding'. It is not just a case of learning to identify what trope à writer is using or what poetic form the writer is working in. It is more a case of knowing what a particular poetic form or trope does within the writing, and understanding how it works as a form or trope. This is not just about the rhetoric involved, although that is certainly part of it. It is about using the rhetorical devices as 'parts' to make a 'new machine', in which the linguistic and artistic effects on the reader have been carefully considered.

Praxis

Praxis deals with the elements of re-writing and self-criticism, which inform the actual 'practice of writing'. The term is taken from Friere (1972: 28), who defined it as a combination of transformative action and reflection and from Green (in *College English*, 2001: 154) who defined it as 'the language of use and action, of practice and implementation'. Clearly the 'action' here may be either the re-writing or the criticism, and the 'reflection' may also be applied to both. This makes the term doubly apt, especially since the two sub-processes are so inextricably linked. This self-critical, writerly approach looks at criticism on a number of levels.

Firstly, there is literary criticism, where the writer criticises the work in terms of a piece of literature, addressing what works and what doesn't, but including an element of writerly criticism that attempts to answer the question: How can I make it better? Likewise, this writerly approach extends to other texts and seeks to address questions such as: How does that author achieve his/her effects? What tropes do they use? What can I learn from these texts as a writer?

Yet another level of praxis critically analyses the constituency out of which the writer writes. This may include looking at a variety of literary theories, which may inform the writer's work from a political perspective, but may also look at traditions and movements that provide influences and directions in the writing. Then of course, there is the rewriting of the text to include the results of these critical processes and reflections. Praxis can therefore be seen as a cycle along similar lines to Kolb's cycle, as follows in Figure 8.1.

This cycle links at various points with poesis. The 'toolbox' is brought into play in a further set of steps in between the steps outlined in Figure 8.1, where the writer must ask him or herself 'What tools do I use to make the changes?' 'What tools do I use to decide if I've made it better?' etc. This demonstrates the linkages between the processes concerned with poesis and praxis and also demonstrates the importance of process in the over-arching framework, because process also is inextricably linked to praxis through the creative and critical processes that are brought to bear in the formulation and answering of the questions above and in the aesthetic, artistic, critical and practical decisions reached every time the cycle repeats itself as the drafting process continues.

If one takes Kolb's model (in Jarvis, 2004: 102), one can see that the integration of poesis, praxis and process follows Kolb's ideas on experiential learning very well. In the actual process of writing you have the 'concrete experience' that informs the 'reflective observation' of the writing through the critical processes. This informs the 'abstract conceptualisation' of looking at what various forms and tropes actually do, how they function within a piece of writing and how that understanding can be applied to other new pieces of writing in an original fashion. This leads very neatly to the 'active experimentation' phase of the cycle in which new writing is generated in light of these new understandings, and this in turn leads back to more 'concrete experience' in the process of writing the new or improved text.

This repeating cycle also fits remarkably well with John Dewey's (1997: 33–34) theories on Experiential Learning, especially his idea of the experiential continuum that allows learners to decide for themselves what experiences are educationally worthwhile. This operates within the model I describe through the questioning process at each stage of the cycle. It becomes an experientially selective process through the students applying

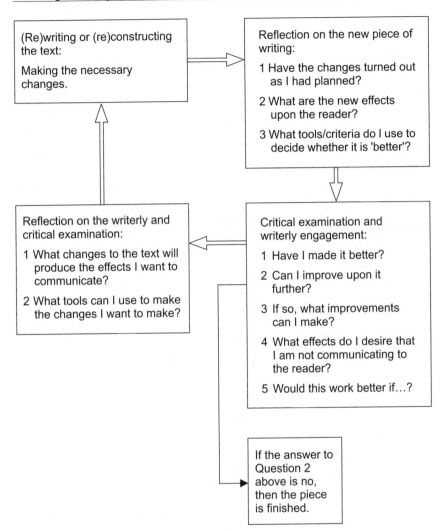

Figure 8.1 The cycle of creative writing praxis

knowledge they have gained through previous operations of the cycle to dictate the choices they make in succeeding operations of the cycle. They may then decide that certain operations are educationally less worthwhile since they have been tried before under similar circumstances but proved unsuccessful. It is to be remembered, however, that this operates along a continuum of usefulness. Strategies that have proved unsuccessful for one endeavour may prove successful for different types of endeavour and students must decide whether the strategy is educationally useful for the purpose they have in mind. Any decision the student makes will also be influenced by the experiential learning the student has built up regarding the strategy under consideration; and the decision may well change over time.

The basic philosophy that informs these views might be described as a type of constructive alternativism, as outlined by George Kelly (1963: 15), in that it assumes that *'all of our present interpretations of the universe are subject to revision or replacement.'* It depends on both the student and the teacher being open to changes in artistic and critical perception, which may occur through the processes of experiential learning. Or, to go back to our model in Figure 8.1, we must be open to the fact that the tools we use to solve the problems we identify in the writing are chosen from alternatives that are unstable and may change depending on how our artistic and critical perceptions change. We should, as writers and teachers, be aware of the processes involved in these changes.

Process

Process is concerned particularly with looking at methodologies that help the creative processes work better. This element concentrates on finding ways to make writing happen. It explores a variety of theoretical viewpoints on what the creative process actually is, and which triggers are of most use to the writer concerned. These processes, if properly understood can become a way for students to overcome problems they face in their writing. For us, as writers and teachers, they are also useful ways of finding creative solutions to pedagogical and critical problems that may present themselves. The key thing for the student is to understand how the creative processes operate on an individual basis in order to find ways in which they can help make what Heaney referred to as 'the gift' (quoted by Brown, 1986: 34) happen. Some students respond better to different types of stimuli than others – it is rather akin to being a visual, auditory or kinaesthetic learner. Some students will find that visual, verbal, tactile, olfactory or auditory triggers will work best for them. The teacher's job is to be aware of all the various types and to have a bank of triggers that can be used in order to help the student discover how the creative process works for them.

In breaking down the creative process, one must be aware that the process extends back beyond inspiration to the process of observation. Without observation (and here observation includes apprehension by any of the senses and apprehension through reading), there can be no trigger for the inspiration. In the Irish language the word for poet is *file* (pronounced fil-le) it takes its derivation from the verb 'to see' and its root meaning carries the nuance of 'a seer into things'. It has a sense that describes the beginnings of poetry, if we define that essence as the revealing of new ways of seeing things, perhaps in terms of other things, and perhaps more clearly as themselves. So learning how we observe, and learning to look at things and to 'see into them' is clearly a skill we should be teaching students to develop. How do we do this? One way is an object-based workshop. For this we can choose objects that are interesting in a number of different ways – something that appeals to as many senses as possible. I remember vividly, even now, the smell of a pipe given to me in a workshop and the bitter sting of the tobacco residue in the shaft when I put it between my lips. It looked interesting too. It was caked with cement. I felt the different textures, the weight of it. From all of these observations, a story began to weave itself in my head. The outcome was a sonnet, later published. This just goes to show how important it is to get the 'right' trigger exercises, and to find the 'right' trigger.

In Creative Writing an element of play is particularly important. Students should be free to take an initial trigger and play with it until it becomes something interesting, something more original and something the student owns. An example of this type of exercise might be giving out pieces of paper with clichés written on them and asking the student to re-invent the cliché and write a poem around the new central image. One might also offer the last line of a poem and ask students to take it as their starting point. Both of these exercises teach, in a very hands-on way, elements of Bloom's *Anxiety of Influence* and can be useful in demonstrating what exactly is meant by terms such as 'Clinamen' or 'Tessera' (Bloom, 1997: 14)

The next part of the process often centres on the ability to 're-visualise it all' as Gary Snyder (1980: 32) puts it. Such a system of creative visualisation is part empathy and part examination. It is necessary to see the thing from the inside and the outside simultaneously in order to get a view of the energetic 'shape' the thing makes in the world and how it feels to put on the essence of the thing. This touches on Hopkins' (1994: 1–6) theories of inscape and instress in very interesting ways. What the poet is endeavouring to do is to get as exact an apprehension as possible of the thing to be described in order that that apprehension can be communicated to the reader in as complete a way as possible. In the trigger exercises, students can be asked to provide images that describe the object to which their attention is directed from as many different sensual and abstract perspectives as they can and then to work these up into a poem.

These processes also have their own elements of praxis that require reflection on the actions carried out in order to help the writer and teacher decide just how useful such exercises are and if they can be improved upon. When one brings the learning cycle to bear on the creative process from this perspective, one gets a much more critically-aware engagement with the processes that the writer causes to work on his or her material. It can also help individuals to question, understand and hone their own creative processes to make them much more efficient. It can also broaden the creative processes through experimentation and reflection upon new techniques, which can then be analysed for usefulness. As teachers we can present these techniques to our students with some confidence that at least a proportion of those students will find them useful. Over time, we, as teachers, can also develop some guiding principles as to the type of students who might find a particular technique useful. It becomes a process of addition of 'specialist creative tools' to the toolbox rather than a reliance on the creative equivalent of 'Swiss army knives', which work to some extent for everyone and in all situations.

Pedagogy

In considering how pedagogy is integrated with poesis, praxis and process, the different types of pedagogy must be broken down into their constituent parts. In the first instance, the pedagogy of poesis consists of teaching the techniques, forms and tropes used in the writing of poems. It is also necessary to teach reflective understanding of these and this means teaching the student to critically engage with the forms and tropes from a writerly perspective. The student should be challenged to consider what each particular form or trope does; what it may be useful for; and what problems or issues the use of the particular trope or form raises from a writerly perspective. This engagement can then be tested through the production of pieces of 'writerly critical understanding' alongside the creative work in the assignments. This, ideally, should show that the student has made an informed conscious decision to use a particular form or trope and the artistic reasons behind it as well as a consideration of problems faced and some analysis of how these problems have been engaged with and reconciled.

In teaching praxis, a similar mix of theory, practical technique and writerly critical engagement can be taught. The student can be asked to study the drafting process, and how the poem changes through the process, giving sound artistic reasons for the changes made, which have stemmed directly from the reflection–action cycle. This can also safeguard against plagiarism, since the students will be asked to engage with and study the work as it is being produced and report back on the processes concerned. Similarly, when examining the creative process, students should be challenged to analyse the process, both from a theoretical and practical standpoint, thereby elucidating how the creative process works for them and learning about the creative processes involved in a much more experiential and therefore 'deep' way, rather than just reading about what others have said and regurgitating that 'surface' engagement.

In looking at the last piece of the jigsaw, the pedagogy of pedagogy, all of the above must be integrated in order to enable students to develop structured and comprehensive syllabi and courses that teach Creative Writing according to a philosophy that is compatible with the structures within the prevailing educational milieu. In my case, this generally means within adult, further and higher education in general and at university level particularly. The philosophy I espouse is constructionist and student-centric. I seek to enable students by providing structured learning environments within which they may be enabled to pursue their own development as writers, critics, editors, teachers and, most importantly, individuals.

Working on the principle that the university term is only so long and that one can't cram everything into level one, this means that certain elements must, of necessity, be prioritised at different stages. The structure I prefer is one where the concentration in Level One of the BA is very much on poesis since this forms the basic tool box that allows the writer to write. I see understanding of the various forms and tropes as crucial groundwork the writer must possess before moving on to the more complex issues drawn out by the examination of praxis and process. These elements are present from the beginning certainly, in that the students are asked to look at their drafting processes and the triggers and inspiration behind their work. But even here, the focus is very much on the changes to form and trope and the 'why' of choosing particular forms etc.

In Level Two, the focus changes somewhat, I expect the students to have a reasonable grounding in the basic poesis and I shift the focus more towards the praxis and process elements. Praxis becomes more dominant. I expect more detailed analysis and engagement with the drafting process (along with correspondingly more 'polished' work). Poesis is still a consideration, and process starts to become more important: the students are challenged to examine their own writing processes more and over a longer period of time and through a greater variety of theoretical and critical 'lenses'. The student at this stage should be able to construct clear writerly critical texts that accompany and inform the creative work and should be able to tackle questions of process and praxis as well as poesis within the construction of the text in a coherent and integrated manner.

Level Three tends to shift the focus again, so that writerly, critical and theoretical concerns take precedence over the more practical concerns. This tends to mean that the students are asked to examine the constituencies out of which they write and the theories that inform their writing and to analyse how these engage with and inform their writing processes as they go about the construction and reconstruction of the text of the poem. At this stage, the students would be expected to be able to critically examine their own work and the work of others and draw out complex theoretical concerns, making suggestions for improvement to the writing if necessary. They would also be expected to be able to take a variety of such views on their own work and synthesise a creative and critical response to them, either in defence of their work (or the work of another) or to select appropriate advice which they feel to be correct, and explain why they feel it to be so. The students should be able to use this faculty to demonstrate in the writerly critical accompaniment to the creative portfolio, that they are able to draw together the various strands of poesis, praxis and process into a coherent writerly critique of the creative text.

At Postgraduate level, the development of the structured system continues. At MA level, one would expect that the students being encountered are reasonably accomplished writers with a wide understanding of poesis and a solid understanding of their own praxis. Students at this level usually want to be published or 'professional' writers and some of those also want to go on to teach the discipline. Masters degrees in Creative Writing and their variants tend to fall between two stools, in that it they are not really 'taught' degrees, although they often sail under that flag of convenience. They are not totally research degrees either, since certain very important elements are taught. At this level the concentration becomes more individualised, students become more mentored than taught, but in general, elements of process and praxis tend to be fore grounded (although pedagogy is becoming increasingly important).

This is not to say that poesis is not important at this level. But one would expect it to be a much more individualised 'gap-filling' type of teaching, which takes a skills audit of the student, identifies deficiencies and sets about helping the student fill these gaps as quickly and efficiently as possible. In the future, I expect that modules on pedagogy will increasingly be included in Masters' level Creative Writing degrees, and more and more, the workshop will become a place where students not only analyse writing, but also analyse group dynamics, teaching methodologies and trigger exercises. Students and teachers will analyse these methodologies and exercises for fitness of purpose, try to find ways to improve them and experiment with new variants and reflect on this experimentation. They will, in fact, produce a poesis and a praxis for the pedagogical process. And so the system will re-integrate and come full circle. Perhaps soon, there will be a further concentric circle to our original model. That of the teacher of the teacher of writing, and so, what Myers (1996) called 'The Elephant Machine' will enter a new level of complexity.

All of the above strands are present throughout the BA and MA programmes I have put in place. Most of our students will have come through A-level English and will find the writer-centric, 'elephant's view of zoology' (Myers, 1996: 8) approach difficult to come to terms with. The students are used to looking at poems as artefacts which may be read from a number of viewpoints and which may be used as evidence to back up assertions about themes and issues. We ask them to get underneath the bonnet and see what happens when we start tinkering with the engine, we ask them to look at how the text is constructed, and what other ways it could have been constructed and to strip it down for parts to build a whole new engine. This approach allows the student to become actively engaged with the tools and processes of writing in such a way as to stretch and challenge them, and to allow them to challenge themselves. It is directly related to what Biggs (2003: 26) referred to as creating 'a balanced system in which all components support each other, as they do in any ecosystem'.

This approach also tends to instil in the students a sense that their learning is active and self directed, that in fact they are participating in what Knowles referred to as an 'androgogic' process rather than a pedagogic one. The approach fits very well with Light and Cox's (200: 58–61) description of androgogic learning in that it is very much problem-oriented and students have commented how they have gained not only in knowledge and understanding of their subject but also in self-esteem and confidence. As one student put it 'I had considered myself incapable of anything over about mid-60s up until today ... thanks for inspiring my belief in myself, and helping me to mature as a writer.' I try to instil in the students a belief that in the end, it's not about the mark, it's about the writing. If the writing is made to work and we understand what we're doing and why we're doing it, the mark will follow.

References

Biggs, J. (2003) *Teaching for Quality Learning at University*. Maidenhead: SRHE & Open University Press.
Bloom, H. (1997) *The Anxiety of Influence: A Theory of Poetry*. Oxford: OUP.

Brown, T. (1986) A northern voice. In H. Bloom (ed.) *Modern Critical Voices: Seamus Heaney.* New York: Chelsea House.

Dewey, J. (1997) *Experience & Education.* New York: Touchstone.

Friere, P. (1972) *Pedagogy of the Oppressed.* Harmondsworth: Penguin.

Green, C. (2001) Materializing the sublime reader: Cultural studies, reader response and community service in the Creative Writing workshop. *College English* 64 (2).

Hopkins, G.M. (1994) *The Works of Gerard Manley Hopkins.* Ware: Wordsworth Editions Ltd.

Jarvis, P. (2004) *Adult Education & Lifelong Learning: Theory and Practice.* London: Routledge Falmer.

Kelly, G. (1963) *A Theory of Personality: The Psychology of Personal Constructs.* New York: Norton.

Light, G. and Cox, R. (2001) *Learning & Teaching in Higher Education.* London: Sage.

Myers, D.G. (1996) *The Elephants Teach.* Englewood Cliffs: Prentice Hall.

Snyder, G. (1980) *The Real Work: Interviews and Talks 1964–1979.* W.S. McLean (ed.). New York: New Directions.

Chapter 9

Gonzo-Formalism: A Creative Writing Meta-Pedagogy for Non-Traditional Students

NAT HARDY

Introduction: The Grotesque Carnival of Gonzo-Formalism

To help students gain a deeper understanding of literature and the creative process itself, Creative Writing teachers must experiment with a variety of pedagogical methods and approaches. Armed only with a well-furnished mind and some bookish wisdom, this literary enabler is no exception to the tradition of instilling artful technique and interpretive understanding into the initiates of creative and literary studies. After many years of pedagogical exploration and discovery in a wide variety of academic settings, regions, countries and demographics, however, this pedagogue has developed an unorthodox workshop methodology best described as 'gonzo-formalism'.

By borrowing from the less-stale pot-pourri of literary theory, this meta-pedagogical method blends and adulterates a variety of theoretical models, creative and critical, in an attempt to guide students through the precarious corridors of the literary imagination. In a non-traditional and even absurdist fashion, gonzo-formalist pedagogy is a transformative meta-pedagogy; a progressivist model that begs and borrows from Bakhtinian formalism and gonzo-journalism.

Although perhaps more radical than traditional teaching methodologies, gonzo-formalism cannibalizes useful concepts and strategies from pedigreed writers and theorists in an attempt to facilitate a deeper understanding of the literary aesthetic in form, function, and practice. And, just as other Creative Writing pedagogies emphasize both reading and writing as a necessary path to enhancing the creative process gonzo-formalism is in sync with that time-honoured tradition, yet innovative and more egalitarian in its execution.

At its pedagogical core the modus operandi of gonzo-formalism is arguably dualist: its interpretive lens dialogically Bakhtinian, its workshop method absurdly and grotesquely Thompsonian. Though not fanatically bound in any sense to the cult of Bakhtin or Gonzodolatry, this pedagogical hybrid is Rabelaisian and freewheeling in spirit: a method that sustains a productive and carnivalesque environs for students and professor. As David Lodge puts it in *After Bakhtin: Essays on Fiction and Criticism* (1990a) – 'What is carnival but a licensed communal waking dream?' – in cross-fertilizing the dialogical with unconventional gonzo-formalism, the critical mind of the workshop attempts to collectively mirror the idiosyncrasies of the creative mind. Collaboratively then, the carnivalesque workshop is a 'communal' environs of professor and students who actively interpret, rework and refine the creative text under a hermeneutic of suspicion.

While rhetorical and composition pedagogues use Bakhtin's theories and ideas widely, it seems that few Creative Writing teachers, apart from David Lodge, muse upon the pedagogical possibilities of Bakhtin's interpretive methods. Bakhtin's insights and genius are, therefore, largely condemned to the critical rather than the creative realm. Although Lodge (1990b) explores the creative and critical possibilities of literary theory, some literary critics[1] predict the inevitable abandonment, reinvention, or even lingering death of theory. The residual effect that radical theoretical change might have on Creative Writing pedagogy is impossible to determine. From a creative writer's point of view, however, what can be predicted is the continued pooh-poohing of theory in all of its manifestations.

While some critics contend that theory has been theorized to death, many literary artists consider critical theory itself not only repugnant, but even harmful to the creative process. Theoretical rejection among authors is not a new phenomenon. Verbal disdain for literary theory is endemic, even fashionable, among some creative writers, so much so that some of these paradigm haters indulge in satirizing and parodying literary criticism and critical theory (see Kratzert & Richey, 1998: 93–111). Even Lodge's academic comedies, *Changing Places* (1979) *Small World* (1995) and *Nice Work* (1989), poke fun at criticism by fashioning archetypal characters that are the embodiment of a particular literary theory. That said, however, even Lodge's (1990b) pedagogical, *The Practice of Writing*, avoids literary theory for the most part.

As a writer, one can appreciate the fear and loathing of theory. As a scholar, however, one can, by avoiding orthodoxy or 'literary fascism,' to use David Carroll's (1998) term for some French theorists, benefit from theoretical insights and their applications to the writing process. Perhaps this hostility explains why few writers who teach Creative Writing engage in or at least deny the slightest hint of theoretical praxis. Unlike the anti-theory pedagogues whose attitude represses the Lacanian or Eagleton within, gonzo-formalism indulges in the illuminating possibilities of theoretical insight.

For those of us who have trained in and practiced creative writing and scholarship, a precarious tension bubbles and festers between creativity and theory. Intellectually, the creative/scholar types are condemned to some sort of paradigm not only for interpreting but for teaching Creative Writing. Like it or not, theory in some shape or form unavoidably comes with the pedagogical territory of teaching literature and the art of writing. As H.L. Mencken (1996: 5) put it best: 'A professor must have a theory as a dog must have fleas.' Thus even for those who consider theory a literary parasite or a disease carrier that literally 'plagues' interpretation and invention, Creative Writing teachers cannot help but scratch their paradigms for instructional effect.

The Carnival Workshop: Pastiche Theory in Praxis

With respect to its meta-theoretical bent, then, gonzo-formalism does not take an orthodox approach to either Russian formalism or Bakhtin, or to Thompson's firebrand version of literary cubism[2] for that matter. The meta-pedagogical method simply cannibalizes useful methods of interpretation and invention out of Bakhtin's theories and Thompson's creative genius.

Though university students of any background can benefit from this inventive teaching approach, experience dictates that mature students are best suited to pedagogic rigors of gonzo-formalism. On an interpretive level, adversity and lived experience enable mature students to better digest and appreciate the unvarnished truths of great literature. The older student is more immune and even appreciative of explicit or implicit adult content, subject matter that might very well shock or awe younger readers with less-seasoned sensibilities.

In a Bakhtinian respect, the meta-pedagogy loosely explores the interpretive potentialities of Bakhtin's three global concepts: 'prosaics',[3] 'unfinalizability',[4] 'dialogue'.[5] While Bakhtin's theories and concepts are admittedly complex, indeed, his association with Russian formalism is considered tenuous for some theorists such as Radu Surdulescu, the purpose here is not to debate the finer points and nuances of Bakhtinian theory, but to methodologically adopt some of the theorist's more useful concepts into the Creative Writing workshop.

On a symbolic level, the workshop also embodies the 'death of the author' notion, because the monological author must restrain any response to criticism until the critical mass has concluded its interpretive, or polyphonic, review. For any author, donning the scold's bridle for the duration of workshop dialectic is the most difficult, nay emasculating, part of workshop. Verbal castration sounds excruciating, and, for the silenced writer, it is as if he or she must quietly endure a discriminating panel of critics who cast their literary judgments on the author's work. Though painfully discerning at times, the carnival of criticism is self-policing because the workshop critics understand that they too will have their turn in the hot seat of authorial suppression. This unwritten code or honor among writers ensures that interpretive scrutiny remains aspersion free, vigilantly critical but not hostile. Once critical discussion of the creative work has concluded, the author can address his or her live audience to clarify ambiguities, ask questions or, in some cases, beg forgiveness.

Having clarified the 'formalist' dimension of gonzo-formalism, this treatise shifts its Russian focus to a more American locus in order to address the Thompsonian or 'gonzo' features of this meta-pedagogy. If we consider Thompson a postmodern Rabelais, Bakhtin's concepts offer an ideal paradigm for a critical understanding of Thompson's unique style and form and how these concepts can be usefully employed in a writing workshop. While naysayers might argue that Thompson was not a textbook pedagogue in any sense of the term, Dr Gonzo PhD did offer a wealth of helpful suggestions for writers on university campuses across America. Indeed, Thompson's university lectures established an *esprit de corps* among disillusioned student writers, intellectuals and his growing readership. Thompson's influence on American literature is undeniable and, since his suicide, membership in the Gonzo Cult continues to expand. One would think even Bakhtin would concur: Thompson remains America's own postmodern Rabelais: carnival by nature, grotesque in execution and style.[6]

In *Rabelais and His World*, Bakhtin (1984b) addressed the concepts of 'carnival' and 'grotesque realism' as they functioned in the work of Francois Rabelais: carnival representing the social dynamic (for our purposes, the workshop) and grotesque realism representing the literary mode (critical discourse within the workshop) – these concepts figure prominently in Hunter S. Thompson's work and in the gonzo-formalist workshop. Of course, yoking Thompson with the carnival and grotesque is not an entirely new conceit. Indeed, one only need revisit Kurt Vonnegut's insightful review of *Campaign Trail '72*. According to Vonnegut, 'Thompson writes the way he does – violently and grotesquely, using words a carnival mirrors' (*In Our Times*, 2006: 1). As Vonnegut and other critics suggest,[7] Thompson's grotesque realism offers a visionary speculum – a Rabelaisian cavalcade of violence and savagery that flatters not. For all its visionary hedonism and celebratory law breaking, however, the more 'grotesque' elements of the carnival also pervade Thompson's creative work.[8]

While Thompson's canon is intrinsically carnivalesque – his work and cultural criticisms defiant and unapologetic – these elements and techniques provide a wealth of literary strategies that are useful in the gonzo-formalist workshop. Minus Thompson's irreverence and penchant for the excremental, the gonzo-formalist pedagogy engages in its own unapologetic critiques because half the truth is often a whole lie. Like Thompson, the workshop tenor demands that readers keep their criticisms constructive, though critically honest. In a meta-pedagogical sense gonzo-formalism adopts a tempered version of the carnivalesque and grotesque realism. Where Bakhtin associated the carnival with the collective voice (Clark & Holquist, 1984: 302) for our purposes, the writing workshop, the corresponding overturning of authority that accompanies the carnival is evidenced in the more collegial though critical role of the professor as compeer rather than as all-knowing Übermensch.

During workshop discussion of published works and student writings, the ex-cathedra notion that supreme knowledge emanates exclusively from the authoritative genius of the monologic professor is, to a considerable degree, displaced by 'collective' interpretation and revision. The professorial panoptic and authoritarian models of pedagogies past are, therefore, replaced by gonzo-formalism's more egalitarian paradigm. Through the workshop dialectic then, monological truth is superseded by a dialogical collectivity of writers who work hermeneutically and intertextually to not only explicate but to refine the text under consideration. Instead of the professor dominating and guiding discussion, as is typical in lecture format, students take a more proactive role in determining the interpretive and instructive course of the class. While student engagement is vital in any workshop, it is especially necessary for gonzo-formalism's carnivalesque approach. To encourage student participation and attendance 30% of their final grade is based on workshop critiques both written and oral. In order to succeed in the course and improve their writing (the *raison d'être* of the course), grade-driven students have a vested interest in maintaining a visual and a verbal presence in the workshop.

Bakhtin's notion of grotesque realism as a literary mode and Thompson's cubist impulses also figure prominently in gonzo-formalist pedagogy, albeit in a somewhat diluted form. In its own carnivalesque spirit, the meta-pedagogy adopts Thompson's unconventional and subjective style into the workshop. For gonzo-formalism grotesque realism is, simply put, critical honesty or the ugly truth of how literature succeeds or fails. Since constructive criticism demands critical distance but, above all, honesty, workshop critique can descend into the realm of the grotesque. Through critical reading and commentary, engaged readers must provide writers with naked or gospel truths, a demonstrated capacity for careful observation and appropriate editorial commentary. Not necessarily 'brutal' truths that might destroy the aspiring writer, but an honest and delicate balance between half-truth and pre-libel. The golden rule for helping aspiring writers improve their craft is to maintain honesty in a productive critical exchange without, of course, offending even the most sensitive creature.

While the more enthusiastic writers will take criticisms in their stride to enhance their art, other writers sometimes take workshop critiques personally. The wounds of truth can indeed be painful for the more thin-skinned writer as Thompson (1998) himself reminds us in *The Proud Highway* – 'For every moment of triumph, for every instance of beauty, many souls must be trampled' – thus, some soul trampling unavoidably occurs in workshop, never out of spite but in the pursuit of improvement. In time, of course, a critical callus will form a protective barrier to protect the author's fragile ego and, by the end of term, even the most vulnerable writers will concur that their work benefited from the informed and engaged criticism of the workshop experience.

As a carnival of critical and non-hierarchical discourse, therefore, the gonzo-formalist workshop, in theory, is never subdued or muted, but rather a grotesque arena where literature is re-imagined and ultimately refined by an uncensored audience of peers and preceptor. Another essential feature of this so-so-Socratic method is its call-and-response tactic, a challenging rubric that imposes on both student and professor the rigors of close reading and constructive criticism. In this dialogical matrix, students and teacher generate a broad range of creative suggestions and, often, visionary possibilities for the student writer. Like other less-conventional pedagogies, the gonzo-formalist workshop fosters an arguably strange affinity for unraveling and appreciating uncertainty, and sometimes absurdity itself, that illusive essence of the literary imagination that the Beat poet, Lawrence Ferlinghetti (1968: 30) muses upon in his reflexive *ars poetica*, 'Constantly Risking Absurdity.'

As a meta-pedagogy the discursive mode of the workshop is lucid and speculative, its collective interpretive method arguably absurd in ambition. Given the fact that all writers, great and small, are haunted by some 'ludicrous' muse, gonzo-formalism considers the creative process itself 'absurd'. To understand the inner-workings of literary creativity thus requires a somewhat less rational and more speculative approach to enlightened interpretation. In this controlled anarchy of voices or 'critical polyphony', a somewhat chaotic dynamic emerges as students take a poetic leap of faith in explication, what Coleridge defined as 'that willing suspension of disbelief' to interpret creative thought and how literary expression might be enhanced aesthetically. In their role as workshop critics, students can dismember the text on an interpretive level, in their capacity as creative writers, however, these aspiring authors have an insider's understanding of the muse, an armchair psychiatrist's understanding of creative process. In this freewheeling, *in medias res* environment the gonzo-formalist paradigm fosters fruitful and, as the course progresses, sublime discussion because its lucid method discursively seeks the absurd nature of creativity and literary meaning(s).

Pedagogical Risk Knowledge: Gonzo-Formalism and the New Humanities

Teaching Creative Writing, much like the intelligent design of this essay, is an evolutionary work-in-progress. Throughout their careers, Creative Writing professors sharpen their craft along with their students or risk personal tedium and obscurity in the process. In order to succeed, teachers, much like their students, must not only improve, but also adapt to their transformative environment. A failure to acclimatize to the change in workshop temperament renders the teacher ineffective at imparting knowledge, learning, and the mellifluous art of tossing words methodically onto a page suitable for publication. And, last but not least, teachers are obliged to improve in order to avoid the sedimentary folds of professional extinction.

Any seasoned professor should readily admit we few, we happy few are not infallible demigods. Over the course of a career Creative Writing professors will experience their finest hour, and their 15 minutes of infamy. To forestall pedagogical disaster, embarrassment and out-dated methods, gonzo-formalism adopts a bold communal approach to learning because pedagogies and disciplines advance only when they are challenged. Like other meta-pedagogies, gonzo-formalism is, of course, not without its risks. Any provocative and reflexive pedagogy that goes against the grain of convention with a more student-centered approach is fraught with contretemps but then what is 'evolved' teaching without some inherent risk?

Pedagogical risk taking can be profoundly empowering for both the teacher and the students. The pedagogical risk is not only transformative but, in a sense, shared as most also engage students, along with their professor, in carnival dialogue, 'constantly seeking', the absurdities and the sensibilities of literary imagination. As they threaten tradition with more experiential pedagogies teachers who refuse to surrender opportunity for security will inevitably benefit from what Gilda Segal and John Oversby define as 'pedagogical risk knowledge' (Oversby & Segal, 1998: 1). As a meta-pedagogy that involves 'thinking creatively in front of a class in addition to admitting mistakes when these occur' and 'think[ing] creatively in front of their class in the ways that they would urge their students to think' (Oversby & Segal, 1998: 1), the gonzo-formalist instructor is candid in method and exemplary in temperament as he or she encourages students to take risks in their writing and in their written commentary and workshop dialogue. This open and honest engagement with the material demands that students become actors and characters within the workshop, a progressive mechanism that builds student confidence through collaborative learning and constructive criticism.

In what might appear as 'un'disciplined or absurd praxis by virtue of its carnivalesque method, as a meta-pedagogy gonzo-formalism is ideally suited to the emerging meta-discipline known as the 'new humanities' which embraces a fresh global and pluralistic approach to learning in a destructive age of globalization – a paradigm that Creative Writing and other liberal arts disciplines should pursue with a similar vengeance. In *Creative Writing and the New Humanities,* Paul Dawson (2004) explores the future or 'new humanities', and specifically creative writing's role in this emerging discipline. Dawson's telling and insightful study examines vital pedagogical and systemic questions of the academy (the cross-disciplinary chasm between the critical and the creative), an issue that can no longer be ignored by educators or curriculum administrators or students if university classes are going to, in fact, engage in critical thinking, dialogue and creativity. Literature, out of all the liberal arts, offers artists the most rhetorical and revolutionary aesthetic. Creative Writing can, according to Dawson, play an intermediary role in bridging the inter-disciplinary chasm that the New Humanities confronts.[9] In its discursive and ultimately theoretical mien, Creative Writing and its pedagogical discontents, namely the gonzo-formalists, have an opportunity to help refine and even redefine the *beaux-arts* of writing through the interdisciplinary approach of the new humanities.

As it continues to evolve and explore the complexities of the literary imagination and interpretation, gonzo-formalism will be best defined as a pedagogy of discovery rather than a paradigm of conformity or restraint. By ideology and design the gonzo-formalist paradigm refuses to impose a dogmatic litany of creative rules and practices. In its doctrinaire stead, gonzo-formalism's carnivalesque workshop promotes and encourages a diversity of commentary and insight, those 'haphazard winds of group discussion,' that Joseph Moxley (1989: xiv) addresses in *Creative Writing in*

America: Theory and Pedagogy, a dialogical method that enables students to make those crucial connections between the creative and the critical either through collective interpretation or on their own. And finally, on a global level, gonzo-formalism also challenges the foundation of English literary studies by embracing not only the canonical but emerging literature as well – not simply the literature of English-speaking nations but international literatures of all nations, published and forthcoming. Pedagogical risk knowledge imparts literary and cultural knowledge as well as a deeper understanding of the writing craft in all its complexities for professor and student alike.

Admittedly, to the uninitiated educator, the gonzo-formalism might seem an unconventional strategy to adopt. But given the atypical, uncertain, and often unpredictable nature of the venue – the lunatic fringe of collective creativity, or, what we teachers affectionately call 'the Creative Writing workshop' – this perhaps heretical method has garnered many more successes than failures and, one hopes, spawned a gaggle of future Pulitzer and Whitbread Prize winners.

By design the gonzo-formalist method is hell bent on developing and evolving the students' own creative genius, a meta-pedagogical departure from the traditional approaches of emulation and imitation, or, as this professor calls it – the MSR or 'Murder-She-Rote' method. Mechanical repetition has its place in the factories of Harlequin and Hallmark, not in the industrial meta-imagination of gonzo-formalism. By harnessing and embracing their own budding ability to understand and master the qualities of genius, students will ultimately become better, and through hard work, possibly greater writers. Exposing students to a variety of literary traditions and movements provides the acumen of cherry-picking the more masterful tropes and qualities of genius as opposed to simply mimicking great literature to the letter, as imitation tends to do. In this sense mimesis is superseded by less derivative and in some instances, more original thought than formal emulation permits.

In the end, however, 'All a teacher can do,' as Wallace Stegner (2002: 12) suggests in *On Teaching and Writing Fiction,* 'is set high goals for students – or get them to set them for themselves – and, then, try to help them reach those goals.' Creative Writing teachers are only enablers, and, at their best, literary exemplar. In this sense, the gonzo-formalism is uniquely simpatico with other teaching methods that foster interactive or dialogical discourse. Stegnerian as it is stygian, Dickensian as it is Dante-esque – the gonzo-formalist workshop is hellishly helpful, temperamental and for some, torturous.

Gonzo-Formalism: A Non-Traditional Pedagogy for Non-Traditional Students

While some mature students have had to put college on the back burner after dropping out of the Middle School of Hard Knocks, others have transferred from the High School of Life. Before attending college, others had children and families, work commitments, personal tragedies, disabilities, military service, domestic abuse, poverty, homelessness, dependency issues and an entire range of life's savage and unnatural curveballs.[10] These are the 'elder, would-be writers who managed to hold onto their dream for decades before they could actually "clear the decks" enough to act on it' that Jeri McCormick explores in *Writers Have No Age: Creative Writing For Older Adults* (Coberly *et al.*, 2005: 1). As McCormick concurs, mature students make a revitalizing addition to the Creative Writing workshop, not only by virtue of their life experience, but also because they have made a personal commitment and, in some cases, considerable sacrifices to attend college.

While this heterogeneity of age, race and class might culturally divide the class, the diversity, in fact, adds a vital dynamic, a new humanities dimension to the workshop environment. For gonzo-formalism cultural divergence is a healthy component that enhances the workshop carnival, as the monologic insights of the individual become part of dialogic polyphony of the gonzo-formalist workshop. As Scott DeWitt's *Writing Inventions: Identities, Technologies, Pedagogies* points out: 'Even after recognizing such diversity among our students and between our student populations ... there is a common context where we all can begin to think about invention' (DeWitt, 2001: 20). For most Creative Writing meta-pedagogies, gonzo-formalism and others, student variance enriches rather than confines the complexities of creation and invention.

Most traditional students are truly committed to their studies, and fiercely determined to improve their writing and their lives. Their classroom presence enhances the creative environs because unlike their younger adversaries, these elder students have a wealth of life experience at their poetic beck and call. To this end, lived experience offers mature students a distinct content-based advantage in a Creative Writing workshop. As Hunter S. Thompson put it, 'Fiction is based on reality unless you're a fairy-tale artist, you have to get your knowledge of life from somewhere. You have to know the material you're writing about before you alter it' (Leonard, 2005), mature students have the poetic license to alter their material because their creative work 'is based on reality'.

Unlike the bulk of their contemporaries who still struggle in the salad days of their youth, these older undergraduate students, then, offer refreshingly mature insights in to creative expression. The student elders eagerly share their own stories, either through submitted poems or thinly veiled non-fiction parading as fiction (non-fiction is a separate course!). In many cases, the 'adult-oriented' content makes up for the lack of technical skills because the non-traditional student is well-furnished with that Blakean wisdom of experience, an acquired edge that younger students simply do not have as the elder students explore and indulge in what Celia Hunt (2000: 12) refers to in *Therapeutic Dimensions of Autobiography in Creative Writing*, as 'fictional autobiography'. In mining the self, mature students have access to a rich repository of material for writing. Creatively then, students are 'relocating the personal', to use Barbara Kamler's (2001) concept from *Relocating the Personal: A Critical Writing Pedagogy*. Through poetic and narrative self-exploration, the students create autho-ethnographical texts that offer a distinct and often compelling veracity. This autobiographical tinge gives the writing a more vivid emotional and graphic depth: a grits and gravitas perspective.

This professor encourages mature students armed with the lint of living to conjure up not only the fluffy happy times of their lives, but also the all-important *sturm und drang* of their lived experience through poetry and fiction. In helping students transform the walk of life into the writ of literature, workshops can sometimes border on therapy sessions, just as Graham Greene's (1980: 71) suggested: 'Writing is a form of therapy; sometimes I wonder how all those who do not write, compose or paint can manage to escape the madness, melancholia, the panic and fear which is inherent in a human situation.' Through hard work, guidance and productive work-shopping, the novice writer has the opportunity to transform life's baggage into artful poetry or prose. Instead of getting mad, students can often get even with suffered injustices because, as Meg Cabot says, 'The best revenge is to write about it' (Court, 2002). There is a therapeutic catharsis and often closure when students write about the triumphs and tragedies of their own human situation.

Of course, personal catharsis can become public shame. As W.H. Auden (2005: 13) put it, 'Art is born of humiliation.' The gonzo-formalist workshop environment can hover around abasement and humiliation. This is why beginning writers often take criticism personally because the story or poem is torn from a page of their lives. And that is precisely why this professor constantly reminds workshop critics to direct constructive criticism towards the art and not the artist, because we are often sharing in the writer's suffering. Maintaining emotional distance in the workshop is, therefore, essential for a non-violent and relatively tear-free environment.

Having said that, praise alone, even when warranted, is not going to help developing writers improve their craft. Even when writers feels 'attacked' they remember that their emotive labours will not go unnoticed, but rather, tempered and improved through the constructive criticism.

Conclusion

Like the calm and steady hand of an apprentice mohel, learning to write creatively is somewhat like acquiring the mastery of technique in any of the other arts. Aesthetic craft comes through commitment, dedication, diligence, and hard work. While some Creative Writing teachers of the much-respected Iowan Tradition 'do not believe that writing can be "taught" or "learned" in the strict sense of these words' (Wilbers, 1980: 125), this professor and his rebellious meta-pedagogy are of the William Saroyan (2005: 186) school of thought that maintains: 'The writer who is a real writer is a rebel who never stops.' Of course, assiduity, perseverance and proven work ethic do not guarantee the genesis of great literature, but then neither does a salary-drawing teacher of Creative Writing promote the craft of writing when he believes his job is futile and self-redundant.

While there are limitations to any Creative Writing pedagogy, gonzo-formalism incorporates E.L. Doctorow's writing dictum: 'You start from nothing and learn as you go' (Morris, 1999: 101). While Creative Writing students are not *tabulae rasae* in the strictest academic sense, most within a non-traditional campus enter an introductory course with little reading skills and even less technique for writing. Not so much blank slates but virgin canvasses willing to, as Robert Herrick would say, 'make much of time' in dedication to learning the art of writing creatively to beget literature. Unlike their seasoned literary competitors apprentice writers are more willing to experiment and less embarrassed to take chances and that is refreshing trait for a veteran teacher to observe.

As this educator sees it then, our role as teachers, interpreters, critics, and editors, is to instill some 'positive capability' in the novice writer, particularly at the end of term as the students' final portfolio takes shape. This pedagogical strategy can be accomplished by directing their creative works at the end of term with critical and constructive commentary of the grotesque carnival with the tempered expectation that these students will ultimately become better readers and writers perhaps even talented writers like those who have trained in the academy before them. Stephen Wilbers (1980: 127), in *The Iowa Writers' Workshop: Origins, Emergence and Growth*, suggests that writing teachers 'might help others to master the elements of their craft,' however, 'they make no attempt to teach talent.' While this professor generally agrees with this statement, he is of the mind that teachers can impart ability and skill to, as Wilber says, help 'master the elements' of writing.

After a term of committed learning, voracious and careful reading, engaged workshop participation and much writing and rewriting, the onus is ultimately on the student writer to develop his or her talent. Talent, in this professor's humble estimation, is, of course, inevitably up to the individual and his or her muse. 'Talent is helpful in writing,' as Jessamyn West (1986: 73) emphasizes, 'but [it's] guts that are absolutely essential.' If the mature student population has any capacity for plenitude, it has to be intestinal fortitude and ample mettle to convey it in their writing.

Unlike their MTV Generation colleagues and adversaries, these elder learners have overcome adversity and aspire to become students and writers. Through the meta-pedagogical approach of gonzo-formalism, teachers can inspire by example and provide all students, but especially non-traditional students, with the tools necessary for achieving and mastering literary talent. Whether these students build an 'unfinalizable' *Doll's House*, a *Little 'Prosaics' House on the Prairie*, a carnivalesque *House of Mirth*, or a grotesque and scatological *House at Pooh Corner*, the gonzo-formalist method offers these mature and struggling writers a workable blueprint for an original and possibly visionary literary construction.

Note

1. Terry Eagleton's *After Theory* (2003) and Stein Haugrom Olsen's *The End of Literary Theory* (1987) are representative of this appropriately cynical school of thought.
2. Kurt Vonnegut describes Thompson's writing as 'the literary equivalent of Cubism: all rules are broken.' See Hunter S. Thompson's (2007: 227) *Fear and Loathing In America: The Brutal Odyssey of an Outlaw Journalist* Volume II.
3. By appropriating Bakhtin's 'prosaics' approach, the meta-pedagogy reinforces the 'suspicion of explanatory systems' to explain and interpret literature (Emerson & Morson, 1994: 65). In addition to its dialectic meaning the prosaics approach also converges upon the more incidental or 'prosaic' moments – the kitchen sink dramas of everyday life – creative material much more accessible to students than those epic or catastrophic events that Hollywood indulges in, the explosive page-turner or the soft-pornographic bodice-ripper. From the prosaics' perspective mature students have an experiential upper hand in fashioning their own more cultivated literary works, a grist-for-the-mill advantage that wet-behind-the-ears students simply do not possess.
4. Concerning Bakhtin's notion of 'unfinalizability' this global concept figures centrally in the cubist thrust gonzo-formalism. To obscenely oversimplify: no one has the corner on literary truth; interpretation is condemned to infinite reinterpretation. As Bakhtin (1984a: 166) contended in *Problems With Dostoevsky's Poetics*: 'Nothing conclusive has yet taken place in the world, the ultimate word

of the world and about the world has not yet been spoken, the world is open and free, everything is still in the future and will always be in the future.' When applied to a workshop environment Bakhtin's concept demands a future-perfect tenor to the critical dialectic. Workshop critiques and suggestions are, therefore, just that: informed though 'unfinalizable' recommendations for improvement, not necessarily authoritative, but highly advised by the author's tutor and peers. Any creative texts submitted by students thus remain, 'works-in-progress' (one hopes a trimester or two past the embryonic and a semester away from the Byronic), until the works are revised and resubmitted at the end of term in the final portfolios. Much like Walt Whitman's revisionary concept of poetics, as exemplified in *Leaves of Grass* (1995), student works are open to reworking even after submission, or in Whitman's case 'self-publication', as the text lingers 'unfinalizable', at least until it's published in a book or journal of some repute.

5. Bakhtin's third global concept, 'dialogue', which suggests 'that 'all language is dialogic, [that] there are no monologic utterances,' although '"dialogic language" does allow for monologic utterances' (Emerson & Morson, 1994: 65) is also central to gonzo-formalist pedagogy. How this somewhat confusing concept applies to the workshop is linguistically two-fold. On the first level, the 'monologic' voices of the text function as 'polyphony'. On the second level, it is the 'unfinalizability' of each individual or monologic voice that creates the textual polyphony. This polyphony is mirrored in the workshop dynamic of interactive discourse as a critical symphony of collective and competing voices emerging in a staggered chorus, with the professor playing a quasi-choir master sans baton. It is within this fluid matrix of author, text and reader response that the 'dialogic imagination' is manifest. Through this plurality of opinion and commentary – an *e pluribus unum* of explication– the text is anatomized and, with constructive critical intention, refitted with some better working limbs and organs. This verbal interplay of text and collective criticism is the vital force that drives the workshop through the Freudian slips and Jungian teddies of interpretation and suggested revisions.

6. Thompson's (2003: 113) vernacular from the *Kingdom of Fear* – 'I shit on the chest of fun' – epitomizes his grotesque Rabelaisian bent best.

7. Michael Hames-Garcia (2000: 463) has described Thompson's Rabelaisian grandeur as 'Dr Gonzo's Carnival'. In a similar vein Chad Seville (2006: 1) also likens Thompson's style to the carnivalesque: 'The depravity of clandestine behavior in his [Thompson's] work is built into a kind of carnival ride, which backdrops his self-proclaimed quest for the core of the American dream.'

8. As David Petersen (2004: 2) suggests, the 'grotesque hyperbole is a significant element of Thompson's weird attraction.' David Aquarius (2005: 1), in his own gonzo vein contends that Thompson 'painted grotesque portraits of national icons that stuck like vomit on the back seat.' Even the 'splattered inklings' of Thompson's expressionist illustrator, Ralph Steadman (2000: 1) reflect the Thompsonian grotesque as Gregory Daurer's 'The Grotesque and the Gold' argues.

9. As Dawson (2004: 2) suggests: 'Creative Writing functions as a discursive site for continuing debate over some of the foundational questions of literary studies: what is literature, what is the nature of the creative process, and what is the relationship between the creative and the critical?'

10. Jacki Pritchard and Erick Sainsbury's (2004) *Can You Read Me? Creative Writing*

with Child and Adult Victims of Abuse, offers a variety of helpful strategies to enable students to write about and work through abuse.

References

Aquarius, D. (2005) In memoriam: Hunter S. Thompson. *Takebackthemedia.com*, 21 Feb. Online at http://web.takebackthemedia.com/geeklog/public_html.article. php?story=20050221083814402. Accessed 17.6.06.

Auden, W.H. (2005) *The Cambridge Companion to W.H. Auden.* Cambridge: Cambridge University Press.

Bakhtin, M. (1984a) *Problems With Dostoevsky's Poetics* (C. Emerson, trans.) Minneapolis, MN: University of Minnesota Press.

Bakhtin, M. (1984b) *Rabelais and His World* (H. Iswolsky, trans.). Bloomington, IN: Indiana University Press.

Carroll, D. (1998) *French Literary Fascism*. Princeton, NJ: Princeton University Press.

Clark, K. and Holquist, M. (1984) *Mikhail Bakhtin*. Cambridge, MA: Harvard University Press.

Coberly, L.M., McCormick, J. and Updike, K. (eds) (2005) *Writers Have No Age: Creative Writing For Older Adults.* New York: Haworth Press.

Court, A. (2002) All-American success story emerges from teen fantasies: Review of Meg Cabot's 'All-American Girl'. *USA Today*, 3 Dec. On WWW at http://www.usa today.com/life/books/reviews/2002-12-02-all-american_x.htm. Accessed 2.1.07.

Daurer, G. (2000) The grotesque and the gold. *Salon.com*, 1 Sept. On WWW at http://www.archive.salon.com/people/feature/2000/09/01/steadman/index.html. Accessed 12.6.06.

Dawson, P. (2004) *Creative Writing and the New Humanities.* London: Routledge.

DeWitt, S.L. (2001) *Writing Inventions: Identities, Technologies, Pedagogies.* Albany, NY: State University of New York.

Emerson, C. and Morson, G.S. (1994) Mikhail Bakhtin. In M. Groden and M. Kreisworth (eds) *The Johns Hopkins Guide to Literary Theory* (p. 65). Baltimore, MD: Johns Hopkins University Press.

Ferlinghetti, L. (1968) *A Coney Island of the Mind: Poems.* New York: New Directions.

Greene, G. (1980) *Ways of Escape: An Autobiography.* New York: Simon and Schuster.

Hames-Garcia, M.R. (2000) Dr Gonzo's carnival: The testimonial satires of Oscar Zeta Acosta. *American Literature* 72 (3), 463–493.

Hunt, C. (2003) *Therapeutic Dimensions of Autobiography in Creative Writing.* London: Jessica Kingsley Publishers.

In Our Times (2006) Kirk Vonnegut's last days: A review of Man Without a Country. 26 April. On WWW at http://www.journals.concrete.org.au/inourtimes/archives/2006/04/kurt_vonneguts.html. Accessed 15.06.06.

Kamler, B. (2001) *Relocating the Personal: A Critical Writing Pedagogy.* New York: State University of New York.

Kratzert, M. and Richey, D. (1998) De(construction) of literary theory: The rise of anti-theory fiction. *The Acquisitions Librarian* 10 (9), 93–111.

Leonard, T. (2005) Lonely death at Owl Farm for gonzo pioneer. *The Telegraph*, 22 Feb. On WWW at http://www.telegraph.co.uk/news/main.jhtml?xml=/news /2005/02. Accessed 14.6.06.

Lodge, D. (1979) *Changing Places.* New York: Penguin.

Lodge, D. (1989) *Nice Work.* London: Penguin.

Lodge, D. (1990a) *After Bakhtin: Essays in Fiction and Criticism.* New York: Routledge.

Lodge, D. (1990b) *The Practice of Writing.* New York: Penguin.

Lodge, D. (1995) *Small World.* New York: Penguin.

Mencken, H.L. (1996) *Prejudices: A Selection.* Baltimore, MD: Johns Hopkins University Press.

Morris, C.D. (1999) *Conversations With E.L. Doctorow.* Jackson, MS: University of Mississippi Press.

Moxley, J.M. (1989) *Creative Writing in America: Theory and Pedagogy.* Urbana, Il.: National Council of Teachers of English.

Olsen, S.H. (1987) *The End of Literary Theory.* Cambridge, MA: Cambridge University Press.

Oversby, J. and Segal, G. (1998) A study of a tutor responding to the needs of pre-service primary student teachers. Queensland University of Technology Faculty of Education. On WWW at http://www.fed.qut.edu.au/projects/asera/PAPERS/Segal.html. Accessed 14.6.06.

Petersen, D. (2004) Hey Rube: Review of Blood Sport, the Bush Doctrine and the Downward Spiral of Dumbness: Modern History From the Sports Desk. *Bloomsbury Review*, 14 June. On WWW at http://www.bloomsburyreview.com/Archives/2004/Hey%20Rube.pdf. Accessed 12.06.06.

Pritchard, J. and Sainsbury, E. (2004) *Can You Read Me? Creative Writing with Child and Adult Victims of Abuse.* London: Jessica Kingsley.

Saroyan, W. (2005) *Essential Saroyan: Challenges and Practices.* New York: Heyday Books.

Seville, C. (2006) A shotgun, golf ball and cannon. *Fusion/News*, 14 April. On WWW at http://www.purchase.edu/Departments/AcademicPrograms/las/humanities/fusion/hunter.aspx. Accessed 14.6.06.

Stegner, W. (2002) *On Teaching and Writing Fiction.* New York: Penguin

Surdulescu, R. (2000) Mikhail Bakhtin and the formalist theories. In *Form, Structure and Structurality in Critical Theory.* Bucharest: Editura Universitatii din Bucuresti.

Thompson, H.S. (1998) *The Proud Highway: Saga of a Desperate Southern Gentleman 1955–1967.* New York: Ballantine Books.

Thompson, H.S. (2000) *Fear and Loathing In America: The Brutal Odyssey of an Outlaw Journalist* (Vol. II). New York: Simon & Schuster.

West, J. (1986) *The Woman Said Yes: Encounters with Life and Death.* New York: Harvest Books.

Whitman, W. (2005) *The Complete Poems* (F. Murphy, ed.). New York: Penguin Classics.

Wilbers, S (1980) *The Iowa Writers' Workshop: Origins, Emergence and Growth.* Iowa City, IA: University of Iowa Press.

Chapter 10

Acting, Interacting and Acting Up: Teaching Collaborative Creative Practice

JEN WEBB

Introduction

Week one of semester one. I ask the 80/90/100 students in the lecture hall, 'Who has done group work before?' Everyone raises a hand; but no one looks pleased. I go on: 'Who likes to work collaboratively?' No one raises a hand. And then: 'Who thinks they'd work better in a team?' No hands.

It can't be helped. These students are enrolled in a required subject for final-year students in the Creative Writing, Film and Television Production, and New Media Production degrees, and they are about to begin a semester that is entirely committed to group work. Although they've shared subjects in theory or communicative practice, they have had – and seemed to want – very little contact with each other's media, techniques or aesthetics. Some of them have even displayed a sort of disciplinary xenophobia: I've heard, for instance, that writers are navel-gazers who work in a worn-out form; that new media practitioners are elitists who have no idea of the capacity of narrative; and that film-makers have sold out to the commercial world. I don't mean that the School is a hotbed of discontent. As individuals, the students get along as well as any other collection of students. But, as Nietzsche (1968) has pointed out, put any group of people together and you'll get will-to-power. A group, especially when it is participating within what sociologists term a cultural field,[1] is made up of agents motivated and informed by self-interest, and hence given to competition. Pierre Bourdieu (1991: 242) points this out, writing: 'Every field is the site of a more or less openly declared struggle for the definition of the legitimate principles of division of the field.' Our students, on the (admittedly rare) occasions when they badmouth other forms of practice, are simply manifesting conventional field-driven behaviour: the struggle to define the field of creative production and its principles of value.

This semester they will have to suspend this tendency. They will (we hope) acknowledge and value the sorts of work carried out by those in other disciplines, and learn the extent to which anyone practicing at a professional level is dependent upon other parts of the creative field. Instead of being *writing students, media students, film students,* they will become a sort of family, deeply involved with each other's work and forms for the next 15 weeks.

Where We're Coming From

But are they happy about it? Not really. The students look back at me with what seems to be resentment. Someone calls out that this is not what they signed up for when they enrolled in the subject. I reply that if they are to be properly prepared to work within the creative professions, they need to be trained in the actualities of the field of creative production. In part this involves familiarizing writers with the exigencies of the film/television/ new media worlds, and familiarizing students from the latter disciplines with the significance of narrative and genre. Each group needs the other, I insist, if they are to produce work that will reach more than a narrow audience of friends, family and fellow practitioners. I point out that, if they have not been exposed to ways of thinking and seeing that emerge from other creative traditions, they will be less capable of working productively in what the media call 'the real world'. This is because for most creative practitioners, finding a social space and/or an economic space in which to present or perform work is vastly aided by knowledge of cognate fields and practices. I am not convinced that writers need to have high-level skills in, say, animation and other digital media. I am, however, convinced that, unless they know the structure of the field and the shape of the industry, they risk missing out on approaches to creative expression that might drive, or at least inform, both their personal practice and their capacity to derive a professional income or career from their practice.

Until a few years ago, students in our programs were trained to handle the technical aspects of production in their chosen form, to think creatively and critically, to experiment with their own aesthetic, to work autonomously and to take risks. But they weren't explicitly trained to move from the garret to the lab, production company or funding body. They were not explicitly provided with the literacies they would need to step outside the confines of their own practice, and hence to move from a good idea to an achievable product. To remedy this, my (new media) colleague Greg Battye and I developed a research project to investigate our teaching approaches and their epistemological validity. One outcome from this research was the design of subjects intended to give creative students training and experience in (almost) real-life professional practice. Collaborative practice. Our argument for this was that, in the long run, very few creative practitioners actually work alone. The fantasy/fallacy of the alienated genius is a problem with a lot of university training because teaching, learning and assessment tend to focus on the individual student, while in fact it is rare to work purely as an individual in the world of creative production. Scriptwriters and film-makers, for instance, are intimately connected in the making of a work. New media practitioners draw on, or directly collaborate with, other creative professionals – including writers. Even in what is arguably the most solitary of occupations, poetry, there is interaction and collaboration between poet and editor (and, later, the reader).

The film/television and new media production students seem pretty much okay with this. They know, because of the structure of the industries in which their art is produced, that no one works in isolation. But the writers tend to be resistant to the idea of collaboration. They seem more likely to have been imbued with the notion of art as the charismatic representation of a personal vision, and the creative agent as an autonomous artist. This dream of 'the artist' as unique and imbued with a particular charisma is fueled by stories of the tortured and eccentric, yet wildly attractive, lives of major artists: Jackson Pollack and Dylan Thomas as genius-alcoholic; Pablo Picasso and Norman Mailer as genius-sexually excessive; Virginia Woolf and Kurt Cobain as genius-depressive; the poets (Samuel Taylor Coleridge, Jim Morrison) and artists (Howard Arkley, Brett Whiteley) as genius-junkie. And so on: all of them terribly dysfunctional, but terribly romantic, productive, and (capital A) Artistic.

This representation of artists as solitary alienated beings is, of course, comparatively recent. During the Middle Ages, creative workers were simply workers who applied their specialized skills within collectives or guilds (Williams, 1981: 59). Not until the Renaissance did they became alienated from the ordinariness of workers in the general economy, and begin to compete for different forms of capital: particularly those forms associated with distinction in the fields of theory and philosophy (Zolberg, 1990: 10). It took a couple more centuries before artists became the disinterested, transcendent genius of modern discourse. But whatever the discourses, or the stories we tell ourselves, creative practice is and has always been about the beehive of society. Creative work and workers are, like everyone else, defined, determined and delimited by the structures, logic and trajectories of the field and of social institutions and practices. To work effectively in the field, therefore, we must find ways of forming points of connection in the network that is society, that is industry, that is the creative community.

A Question of Pedagogy

This is what I tell the students, partly in an attempt to provide them with a sense of the history of their community and its field, and partly to persuade them that collaboration is appropriate, productive, and even exciting. They tell me it may be true when applied to professional artists, but that it is unfair to make students do group work. They tell me that when they've worked in groups in the past, they were always the only one who did any work, and the others just rode on their shoulders. That their final marks were pulled down by the slackness of their team mates. That they did after all achieve a high grade but their lazy colleagues earned the same grade without lifting a finger, and it's not fair. That they are artists, not bureaucrats or members of the creative industries, and how can they possibly subsume their vision within that of the group?

True, no doubt; in some cases at least. I have a certain sympathy for their points of view, and certainly would be very reluctant to, say, co-write a novel. This is not because I avoid working with others: I have been involved in a variety of collaborative projects. But when it comes to what I frame as 'my own work', poems and prose fiction, I think I prefer to work alone. I think I work better alone. (Though to believe this I must forget the input of friends, co-writers and editors in making the finished work, and then forget that I have forgotten it. Forgetting is, after all, active, 'not something passive, a loss, but an action directed against the past' (Certeau, 1986: 3) – an action that allows me to sustain the sense of my creative autonomy.) I put this aside – I re-forget, and focus instead on what the teaching literature suggests: collaboration is a critical part of effective training.

Collaboration in this context is generally defined as interactive and student-centred learning, focused on generic qualities rather than the accomplishment of a task (Panitz, 1996), which results in graduates educated to generate, rather than simply reproduce, knowledge. David Tait and Robert de Young sum up the general perspective when they write:

> to succeed in the workplace, students need to become independent, critical thinkers who can effectively express their ideas in a collaborative environment. Collaborative learning, with its emphasis on critical thinking, problem solving, personal transformation and the social construction of knowledge is of paramount importance in areas of education and employment. (Tait & de Young, 2000: 193)

This is what we are aiming at, in developing this new area of training in collaboration: to ensure that graduates are better positioned to practice effectively.

It is not easy. The university system is not set up particularly well to accommodate the sort of 'messy' or 'wild' teaching we apply in this subject. Collaborative production teams don't follow set timetables, and students don't necessarily cooperate immediately in taking the work on as a learning experience. The cannier among them find ways of circumventing the subject's goals, or making it less painful – for instance, by organizing themselves into groups based on friendship, with the idea that it will be easier than working with strangers, or with people they don't like. We convince them that this is not how it works, usually: that groups must be formed on the basis of the extent to which an idea can be brought to life, and on the sweep of professional skills needed to realize a creative project. Certainly sometimes luck or opportunity may allow one to work in a team made up of friends, but just as often the experience is of cool respectful professionalism – or, at its worst, mutual loathing. It's not ideal, but it's all right. Just as long as each member works as a professional – that is, with courtesy, being reliable, participating actively, thinking creatively and practically, and being open to negotiation about how the project unfolds. Just as long as everyone in the group remembers that no one owns the idea. Just as long as everyone in the group has a right to involvement and discussion about what is being done, and what form and curve the idea will take.

So they pitch their projects, and organize themselves into groups. They will make animations, television advertisements, online magazines, short films, experimental poetry, site-specific installations, games ... anything that takes their fancy, is do-able, and meets the subject's objectives: to come up with a product of professional standard that can occupy a place within the creative field. Poets settle down with animators; photographers work alongside editors; everyone finds a home and something to do. How they divide up the work is up to the group. Just as long as they can start work on the project.

The Idea of Collaboration

They still aren't necessarily very happy with it all. There is always someone left out of a group, someone with a certificate excusing them from the stresses of group work, or with such heavy work or family commitments that they don't feel they'll be able to contribute. We discuss it. We find points of compromise. I remind them of the realities of creative professionalism. I remind them that it's in fact impossible to work in pure isolation: even a single person is not solitary, as Gilles Deleuze and Félix Guattari (1998) point out ('Since each of us was several, there was already quite a crowd'). Then I expound the benefits of collaboration (Thagard, 1997), which include:

- *clarification:* members are more likely to notice mistakes because they are not as buried or invested in the whole project as they would be in something that is their work only;
- *variation:* members are likely to use different techniques in solving a problem, thus speeding up the results and strengthening reliability;
- *lateral thinking:* members are more likely to come up with experimental and innovative designs and ideas (many brains make light work);
- *synergy:* collaborations bring together ideas and approaches that would otherwise be isolated, and draw out the strengths of each;
- *professional courtesy:* members show greater dependency on each other because they aren't trained or skilled in each other's methodologies; and this facilitates the development of respectful and collegial working conditions;
- *flexibility:* collaboration helps the development of problem-solving skills because each collaborator must work out how to fit together the parts that make up the project;
- *verification:* collaborative practice strengthens the justification process because collaborators must explain and justify their ideas and approaches to their partners;
- *specialization:* collaboration offers the benefits of shared load through division of labour, and hence a more efficient production.

They aren't going to lose, I assure them. They will gain. They don't necessarily believe me, but they give up the argument at this point. My teaching colleagues and I provide them with information and principles we hope will help mitigate some of the inevitable problems attendant on more than one person being in a room at the same time. It is unlikely to be painless, we know: collaboration can be intensely difficult. Conversations at conferences and parties provide many anecdotes of how it can all go wrong – of major rows between collaborators that proved insurmountable, of major but surmountable rows. But there are also stories of genuinely pleasurable experiences, one of which comes from Australian writers Tess Brady and Donna Lee Brien. They described their experience in a very useful article (Brien & Brady, 2003) that also sums up some technical and practical aspects of collaboration, and lists models of collaboration. I set these out for students in the first weeks of semester. I tell them they need to select the model most suited for the project on which they will be working – and that by the end of semester they will need to be able to analyse that model and evaluate it against others, and against how effectively it worked in their experience. The models include:

- *The contribution model*, the most common approach. Various people work on the same project, making discrete contributions to it: for example, a director, scriptwriter, camera operator and sound engineer all work on the same movie, with occasional group discussion.
- *The cooperative model.* Here one team member begins a task, and circulates it among others for their contribution. Again, the film world provides an example: one person crafts the script treatment, the next fleshes it out, and it goes on through many hands to end up as a film. In this model, there is often little discussion between team members, but the director has the overall vision and is the point of contact for all the other members.
- *The synchronous, or mutual model,* also known as joint collaboration. A difficult one to achieve, because members work closely side-by-side on each aspect of their project, and the finished project belongs to them all. It is a model likely to be used by new media practitioners and writers, who must sit together in front of the monitor, discussing, planning and realizing each step. It requires reserves of patience and grace if the work is to be achieved without resorting to violence or vitriol.

There are other models too, though they require fewer skills in collaborative practice. One is *secondary collaboration*, where one person makes a product, and the next finishes it (for instance, a writer handing a manuscript over to an editor, who brings it to the point of publication). Another is the counter-intuitively named *dictator collaboration*, where one person is in charge of the project, and makes the decisions, while the other members carry out their designated tasks. Then there is *mentor collaboration*, where an apprentice artist works with a more experienced artist or mentor to produce a work between them; and *discrete collaboration*, where each member completes his or her element independently, and all parts are combined for the final product – suitable in the production of, say, a magazine. The nominative and taxonomical impulses that seem to drive all humans, and especially academics, cause the names and subtly-different descriptions of each model to ramify. And like all taxonomical games, the barriers between each type are permeable and temporary. It is rare, Brady and Brien write, for a collaborative project to fit just one model, and remain in that form for the duration of the project. At different stages in a project, the members are likely to move in or out, take more or less responsibility. The work being undertaken, the processes followed, and the composition of the group all have an effect on what is required and expected of each member at various points along the way. I tell the students this; I tell them to expect, and indeed plan for, changing practice and changing levels of input. I urge them to talk about it with each other and, before things become too difficult, with their tutor.

Duking it Out

Before the mid-semester break the groups have consolidated and begun to produce work directed towards their chosen projects. If problems are going to emerge, this is the time they'll surface. To encourage students to approach their own ideas with fluidity and grace, I return to Nietzsche, who pointed out:

> Over immense periods of time the intellect produced nothing but errors. A few of these proved to be useful and helped to preserve the species: those who hit upon or inherited these had better luck in their struggle for themselves and their progeny. Such erroneous articles of faith, which were continually inherited, until they became almost part of the basic endowment of the species, include the following: that there are things, substances, bodies; that a thing is what it appears to be; that our will is free; that what is good for me is also good in itself. (Nietzsche, 1974: s110)

This demands of students some fancy footwork in the area of thought and ethics. Clearly Nietzsche is pointing out the problematic of 'good' and the terms of its definition. 'What is good for me is also good in itself' can be justified by sloppy postmodern thinking, which might argue that in the absence of a transcendent referent or final principles of legitimation there cannot be substantive common good (Mouffe, 1992: 229); that 'good' remains a contingent term, determined by the demands of specific contexts and by negotiation between agents in those contexts. That therefore anyone with the power to say 'what is good for me is good in itself' has a powerful argument. This is not a productive basis for collaboration, because it suggests a struggle for the authority to say 'that's good!' rather than a genuine commitment to the project. Students – or indeed any practitioners in any sort of collective – may elect to take this latter approach, and claim the right to craft an evaluative landscape for everyone else. But to achieve the benefits of collaboration, we urge them, it is more useful to pause at the point at which one is tempted to say 'what's good for me is good', reflect on this position, and consider whether it is really a good-in-itself (i.e. valid) position or just 'good for me'.

Of course there are more mechanical, or practical, ways of avoiding conflict. Both the literature and anecdote indicate that major difficulties can be avoided if the groups are small and comprise a diversity of members

(Thagard, 2002; Dillenbourg & Schneider, 1995). The smaller the group, the more likely it is that everyone is actively engaged, and that no one either feels left out, or is able to slack off and leave the work to everyone else. Difficulties are also avoided more easily if the group is not entirely homogeneous. The more alike everyone is, the less capable the group will be of garnering the benefits of collaborative practice. There should be some degree of difference in knowledge, viewpoints, attitude and politics, because this will kickstart interaction and discussion, and also introduce the possibility of passion directed towards the project goal.

It is in these early-to-middle weeks that students can be reminded too that there are identifiable phases in working collaboratively, of which Belle Alderman (2000) lists five:

(1) *engagement*, when members gather information, and together build a foundation for their project;
(2) *exploration*, during which members have unstructured time to explore their ideas and the information they have gathered;
(3) *transformation*, later on in the process, when the members clarify, elaborate and refine their information and ideas;
(4) *presentation*, at the end of semester, when they exhibit their work to an informed audience; and
(5) *reflection*, again at the end of semester and ideally for some time subsequently, when members reflect on what they have done and learned, and perhaps move on to the next phase of that project, or to a new collaborative project.

Armed with this knowledge (we hope), the students within their groups can reflect on what might be happening, and be expected to happen, at each stage of the process; and can use this knowledge to calm themselves and their group members if things seem to be getting a bit out of hand. Not that we encourage students to tick off boxes according to an arbitrary, bureaucratic timetable. Rather, we encourage them to observe and analyse the processes through which they are making the work, and the implications of the process chosen. We point them to the early pages of *A Thousand Plateaus* where Deleuze and Guattari (1988)describe issues related to collaborative practice, the process of making, and the models of collaboration. The first is an arbitrary and bureaucratic form, one designed to reproduce 'truth' and knowledge rather than to experiment and innovate. This is what they call the 'root-book'. Visualized as the single root and trunk of a tree, it describes a process and a product that is grounded in realism, in both form and content, and that papers over any distinction between story and substance. It is hierarchical and linear, with little if any allowance made for alterity.

Start at the bottom, this model implies, go on until you reach the top, and then stop. As collaborative process, this seems to countenance something like the dictator model – little room for independent thinking.

The rhizome model is set against this. It lacks the order of the root-book, lacks the beginning-middle-end pattern, lacks the uniformity and focus of its alternative. But what it offers is pretty attractive in that its untidy, non-linear, relatively unfocused shape allows the flow of thought, difference and potential, allows room for serendipity, allows points of connection that are quick light touches rather than legally-binding associations, ways of coming together and apart, together and apart. This is a promiscuous vision of production and practice, but a potentially rich one. It is not tightly controlled, of course, which can be alarming for students seeking a comfort zone or the assurance of a good grade. After all, a rhizomatic structure may result in a beautiful lawn, or field of flowers, but it may equally result in a tangled mess of weeds. We discuss this with the students. We point out that we expect work to be done in a professional manner, submitted on time and legibly, and in accordance with university standards. But we assure them that we are alive to the extent to which the rhizome model of collaboration provides the sort of open space, breathing space that helps to avoid anger or a sense of helplessness; that lets each member get on with his or her part and come together at appropriate moments to advance it; and that may allow something extraordinary and unexpected to emerge from the collaboration. We remind them that creative work is – or can be – an experiment in meaning making, and in the experience of time and space. We quote Deleuze and Guattari (1988: 5) again: 'Writing has nothing to do with signifying. It has to do with surveying, mapping, even realms that are yet to come.'

Return on Investment

That's all very well, say some of the students, but how much do they risk, in terms of grades, if they forgo the assurance and clarity of the tree model for the chaos of the rhizome? This is particularly a concern given that they already feel vulnerable, dependant on the efforts and skills of their team members, not just their individual capacity. So we discuss the issue of assessment.

The most common approach in assessing group work, according to Michael Sergi, is to distribute a group mark equally across all group members. Students are often unhappy about this because of their perception that members may receive equal marks for unequal input (Sergi, 2002: 107). To avoid this, we focus on the assessment of process for group components, and assure them that assessment takes into account not just the professional quality of the product, but the process they have experienced, and their critical reflection on that process. This is underpinned by research into pedagogies directed at adult learners. Oldfield and MacAlpine (1995: 125) write, 'One of the indicators of quality in undergraduate education is the extent to which self-learning ability is nurtured in the participants.' Self-learning, particularly that geared towards professional practice, incorporates an element of self-evaluation, and the capacity to judge work and the practice of peers. This is necessary because in the 'real world' of creative practice, peer assessment is ongoing, and critical for career development. So, though peer assessment is notoriously unreliable as a method of evaluating students' work, we build into the assessment a small weighting for peer- and self-evaluation, mainly to give the students an opportunity to practice and develop confidence in this aspect of professional life.

Of course, they have the opportunity to evaluate the subject as well. What we have found in the evaluations is that students think there is something to be said for collaboration in terms of pedagogical outcomes, professional outcomes, personal transformation and aesthetic innovations. Certainly it is tricky to teach, and sometimes agonizing for group members. Certainly it runs counter to the Romantic story of art, and to the underlying premise of the hegemonic system in which we live: neoliberalism and its doctrine of individual achievement. It rounds counter too to what we know of the politics of practice in any field, particularly that perspective summed up by Ernesto Laclau and Chantal Mouffe in their assertion that society is impossible. This is because, they argue, 'There is no single underlying principle fixing – and hence constituting – the whole field of differences' (Laclau & Mouffe, 1985: 114). Rather, society (or 'society') is an aggregation of individuals and small collectives predicated on antagonisms, competitive practices, fragmented identity and disparate interests. If they are right, and society is indeed predicated on antagonism, how can a small group of self-willed practitioners, motivated by training and predilection to commit fully to their own vision, put aside self-interest and competition to make a collaborative work? We know they (we) can, because it happens – and I suspect it happens in the same way that society works, despite its 'impossibility'. In limited, contingent moments when disharmony and dissimilarity are put aside; in temporary acts of suturing that allow us to achieve a localized and temporary shared goal. So we might lack a guarantee of final truth or perfected community, but we do have practice. Rather than being dismayed by the ontological lack at the heart of the words 'society', or 'team', we can put the term to work as a temporary truth that affords a space for production, and for practice. The better students are often the driven students, and hence perhaps more competitive than their peers; but

at least for the length of the semester, they seem capable of finding ways to be collaborators, complicit in the idea of community, of team, and able to put their energy into the shared vision of their project.

Conclusion

By the end of semester the projects are finished. Each group presents it to staff and other students, members write their assessments of each other's practice, and submit these with their personal production diaries and reflective statements on collaboration and cross-media practice. The groups disband. They may never have dealings with each other again. They may however spend the June break plotting and planning how they will develop this project further, or start something new together. From this point on, it's up to them. But still, I look again and again at the submissions students have offered, and am taken again and again by the richness that even the most cursory of projects has achieved, compared with what I have seen many of them do as individual practitioners.

I don't want to overstate the benefits of collaborative work; after all, as a radio announcer said recently, 'There's no I in "team": but there are five Is in "individual brilliance"!' A fair point. Still, working collaboratively has its values. Importantly, it has the capacity to change those involved in the process – even those involved on the edges, as we are when engaging only as teachers. It crafts a context where we are continually reminded that we are not in control of the situation, that there are things we don't know, that outcomes are not pre-determined. And it has broadened my knowledge and my horizons: I still don't know how to make an animation or a computer game; I still don't care much about video clips for boy bands or angry mags for grrrls. But my tastes and interests have been inflected by my students and their projects. Lately I've begun dabbling in new media and public space projects, and viewing that part of the field with a different set of eyes. The biologists insist that human beings are simply cognitive elements of a greater whole, continually interacting with, changing and being changed by our environments. That sort of interaction, and that alteration, become very visible when teaching and/or participating in collaborative practice.

Note

1. Field, for Pierre Bourdieu, refers to a relatively autonomous social system, and its structures, discourses, internal logic and rules of behaviour (Bourdieu, 1993: 162). Fields are cognate with the traditional 'social institutions' – education, government, law – but extend into other, and more specific, areas of practice; particularly, for my research interest, the field of cultural or creative production.

References

Alderman, B. (2000) *Get Real!* Collaborative learning in higher education. *TEXT* 4 (1). On WWW at http://www.gu.edu.au/school/art/text/april00/alderman. htm. Accessed 27.5.02.

Bourdieu, P. (1991) *Language and Symbolic Power* (J.B Thompson, ed.; G. Raymond and M. Adamson, trans). Cambridge: Polity.

Bourdieu, P. (1993) *The Field of Cultural Production: Essays on Art and Literature* (R. Johnson, ed.). Cambridge: Polity.

Brien, D.L. and Brady, T. (2003) Collaborative practice: Categorising forms of collaboration for practitioners. *TEXT* 7 (2). On WWW at http://www.gu.edu.au/school/art/text/oct03/bienbrady.htm. Accessed 28.4.04.

de Certeau, M. (1086) *Heterologies: Discourse on the Other* (B. Massumi, trans.). Minneapolis, MN: University of Minnesota Press.

Deleuze, G. and Guattari, F. (1988) *A Thousand Plateaus: Capitalism and Schizophrenia* (B. Massumi, trans.). London: Continuum.

Dillenbourg, P. and Schneider, D. (1995) Collaborative learning and the Internet. School of Psychology and Education Sciences, University of Geneva. On WWW at tecfa.unige.ch/tecfa/research/CMC/colla/iccai95_1.html. Accessed 2.06.02.

Laclau, E. and Mouffe, C. (1985) *Hegemony and Socialist Strategy: Towards a Radical Democratic Politics*. London: Verso.

Mouffe, C. (ed.) (1992) *Dimensions of Radical Democracy: Pluralism, Citizenship, Community*. London: Verso.

Nietzsche, F. (1968) *The Will to Power* (W. Kaufmann and R.J. Hollingdale, trans.). New York: Vintage Books.

Nietzsche, F. (1974) *The Gay Science: With a Prelude in Rhymes and an Appendix of Songs* (W. Kaufmann, trans.). New York: Vintage Books.

Oldfield, K.A and MacAlpine, J.M.K. (1995) Peer and self-assessment at tertiary level: An experiential report. *Assessment and Evaluation in Higher Education*, 20 (1), 125–32.

Panitz, T. (1996) A definition of collaborative vs cooperative learning. *Deliberations.* On WWW at www.lgu.ac.uk/deliberations/collab.learning/panitz2.html. Accessed 2.06.02.

Sergi, M. (2002) Using long-term peer assessment to derive individual marks from group work. In A. Arnott, J. Cameron and G. Shaw (eds) *Tertiary Teaching* (pp. 105–118). Darwin: NTU Press.

Tait, D. and de Young, R. (191–204) Displaying the law: A cross-disciplinary learning experiment using the Internet and multimedia technology. *International Review of Law Computers and Technology* 14 (2), 191–204.

Thagard, P. (1997) Collaborative knowledge. University of Waterloo, Ontario. On WWW at cogsci.uwaterloo.ca/Articles/Pages/Collab.html. Accessed 27.9.02.

Williams, R. (1981) *Culture*. Glasgow: Fontana Books.

Zolberg, V. (1990) *Constructing a Sociology of the Arts*. Cambridge: Cambridge University Press.

Chapter 11
Writer as Teacher, Teacher as Writer

AILEEN LA TOURETTE

I'm going to begin this chapter by talking from the point of view of the taught rather than the teacher. My subject is the effect of the teaching of Creative Writing on one's own creative work. Part of my reason for beginning with myself as Creative Writing student is to identify first hand what *can* be taught, and part is to pay tribute to a few outstanding teachers.

It's easy to say that *craft* can be taught, as many Creative Writing teachers do; it's an honourable way out, and certainly craft must be taught. But 'craft' doesn't come in isolation from something else that we also seek to teach, and learn; and the teaching and learning are as inseparable as are the craft and the *art*; for surely that is the word? But art is unteachable; surely that is also true?

'We teach our children one thing only, as we were taught: to wake up. We teach our children to look alive there, to join by words and activities the life of human culture on the planet's crust'. That's Annie Dillard (1984:97), American mystic (for want of a better word) and writer on spiritual matters – again, the language falters. Read Annie Dillard, decide for yourself what she is. But 'waking up' is definitely what there is to do, to teach, to be taught. What is literature for, if not to wake us from the sleep of habit and routine, to remove the film they place and re-place over our senses, feelings, thoughts? And so we teach students about hooking readers with their first line and not letting them go to sleep – to sleep on your feet is the thing to flee, to dream while waking is the thing to court and conjure and command. All our techniques are bent towards this, all our craft is to compel it.

Craft and technique involve negative effort as well. In *The Writing Life*, Annie Dillard quotes Henry James from *The Spoils of Poynton* on the Via Negativa of writing, in what she calls:

> ... a comical pair of sentences that rises to a howl: 'Which is the work in which he hasn't surrendered, under dire difficulty, the best thing he meant to have kept? In which indeed, before the dreadful *done,* doesn't

he ask himself what has become of the thing all for the sweet sake of which it was to proceed to that extremity?' (Dillard: 1989:5)

To take out the self-regarding sentence, to remove the over-explicit paragraph, to pare down, to leave space for the reader's own imaginative leap; these are also part and parcel of what we do, or try to do.

So it would seem, using Dillard and James as mentors, that we need to learn to wake up and also to leave out, remove or destroy something beloved but intrusive and cumbersome. These are the positive and negative charges of learning to write. How do we learn these things, and how do we teach them?

Two teachers gave me my initial lessons in how to write – and also, though I didn't know it at the time, in how to teach writing. They were both nuns. The second of the two was a Dominican in a white habit, a shrewd poet who taught on the first formal Creative Writing course I ever took, as an undergraduate. She ran a very structured course, beginning with an Abecedary: we were to take the alphabet and use it in a poem or a piece of prose. We could use any style, any form, but it had to be consistent. It was a return to childhood, in a sense, even a return to a fictitious childhood where we had learned the alphabet. I certainly did not remember the actual childhood moment when I had actually learned it, beyond a dim memory of kindergarten chanting.

I also recall a James Dickey poem she gave us that was based on a true story of a stewardess who was sucked out of a plane. She removes her clothing as she falls, and her trajectory is described in detail. The poem links in my head now with the Falling Man from the North Tower on September 11, 2001, and the other jumpers. At the time, it was not what we expected from a rotund Dominican nun, and I'm sure she was aware of that. She had guessed that we were all in the process of 'falling' and discarding clothing as we went, sucked into our first sexual experiences. She was giving us permission to be where we were, mid-air, enjoying the fall. She was also telling us that writing involved a similar fall to earth and removal of layers along the way.

Further back there was Mel Loomis, SHCJ, as she now is. At the time she was Mother Christopher Mary and had not yet appeared re-incarnated in lay clothes and her real name. But she loved literature, and she gave us space to find our own literary loves. It was during this period that I discovered Eliot. The recognition of something essential and urgent in the work of a writer – the feeling of a hunger, unexpressed and perhaps unacknowledged, satisfied – is overwhelming. Those people who point us in the right direction and then stand back cannot be thanked enough.

I heard Toni Morrison speak at the ICA in London in the 80s, back when she was still a Random House editor dressed in expensive high heels and New York suit. She described the process by which she came to writing by saying that she wrote the books she needed to read, books that did not exist until she wrote them. Morrison related this lack to the fact that all the books that did exist had white males as their central characters or, or if not their central characters, as primary and pivotal characters: husbands, sons, brothers. Her books were the first she found that did not place the white male at the centre of experience.

In a way, I think what she said is true for every writer; we all write the books, poems, stories and plays we need. I read Eliot at 15, thanks to a nun who was discovering literature for herself; and the hunger he satisfied awakened another. He came the closest to saying what I needed to hear, which made me know that I had never, actually, heard it. Even in him there was something left out, something essential and urgent. He nudged me towards it, emboldened me to find the words myself.

We all know reading and writing are utterly inextricable, in teaching and in writing. The only absolute rule for writing is that you must read. Every other rule can be broken, every other technique is up for grabs. Do workshops work? Are exercises useful? Sometimes yes, sometimes no. But the hunger to read, to find what reading brings, must be there in order to incite the other hunger, to write. We need to find texts for our students. We need to be ready with just this line, this novel, to give just this reference at this moment, perfect as a prescription – or not. In order to do this we need to keep up, to discover new remedies as well as re-visit old ones. That need is one way in which the teaching of Creative Writing enriches and furthers our own writing – by keeping us keeping up. By keeping us reading, by keeping us reading as writers, scouring what we read for what we need.

Beyond these two teachers, when I start to think about it, stand many more. The fact that they all wear habits is an oddity – but not exactly an accident. The nuns who taught me in primary school were woefully untutored and inadequate when it came to science. They struggled with the teaching of arithmetic. But they knew their English grammar. They sent us to the board to diagram (parse) increasingly complex sentences, an exercise I loved. There was craft; there was a method for uncovering the bare bones of written language.

Nothing is as crucial as a firm grounding in grammar. Raymond Carver, in a posthumous book of uncollected writing put together by Tess Gallagher, tells us:

I forget who first passed along a collection of (Isaac) Babel's *Collected*

Stories to me, but I do remember coming across a line from one of his greatest stories. I copied it into the little notebook I carried around with me everywhere in those days. The narrator, speaking about Maupassant and the writing of fiction, says: 'No iron can pierce the heart with such force as a period put in just the right place.' (Carver, 1991a: 125)

This internalizing of the structure of language, the sense of language, comes partly from the formal teaching of grammar itself, but primarily, I believe, from reading. It's as we read that the lesson sinks in. It's an osmotic process, complemented by formal teaching. One last thing about my own schooling that seems relevant is that during these early years in what was a poorish parish school, two grades were taught in one room. The nun would assign work to one grade while she went to teach the other. If you finished your work before she returned, you were free to select a book from the cupboard and read. This reading time was as precious as it was constant. There was no wasted time in the eight years of primary school, because of it. Had my particular bent been for science or maths, I would have been ill-served. But for someone whose focus was language, the education I had could hardly have been bettered. *Seton Poems*, a little book from which we had to memorize and then recite, included poems by Catholic poets such as Joyce Kilmer, but also Keats. It was named for Mother Seton, who founded the Sisters of Charity, Convent Station – who obviously thought poems were important. They were right. Poems are essential; reading is essential:

Literary writing must be located not only in relation to its closest neighbours but also in relation to its models. I mean by models not *sources* ... but syntagmatic *patterns*, typical fragments of sentences, formulas, if you like, whose origins are not identifiable but which make up part of the collective memory of literature. *To write* is to let these models come to one and to *transform* them ...'(Barthes, 1986a: 97)

I like the use of the verb 'located' here. Learning locates something for us, it seems to me, if it works at all. I also like the idea of ' ... let(ting) these models come to one ... ' as a description of a kind of receptivity.

Now to the teaching of Creative Writing. My students are mostly in late youth or some phase of middle age. They have already become readers; or not. They have already internalized the structures and complexities of language; or not. They know that punctuation makes sense of language, pauses the flow of words, halts it, starts it up again, slides a sentence forwards or backwards, holds it steady or pitches it into a continuous stream; or not.

Many of the students I teach come from the 'or not' category. They have not had the privilege of the early, passionate training in language that I was paradoxically lucky enough to receive. Can it be too late? Are the 'or nots' lost to language in some real sense? It may sound like a desperately elitist question, but I know of no one who teaches Creative Writing and does not deplore and at times despair of the lack of appetite for reading on the part of students, the lack of competence in grammar and sentence structure. How do you pass on the most fundamental thing(s) of all?

I'd like to talk about teaching creative writing in Belmarsh Prison in 1991–92. Belmarsh had just been opened, which made it, according to the inmates who'd been inside before, and that was most of them – a strange nick, lacking in atmosphere and 'prison culture' – their phrase, not mine. Belmarsh had not yet become famous, or infamous, or associated with lifers, with terrorists, with Category 'A' prisoners in general.

At any rate, I worked with Category 'B's and 'C's. 'A' Wing was sealed off and separate, a prison within a prison. 'B' Wing housed everybody, violent or non-violent. Many of the men were on remand, there for short periods of time before being sentenced and shipped somewhere else.

We had a restless, changing, agitated population for our three-hour sessions. Three hours is a long time. No smoking – except that the men stood by the windows and smoked, sometimes tobacco and sometimes dope – I stood by the window after a class one afternoon and realized that, the longer I stood there, the higher I got. But to the punch line. I was naive and experimental and what I found worked, above and beyond anything else, was war poetry – Wilfred Owen, especially - and *Macbeth*. A little bit of Yeats, I had success with – 'The Song of Wandering Aengus', for the druggy music – or at least that's how it was heard.

But those guys loved Macbeth. They taught it to me. They got it more intimately than I ever had. They identified the fault line the witches pressed on. They wrote their own version, which they called *MacCrack*. The three witches were replaced by the Pipe Oracle – and as we were rehearsing, getting into the swing, the core group was shipped out – whether by sheer bad luck or out of the system's malice, I never knew.

I think what I'm saying, or trying to say, is that there's a power in language that can overcome limitations, even huge limitations, if it gets a chance. There's a way that language can leap right out and seize people by the throat, Wedding Guest-like, and pour out stories that make a mark even if they don't entirely make sense. After all, most of us have a feeling about words before we quite *get* them. We have a dim sense of what they can do. We have a hungry sense of what they can give us. Then, somehow, we find ourselves taking them in and giving them out.

This process can happen at any stage of life. I am convinced of that. It might be against more odds, it might be harder and more piecemeal when the process happens late on rather than early. But – like the learning of languages per se – it does not become impossible; only more of a struggle, more of a conscious, willed process rather than one that simply happens.

The effect of watching the process at Belmarsh was electrifying. Over and over again, words seized hold of men who were surprised to find themselves in the headlock of language. They might be reminded of poems or stories they'd loved and all but forgotten; but not forgotten. Never entirely forgotten or entirely gone. How to trigger the wisp or bleep of memory, the trace, the sense impression – that's what our endless workshop exercises are for. That, and fantasy – getting a glimpse or a snapshot of what goes on in the imagination. When people do remember, and/or imagine, in the blurred and overlapping processes that these words define, we're amazed. That amazement is itself an amazing thing. It can feed your own work, remind you why you do it. The hard, driving process of arriving at it can, of course, deprive you of time and energy *to* do it. Motivating vulnerable and difficult people is a hard task, sometimes a draining one. I learned deep relaxation techniques when I taught at Belmarsh. I had to. I came home frozen stiff with tension, unable to relax.

To get to that amazement, you have to take risks. You have to hand out texts that might work or might not. You can't condescend and make assumptions. Students may understand your beloved texts better than you do. Or they may reject them, trample them underfoot. Either way, you have to risk them; and keep finding new ones.

When I was Writer in Residence at HMP (Her Majesty's Prison – full British title of such places) Ford, I learned to go back to my Bed and Breakfast and cry. There is also the problem of detachment and engagement, of finding the delicate line. You can bring too much home with you. You can be distracted, pulled from concentration, left without the necessary ruthlessness to get your work done, physically and emotionally exhausted. You can be depleted by needs and demands you can never meet, overwhelmed by the spectacle of need, by the sheer dimensions of the problems people face. You make terrible discoveries – the dark side of amazement. Like the fact that people can be too damaged to accept praise for a piece or, in workshop jargon, 'positive feedback' – that sometimes you have to find tactful ways of doling out the positive, rationing it, like giving food to starving people. You have to find strategies to make good things acceptable – bad ones go down easily.

A bit of a tangent, but not really. Because lessons like that are learned dramatically, and the drama of learning them takes a toll. Creative energy increases exponentially, to a point – then it collapses. Energy is energy, on some level. Distraction – exhaustion – would that everyone who employed you as a teacher of Creative Writing cared that your own creative resources were fed, enhanced, protected. Most don't. They see you as a resource, as a tool in some sense of the word – to till their fields, not yours. How do you assert your own need to write? With difficulty – or not at all. You don't assert it, you just do it. Beg, borrow, steal the time and energy from other pursuits, from other people, from your students and your children and your partner and your friends. Cheat on them all, with your muse – or don't, and take the consequences.

And so to the academy. The refuge, the sanctum. It is and isn't, as we all know. Coming on the heels of far tougher places, it feels like a haven. People are interested in your work. They encourage it. Colleagues share your difficulties and frustrations. You are less alone. Isolation is one of those Catch 22s we all face. Necessary; destructive. Define isolation. Does it mean solitude, or loneliness? Drenched in silence, or drowning in it? Another fine line must be found, and lost, and found, and lost, over and over again. Working with groups leaves you in need of two things – being alone, and also having relationships to sustain you, outside the groups.

Some of the tensions fade, at least, within the academy. The students are there voluntarily – a big plus. More concentration can go on text. The joy of looking at text – concentrating on it, digging into it – is enormous, and feeds your work like nothing else. Entering into a dialogue with a student's text, rather than with the student, is a pristine sort of practice that enhances and refreshes your own critical skills, your sense of what writing and words *are*, or can be, as you go along.

It isn't always pristine. Marking periods come along and you are buried in an avalanche of scripts. What chance for close encounters of a literary / textual kind then? It is, for me at least, impossible to write during a marking period. You can hold on to writing while you teach, if only just. You can't hold on to it while marking. The concentration involved is simply too great. You have to put your own work absolutely on hold for two weeks, or however long it lasts. There is no choice here, no option of sneaking off for an hour or two. Your fallow hours are vegetative, spent languishing in front of the TV or asleep. You might manage newspapers and magazines. Otherwise, even reading is too much.

But the environment is a sympathetic one, and the students are not so desperate that they are both difficult to come to and difficult to leave behind. Their basic motivation is in place, and motivating people is the thing that takes it out of you. They may require specific motivation to go further, re-draft, edit more finely, imagine more powerfully. But although teaching can be draining and students demanding, you are not operating in the absence of an intention, even a desire, to write. You do not have to create that desire before you can start, and re-create it every time you arrive on the scene.

And even marking is made of concentration on text – what else? Dialogue with the written word, finding the pitfalls, identifying the strengths and weaknesses in a piece of student work, must boost the critical powers. Finding yourself unresponsive to a piece in *that way* that makes you think the problem might be in you and not in it and having a colleague at hand to discuss and debate it with, is invaluable if not always comfortable. Someone else may hold the key that unlocks the door, and once the door is open you can walk in and see what's there. Another room is added to your own house of fiction.

There can and should be a connective current between Creative Writing departments and full-time writers. I work with two full-time playwrights on my first year Introduction to Dramatic Writing module. They make a living at it, or at any rate survive on it. If there is a degree of envy that operates between us (and I can only speak for my own intermittent envy of their freedom to concentrate all their energies on their writing, while I imagine that they might occasionally envy the relative security of my position and the ability to teach in one place rather than scramble around the city, as they do) we both have everything to gain from our engagement with each other, and the students have even more to gain from their contact with all of us. Our Royal Literary Fund rents out writers to institutions of higher learning – paying the rent itself, giving the writer some income and giving the institution a writer whom students can consult on a one-to-one basis – invaluable. The Fund's fellows have contributed a great deal to the ethos of our department, as have the guests who come and go, contributing workshops and readings to the MA and MPhil programmes. The academy has to invite in the world and also go out into it as we do with our students, trekking them into Wales on writers' retreats, taking them away from the familiar and the mundane.

All of these things – arranging the visits, the speakers, the residentials, organizing part-timers –take effort, administration, planning. Guests require entertaining, which can be costly in terms of sleep, concentration, discipline, sobriety – these are all factors that can detract from your work and your ability to complete it. To bring something to a finished, polished state of completion, whatever that means –and we all know it means something – is not an easy task. Skip a step in the process and the work shows it. Writing is a jealous god who says *Thou shalt write* and very little else. Perhaps, *pace* Henry James, the word comes down from on high to get rid of something in one's writing as well, to sacrifice cherished sentences, paragraphs, pages, chapters and volumes. But the jealous god must be listened to and listened for, and the list of activities I have just described can also serve as static to jam the messages and prevent them coming in, to blur, distort or simply drown out the one voice that we need to hear,

Festivals – what a nightmare! Papers, conferences, meetings of various kinds – what a whirlwind of activity surrounds each one. More entertaining, more distraction. Books like this. Why am I writing about writing, instead of writing? When I think about it – all of it – I come back again to text. We read and re-read. We search and search again. We consider and re-consider. What a way to make a living, investigating text. It has its contradictions. How do you investigate what makes the mermaids sing? Eliot worked in a bank, Larkin in a library. Pablo Neruda was a politician and member of Salvador Allende's cabinet, as well as a poet. Depression, long considered an occupational hazard for writers, might have something to do with isolation and lack of structure. Sylvia Plath was arguably more balanced while she was teaching than after she gave up. Perhaps her students kept her in touch with some kind of daily reality and prevented her from focusing too obsessively on her own demons. Much as writers slaver for time, time can be quicksand. There are inner obstacles as well as outer ones to overcome and for some of us, at least, the inner ones are more ferocious and less easy to combat. We can deal with the occasional teaching or marking overload. Psychic overload, being stranded from a sense of usefulness and contact with other human beings who struggle with the same dilemmas we face, can be a lot more unwieldy.

The first course I ever taught was in the aftermath of first novel publication, as it is for most people. It was a fairly steep learning curve. You had an ill-assorted group of people who wanted something from you. In the end, it's your ear. Your ability to listen, to hear the right note or the wrong one in their work. You learn to listen hard, to identify quickly what's going on, what's not happening, what chimes and what clashes. You learn more and more about the most precious of all human powers, the power of concentration. You teach concentration, in a sense. Our exercises are intensive in order that students can concentrate without distraction, without having time for anxiety or second-guessing. They go at writing in one go, and see what emerges. At best, they surprise themselves. Something is captured. A flicker, a flare, nothing finished or definite, but something with a hint of life.

Then, of course, the work begins. We all know the danger of living for what Adrienne Rich (1967: 24) calls 'glitter in fragments and first drafts'. Taking it away and putting it in final shape is the next task, and it spawns a million other tasks of drafting and re-drafting, reading and re-reading, editing *ad nauseam*. How much easier to admire the sudden gleam of phrase in an exercise, to read it out to startled admiration and leave it at that. We live with the same temptations as our students because we do the same workshops. We face the same choices they do. We are with them in a community of writers that links us to the long-dead and the still-to-come.

> A good creative writing teacher can save a good writer a lot of time. I think he can save a bad writer a lot of time, too, but we don't need to go into that. Writing is tough and lonely work, and wrong paths can easily be taken. If we are doing our job, creative writing teachers are performing a necessary negative function. If we are any good as teachers, we should be teaching young writers how not to write and teaching them to teach themselves how not to write. (Carver, 1991b: 132)

If we're good learners, we'll be learning how not to write at the same time, and saving ourselves some time, too – maybe evening out the time we spend teaching and not writing. After all, if we're really good teachers, we'll be like Barthes' great teacher Christian Metz, who ' ... always demonstrates ... that *he is teaching himself* what he is supposed to be communicating to others' (Barthes, 1986b: 177).

The publishing industry is changing, failing writers and writing as the market takes all. When Graham Greene died, someone wrote in the daily press in answer to a comment that there would never be another Greene that no, there would not, for the simple reason that Greens' publisher had allotted him the time and space to develop as a writer, without undue pressure to produce or sell. Writers were no longer granted such indulgence; hence there would be no more writers like him.

Surely we must take up the slack and nurture writers, including ourselves. We must provide the salons, the opportunities for conversations with other writers, the rich mixtures of people on which writers thrive. We must provide them for everyone who wants them. It is not easy to claim the territory of writer, to claim the name, to take one's own ambitions seriously. As Eavan Boland maintains in her wonderful essay 'In Defence of Workshops', it is not true that talent will out:

> The truth is that there is such a thing as societal permission to be a poet. Even the notion offends many sensibilities. The idea that a society issues subtle, strict and often ungenerously distributed permissions to exercise an innate gift upsets the contrary elite and romantic view that excellence will out. The sudden recognition of the irrefutable voice. These are conventional, 19th century views of poetic development. They are also male, white and middle class. Langstan Hughes could tell a different story, and does in his autobiography. As does Sylvia Plath in her memoirs and Adrienne Rich in her essays.

There is no area in which a grudging societal permission is a more malign presence than in the elusive distance between writing a poem and being a poet. For many poets this is the beginning of everything. They write a poem; they surprise themselves. And that beginning – the writing of a poem – is interior, graced and free from any pressure. Then complexity enters in, For the sake of the next poem, for the sake of the dignity they should confer on themselves, they need to call themselves a poet and not just a writer of poems. This is where they feel the pressure; absence of societal permission. Instead of putting together the act and the definition of the act, they are tentative, diffident. (Boland, 1991: 42)

We can give permission to ourselves, and our students, to claim this ground. It isn't a once-and-for-all kind of claim. It's a claim we have to make over and over again, with each piece we write. We can legitimize each other's efforts and have our own struggles legitimized. This is the most crucial thing of all, and it's completely a matter of give and take. Permission to take oneself seriously as a writer, despite what family, friends, the publishing industry, may have to say at any given time – this is priceless, and this is what the teaching of creative writing can provide. It isn't the only essential. But without it the rest can get lost, and stay lost.

References

Barthes, R. (1986a) Style and its Image. In *The Rustle of Language* (R. Howard, trans.). Oxford: Basil Blackwell Ltd.

Barthes, R. (1986b) To Learn and to Teach. In *The Rustle of Language* (R. Howard, trans.). Oxford: Basil Blackwell Ltd.

Boland, E. (1991) In defence of workshops. *Poetry Ireland Review* 31 (Winter–Spring), 42.

Carver, R. (1991a) On Where I'm Calling From. In *No Heroics, Please*. London: Harvill.

Carver, R. (1991b) Steering by the Stars. In *No Heroics, Please*. London: Harvill.

Dillard, A. (1984) *Teaching a Stone to Talk*. London: Picador, 1984.

Dillard, A. (1989) *The Writing Life*. New York: Harper & Row.

Rich, A. (1967) *Snapshots of a Daughter-in-Law*. New York: W.W. Norton & Co. Inc.

Chapter 12

The Ladies and the Baggage: Raymond Carver's Suppressed Research and the Apologetic Short Story

ROB MIMPRISS

> We do not claim to rank among the military novelists. Our place is with
> the non-combatants. When the decks are cleared for action we go below
> and wait meekly. We should only be in the way of the manoeuvres that
> the gallant fellows are performing overhead. We shall go no further with
> the —th than to the city gate: and leaving Major O'Dowd to his duty,
> come back to the Major's wife, and the ladies and the baggage.
> Thackeray, *Vanity Fair*, 1877: 275.

'Fires' and the Embarrassed Writer

In his autobiographical essay, 'Fires,' Raymond Carver blames his use of
the short story on an accident of personal history. A father before he was 20,
struggling alongside his wife to earn a living despite his lack of education
and skills (Carver, 2000: 96–97), and forced in his free time to consider the
needs and wishes of his children, Carver found he lacked the energy and
will to invest in any longer narrative form. The attraction of the short story
lay in rapid execution: a story could be finished in a day or two, 'after [he]
got in from work and before [he] lost interest,' and it seems that 'these
ferocious years of parenting' (p. 100) created a habit, a fearful need for
immediate results, that subsequent leisure and critical endorsement were
unable to break. Or this may be the reason he does not write novels; he
thinks so (p. 102).

The almost-insurmountable challenges of parenting and poverty to
writing were famously predicted by Cyril Connolly (1938: 125–127) in
Enemies of Promise. It also seems that they commonly impel writers to the
short story, since the Welsh-language writer Kate Roberts (1891–1985) cites
similar reasons for her use of the form. In an interview included by

Saunders Lewis (1949: 9) in his book, *Crefft y Stori Fer*, Roberts tells him that *'Rhyw un peth yn dyfod ar draws y meddwl, a gweld deunydd stori yn hwnnw, ac efallai, meddwl nad oedd yn digon o amser i gynhyrchu nofel, petai'r syniad yn dyfod'* ['Something comes to mind, and you see the material for a story in it, and perhaps you think there's no time to produce a novel, even if it occurs to you']. Later (Lewis, 1949: 20) she adds that she doesn't think she could write a long novel, *'gan ei bod yn ormod trafferth ysgrifennu'r pethau llanw'* ['since it would be too much trouble writing things in full'].

It is curious that these statements take the tone of apologies, since few novelists would seek to excuse their use of long narratives by an excess of wealth or leisure. As apologies they are also inappropriate to these two writers' achievements, since their stories remain among the finest the form has yet produced. But one notices in both writers the guardedness of the explanation, the 'perhaps,' and one may suspect that more lies behind these writers' choice of form than they are willing or able to say. Kate Roberts's comments about craft and inspiration are hard to reconcile with the stories themselves, and Raymond Carver's pedagogic essay, 'On Writing,' offers few original insights, consisting largely of slogans and quotations which he invites us to record on three-by-five cards (Carver, 2000: 88). Yet his first collection, *Will You Please Be Quiet, Please?* (Carver, 1976) is penetrating in its discussion of the short story and its significance. The heroine of the first story, 'Fat,' describing a day at work to a friend, continues to nag at the hidden meaning of an encounter which her friends and husband tell her is unremarkable or comic (Carver, 1976: 3): a hint from Carver, perhaps, as to the way we should nag at the hidden meanings of his stories. A character in 'Put Yourself in My Shoes' offers his friend the writer various anecdotes he hopes will provide the material for short stories, but the real story lies in the aggressiveness of his demands, the demands of the bad reader for the trite and embittered in short stories (Carver, 1976: 106–110). But perhaps 'The Student's Wife' (1976: 90–96) reveals most clearly Raymond Carver's thinking about the short story form. For it is, very clearly, one of his most graceful designs: covering the hours between night and dawn, and with one major and one minor character, it nevertheless conveys a picture of their life together and a sense of the world they inhabit. Thematically, it is one of Carver's most far-reaching, for the protagonist's solitude and insomnia, her fear of the sunrise, and the brevity and ambiguity of her prayer encourage us to read the story as an exploration of ontological suffering. But it is also thoughtfully modelled on a Chekhov (1998) story, 'The Student,' and the protagonist's experiences recall the main themes in Frank O'Connor's (1963a) study of the short story form, *The Lonely Voice*. My burden in this chapter, presented by a detailed close reading of 'The

Student's Wife,' is that, rather than explaining or defending his use of an unpopular form through his critical or pedagogic writing, Carver – and other writers like him – may encode such an apologetic within his creative practice. Moreover, this apologetic could not otherwise be expressed without embarrassment, for it refers to the less considered aspects of O'Connor's argument: to the experience of 'religion [as] the aspect of depth in the totality of the human spirit' to use Paul Tillich's (1959: 7–8) phrase, on his experience of religion as 'ultimate concern'.

'The Student's Wife' and the Writer as Apologist

When 'The Student's Wife' begins, the student, Mike, is reading to Nan, his wife, from Rilke. Rilke is 'a poet he admired' and we are told that 'he read well – a confident, sonorous voice' that sends Nan into dreams of the Arabesque and exotic while he carries on reading aloud (Carver, 1976: 90). It is when Mike stops to turn the light out that she feels unable to sleep. She is hungry, and asks him to make her a sandwich; she has pains in her shoulders, arms and legs; and she is afraid of being awake on her own. She tells him first about a dream, and then invites him to recall a fishing trip they took in the early years of their marriage, and she tries to persuade him to compare his likes and dislikes and aspirations with hers. She likes food, good books and travelling; she would like the money to buy new clothes for herself and the family; and she would like them to have 'a place of their own' so that they can 'stop moving around every year.' But Mike by this time is almost asleep, and when she asks him to reciprocate, he wishes only that she would leave him alone (Carver, 1976: 94). Still awake after Mike has gone to sleep, she first prays that God will end her wakefulness, and then goes into the other room to look at magazines and to watch the sunrise (p. 95–96). The sunrise is remarkable, for we are told she had never realised 'a sunrise was so terrible as this' (p. 96), and the prayer is also disturbing. For since her request to God to 'please help us' (p. 96) comes at the very end of the story, we will never know whether or not such help arrives, and nothing in the story makes us entirely sure what kind of help is being asked for. Even the pronoun 'us' is ambiguous, for it could refer to the woman and her husband, or to the couple and their children, or even to the whole human race.

Chekhov's 'The Student' is somewhat different. Ivan Velikopolsky, a theology student, is coming home on Good Friday after a day of shooting. The weather turns cold, and he remembers the suffering endured by Russians 'in the days of Ryurik, Ivan the Terrible and Peter the Great' (Chekhov, 1998: 176). He stops to talk with two peasant women at their bonfire, listening to the older woman's memories of her time as a wet nurse and nanny. But the cold and the fire inspire him to describe the events preceding the Passion, when the apostle Peter also warmed his hands at a fire before his denial of Christ. When Ivan leaves the women the older of the two is in tears, and this is not because of his 'gift for poignant narrative,' but because all human beings are linked through the unbroken chain of human history. Ivan has 'touched one end' of the chain, and the other has 'vibrated,' and he goes away affirmed in his humanity and confident in the goodness of the universe (Chekhov, 1998: 178).

Between Chekhov's story and Carver's story, one instantly feels a change in mood. For the allusions in Carver's apologetic short story remind us of the honour and richness of his tradition, stretching back to the work of this older writer and achieving, through Chekhov and through Carver himself, equality with the dramatic and poetic traditions. But Chekhov's story, through which Carver reminds us of this accomplishment, is itself a celebration of narrative, of stories passed down through memory and history in an experience as universal and timeless as the warming of hands by a fire – and Carver himself draws on such ancient narratives, modelling 'Popular Mechanics' on a story of Solomon (Carver, 1982: 103–105; 1 Kings 3:16–28).[1] Writing short stories is no modern aberration, but neither is it mere repetition, and Carver, writing in a feminist and post-Christian age, reinterprets and reuses Ivan's story-telling in 'The Student' to represent, not only the richness and antiquity of the short story tradition, but the manner in which that tradition is disregarded or suppressed.

At the start of Carver's story, Mike is reading to Nan from Rilke: a poet Carver himself may like, and may have come across at college as a key figure in European modernism. He therefore shares with Ivan a sense of culture and heritage, and a desire to pass on this advantage to others: on the fishing trip years ago (he too is a sportsman) he read to her from Browning and the *Rubáiyát* (Carver, 1976: 92). Both men are skilful communicators, for Ivan provides a very vivid account of Christ's arrest and Peter's denial (Chekhov, 1998: 177), and Mike's reading of Rilke, 'now pitched low and somber, now rising, now thrilling,' penetrates Nan's dreams (Carver, 1976: 90). But this communication is always from man to woman, for Ivan is content that the women should be moved but stay silent, and Mike expects Nan first to listen and then to sleep.

The response of the peasant women to Peter's denial of Christ suggests pity, but also repentance. Vasilisa is moved to tears, but hides her face with her sleeve 'as if ashamed of the tears,' while Lukerya blushes as she stares at the student, and her face becomes 'distressed and tense as if she was holding back a terrible pain' (Chekhov, 1998: 178). If these women are aware that it is their sin, like Peter's, that necessitated the scourging and crucifixion of Christ, if they feel that any sin committed in the light of this knowledge is also a deliberate betrayal of Christ, if they are moved to compassion by Peter's agonised repentance and are afraid to sin as he sinned, then their responses are culturally and spiritually appropriate. Their silent devotion is also a Christian response, for one woman in the Gospels wets Christ's feet with her tears whilst drying – or hiding – them with her hair (Luke 7:37–38), and traditionally it is the same woman who is silent before Christ when dragged before him as an adulteress (John 8:1–11). The same spirit is required of women by the Apostle Paul: to learn in quietness and full submission, and not to teach or have authority over a man, for it was Adam who was formed first, and then Eve (1 Timothy 2:11-14).

The response of the peasant women to Ivan, in silence, blushes and tears, perhaps suggests the appreciative silence that Mike expects of Nan. But if so, the narrative of which Mike is a priest, the narrative of Browning, FitzGerald and Rilke, has lost the older narrative's cohesive and emotive power. Devotion has given way to discourse, and where, in Chekhov's story, communication ends, Nan produces a narrative of her own – plaintive, disjointed and inconsequential – consisting of a dream, a memory and list of desires.

In Nan's dream the two are staying at a small hotel by an unfamiliar lake, and since they are on holiday near water and there are no children with them, the dream recalls their earlier marriage as described in the memory that Nan then relates. In the dream, an older couple invite them out in their boat, and since the thwart will seat only three, Nan and Mike each claim for themselves the sacrifice of sitting in the stern. Nan wins the argument, but the cramped posture hurts her legs, and when she is afraid that the boat is being swamped, she wakes up. The dream has been assembled with Freudian realism, for the discomfort which Nan feels, cramped in the back of the boat, is the same discomfort she complains of to Mike when awake (Carver, 1976: 90–91).

But Nan and Mike's friendly argument in her dream perhaps also recalls her memory of the fishing trip as an easier time in their marriage. Nan burnt the food and re-used the same pan, and as the narrator tells us, 'they could never get the coffee to boil, but it was one of the best times they ever had' (p. 92). It seems that physical discomfort has become harder to bear, and that at the same time they have become less supportive of each other. Mike has also forgotten the details of their holiday, remembering only 'loud half-baked ideas about life and art' (p. 92) which he has outgrown along with this intimacy.

Perhaps the time when Mike would have enjoyed bringing his wife a sandwich in bed, the time when life and art at least had relevance to each other, is what Nan spends that evening trying to restore; but perhaps she also wishes to discuss with Mike the daily burdens which she fears could swamp them. Among these would be her duties at the crèche or nursery with the younger children in the Woodlawn Apartments (Carver, 1976: 90), the insecurity, felt also by Carver and his wife, of constantly changing accommodation and work, and of the shortage of money that keeps them in hardship and anxiety (p. 94). All this is a reality that the *Rubáiyát* ignores, that Mike, perhaps, uses his studies to escape from, and which Ivan, though he knows it well, prefers to see transcended by the sufferings of the Russian people and the Passion of Christ.

But Nan's reality also provides spiritual discoveries, and it is in these rather than in culture's great narratives that, in Carver's apologetic short story, the short story should set up its home. Nan likes riding in trains at night and likes the times when she has flown, and there is a moment, when the aeroplane leaves the ground, when 'you feel whatever happens is all right' (Carver, 1976: 94). With some sense of detachment from mundane things, or with some sublime acceptance of danger, Nan has apparently found relief from the worries that threaten to swamp her – a source of comfort that later in the story she addresses as God.

The Submerged Population and the Writer as Teacher

The image of swamping that occurs in Nan's dream recalls one of the major themes in *The Lonely Voice*: the idea of the 'submerged population' (O'Connor, 1963a: 17). For Frank O'Connor (p. 15), the short story expresses the concerns of 'the Little Man', existing, like Akakey Akakeivitch in Gogol's 'The Overcoat,' 'on the [...] level of mediocrity,' and denied access to the privileges that society affords. The short story works best when its writer is in touch with the needs of such people, and speaks on their behalf and on his own. But the short story superimposes such figures – serfs, prostitutes and provincials – on those symbolic heroes, Socrates, Moses, the crucified Christ, and so presents a denial of the values of society and the novel (O'Connor, 1963a: 16–18).

O'Connor's argument in *The Lonely Voice* is one of which Carver, the graduate and teacher, will presumably be aware. Carver will also present himself as part of a submerged population, since his father was a sawmill worker and his mother a waitress, since he himself took unskilled and insecure jobs to support his young family, and since he experienced the utter humiliation of circumstance that only the poor can know (Carver, 2000: 98). Yet subsequent education sets him apart from that sphere, just as under

John Gardner he encounters 'Conrad. Céline. Katherine Anne Porter. Isaac Babel' (p. 111), Browning, FitzGerald and Rilke, and just as his first wife, the waitress and teacher, is replaced by Tess Gallagher, the writer.

If Carver has read *The Lonely Voice* he will know that the short story writer's relationship with his source is intrinsically an unstable one. Katherine Mansfield, the leisured and wealthy expatriate, became too distant from ordinary life to represent it with conviction (O'Connor, 1963a: 127–129), and James Joyce, rather than depicting his submerged population with sympathy or even with fairness, by his pedantry and snobbishness submerged them further (p. 120). If Carver feels drawn away from his roots he may wonder what this means for his writing, and in his pedagogic short story he may embody the conflict he feels in himself in the student and the housewife, Mike and Nan.

But to be drawn away from one's roots is to be lonely, and for O'Connor also the short story is marked by a loneliness from which the writer suffers and towards which he is drawn (O'Connor, 1963a: 19, 165): Kate Roberts the widow also cites loneliness and isolation as influences on her work (Lewis, 1949: 20). But O'Connor also sees the short story as a visionary form, whose writer is aware of a universe extending far beyond the realm of human concerns: an idea he expresses with a quote from Pascal: '*Le silence éternel de ces espaces infinis m'effraie*' (O'Connor, 2004: 19). His insight is not fully clear to O'Connor, but perhaps the connection between the two themes is implicit. For Christ himself disposes blessings on 'the poor in spirit': those that mourn shall be comforted, those who are persecuted shall be rewarded in heaven, and the meek shall inherit the Earth (Matt. 5:4–12). Likewise, in *Varieties of Religious Experience*, William James (1902: 139-140, 145) contrasts the 'healthy-minded', whose competence in mundane things renders them incapable of a cosmic vision and blind to the existence of evil, with those 'sick souls' who feel 'the vanity of mortal things [...] the sense of sin [...] the fear of the universe' (p. 161). And in James's view the sick souls possess true insight, since 'morbid-mindedness ranges over the wider scale of experience,' including those 'evil facts' which are 'a genuine portion of reality' (p. 163). Nevertheless, this ability offers them membership of what O'Connor might also call a submerged population, since to the 'healthy-minded' their desires and fears are 'unmanly and diseased' (p. 162).

For Chekhov's (1998: 179) Ivan all evil is subsumed in good, and to Mike, who fits into the academy because he 'reads well,' his early vocation to art as a life now seems 'loud[,] half-baked.' He hopes to read to Nan from Rilke and then to sleep, but Nan annoys him by responding with her own creative discourse, with a dream, a memory and a list of desires. And if Browning, Rilke and the *Rubáiyát*, Russian history and the Passion of

Christ, represent the mainstream tradition of literature as it is taught, whose champions, as Charles E. May (1994: 134) insists, disregard its competitors, then the fragmentary and inconsequential nature of Nan's discourse will remind us of the short story.

We see, in 'Put Yourself in My Shoes' and 'Fat,' that the suppression of the storyteller is a recurring theme in Carver's fiction, before we begin to suspect that Carver himself is complicit in the suppressing. In one of Carver's later stories 'Blackbird Pie' (Carver, 1988: 91–109), the narrator, a historian with an impressive memory for facts, tries to make sense of the reasons why his wife left him. He is assisted by a letter which she pushed under his study door the night she left, and which recalls many details of their married life which only she could have known. But the narrator insists that the letter was not in her handwriting, and while he is able to quote long sections of it from memory, it transpires that he never finished reading it before it was destroyed.

According to Hilary Siebert, the contrast between historical facts and a mysterious letter represents a contrast between different forms of discourse. Furthermore, the kind of research required of the narrator is just what the short story often requires of its readers, who must 'move from a world in which meaning is spelled out and documented to one in which meaning is felt and inferred' (Siebert, 1997: 37). The narrator leaves the security of his study and his papers, moving 'outside history' (Carver, 1988: 109) into a foggy night where he finds her among the horses that have intruded on their land – horses and fog representing, for Siebert, the intuitive understanding that the short story form demands of the narrator and the reader.

The narrator's longing to be reunited with the woman he loves forces the narrator to reconsider his understanding of the world. In this story, then, the values that the short story itself represents achieve a partial victory. But in Carver's stories such success is not so common. Ralph Wyman, the protagonist of 'Will You Please Be Quiet, Please?' (Carver, 1976: 164–181), an English teacher at a high school in Eureka, is obsessed with an incident that happened two years ago at a party, when he believes his wife, Marion, slept with another man. One evening, when she casually asks him if he ever thinks about the party, he starts to question her about it, and she is forced to admit that the man 'did kiss [her] a few times'(p. 167). Marion is clearly uncomfortable, smiling uneasily as she makes this revelation, and preferring to discuss the dress she plans to buy for their daughter, and the French class she is teaching tomorrow (p. 168). Resisting as well as she can Ralph's insistence on knowing the facts, she finally confirms his suspicions. Ralph immediately leaves the house, returning in the morning when he dismisses her attempts to make peace with the instruction to 'please be quiet, please' (p. 180) – his earlier insistence that she speak, now, ironically, replaced by a demand for silence.

The Lonely Voice and the Writer as Critic

If Chekhov (1998: 178), in 'The Student,' considers the rewards of story-telling, its ability to unite the experience of the fisherman Peter with the experience of two peasant women, then perhaps in 'The Student's Wife' Carver weighs the joy of continuing that tradition against the cost of prac-ticing a supposedly inferior form. For the stuff that forms Nan's narrative to Mike, the fears and longings and deprivations that are also a large part of Carver's fiction, is stuff that a reader of Rilke might ignore, and indeed Mike neither listens to her story nor matches it with his own. Public indif-ference and critical ignorance are the common fate of short story writers who, disowned by their submerged population, and disregarded outside it, find no one whom their work can address. As Andrew Levy (1995: 109–112) points out, Bobbie Anne Mason, acclaimed and published in the *New Yorker*, is regarded as an embarrassment by her own people, who feel she makes them seem 'too much like country people'; yet such public success as she enjoys can sometimes prove temporary. Kate Roberts, similarly acclaimed in her time, is now largely forgotten outside Wales, and read at home with an awareness of 'the poverty and meanness' of the world she describes, 'its slow attrition of beauty, hope and vitality,' and 'the weakness of [her] vision' that causes dark themes to predominate (Jones, 1996: 86–87).

The heroine of 'Blackbird Pie' gains something from pushing a letter under a door; she entices her husband, who remembers facts, to join her with the fog and the horses. Marion, in 'Will You Please Be Quiet, Please?', loses something through her storytelling: although she pads her discourse with talk of lesson preparation and her daughter's clothes, the talk of a submerged population, she is unable to avoid her final confession or her husband's angry demand for her silence. In one scenario the story-teller is heeded, in another she is rejected; and Carver seems embarrassed by his devotion to the form, which he blames on poverty and its habits, which die hard.

Then what should be the content of Carver's confession, and to whom should it be addressed? In 'Fires' and 'On Writing' he proclaims his membership of a submerged population, but in confessing his fear of infi-nite spaces or the sunrise he is cautious, admitting only that a writer should have 'some special way of looking at things,' whereby, as in a story by

Chekhov, 'everything became clear to him' (Carver, 2000: 88). I don't tell my students about being afraid of the universe; I tell them any rubbish but that.

O'Connor, in *The Lonely Voice*, sees to the heart of the short story writer's predicament; but in his own short stories in *My Oedipus Complex* (O'Connor, 1963b) he is, despite the title, comparatively less revealing. His relationship with his characters maintains an ironic distance; it is not so close that it becomes embarrassing. Kate Roberts is honest, for she describes herself as '*[d]ynes groendenau ofnadwy*' ['a terribly thin-skinned woman'], struggling with bitterness, deeply hurt, and she adds that death gives the sudden insight one needs to understand a character, a society, or life itself (Lewis, 1949: 12, 16). Outside my stories I would rather comment on fear and loneliness in others than reveal it in myself, and so a report on my own creative practice becomes encoded as a close reading of a Carver short story.

Nan perhaps speaks for us all. She likes flying on planes at night; there are moments when she suspects that 'whatever happens is all right' (Carver, 1976: 94). Her confession is met with Mike's desire that she would leave him alone, but in this short story there is another room, and it is here that Nan retreats, to read magazines, to watch the sunrise, and to pray. But her prayer is not such that public religion could sanction, any more than Mike would consider her reading matter appropriate. For prayer should arise from constancy and faith or it will not be efficacious (Matthew 21:21–22; Luke 18:1–8), and Christ's own model prayer – reverent, penitent, interceding (Matthew 6:5–15) – is far more purposeful and practiced than Nan's. Rather, her almost-inarticulate cry grows selfishly and from fear 'in one unreasonable' and isolated 'moment of longing' (Carver, 1976: 95).

Without the authorisation of constancy and faith, dismissed by Nan herself as unreasonable, and offered without the support of the Church, her prayer comes to resemble her other discourses – plaintive, disjointed and inconsequential. But Nan prays, as Christ commands 'in secret,' and the help for which she asks God is not for herself alone. If it is the merciful who may expect mercy (Matthew 5:7), then presumably the helpful may expect help – so that Nan, who watches over and cares for her children, and who seeks intimacy with her husband as well as with God, perhaps prays worthily, and her prayer, the last sentence in the story, touches the eternity beyond its last page. Ignored by her husband, denied sleep by God, and submerged in the lowest forms of discourse, she speaks to us with a lonely voice – un-confessed and unheeded, like the short story, but perhaps, like the short story, significant.

Note

1. The Biblical references in this chapter are from *The Holy Bible: New International Version* (1973).

References

Carver, R. (1976/1999) *Will You Please Be Quiet, Please?* London: Harvill.

Carver, R. (1988/1998) *Elephant*. London: Harvill.

Carver, R. (1996) *What We Talk About When We Talk About Love*. London: Harvill.

Carver, R. (2000) *Call If You Need Me*. London: Harvill.

Chekhov, A. (1998) *The Steppe and Other Stories* (R. Hingley, trans.). Oxford: Oxford University Press.

Connolly, C. (1938/1988) *Enemies of Promise*. London: André Deutsch.

The Holy Bible (1973) *New International Version*. East Brunswick, NJ: International Bible Society.

James, W. (1902/1982) *The Varieties of Religious Experience: A Study in Human Nature*. Harmondsworth: Penguin.

Jones, R. (1996) Review of 'Feet in Chains' by Kate Roberts (J.I. Jones, trans.) *New Welsh Review* 34, 86–89.

Levy, A. (1995) *The Culture and Commerce of the American Short Story*. Cambridge: Cambridge University Press.

Lewis, S. (ed.) (1949) *Crefft y Stori Fer*. Llandysul: Clwb Llyfrau Cymreig.

May, C. (1994) The nature of knowledge in short fiction. In C.E. May (ed.) *The New Short Story Theories* (pp. 131–143). Athens, OH: Ohio University Press.

O'Connor, F. (1963a) *The Lonely Voice: A Study of the Short Story*. Hoboken, NJ: Melville House.

O'Connor, F. (1963b) *My Oedipus Complex and Other Stories*. Harmondsworth: Penguin.

Siebert, H. (1997) Ode to history: Lyrical knowledge in the discourse of the short story. In N.H. Kaylor Jr (ed.) *Creative and Critical Approaches to the Short Story* (pp. 35–45). Lampeter: Edwin Mellen.

Thackeray, W.M. (1877/1994) *Vanity Fair*. Harmondsworth: Penguin.

Tillich, P. (1959) *Theology of Culture* (R.C. Kimball, ed.). New York: Oxford University Press.

Chapter 13

A Translator's Tale

GREGORY FRASER

At the University of Houston, where in the mid-1990s I earned my doctorate in Creative Writing, I began what will likely turn out to be a lifelong occupation as a translator. Three of my idols – Marianne Moore, Elizabeth Bishop, and Richard Wilbur – had been translators of French poetry, but my emerging enterprise (should I say *obsession*?) would not involve the rendering of any foreign poetry into English. Instead, I would devote myself to 'translating' the discourses of critical theory into the art and discipline of Creative Writing.

My project originated in a somewhat unlikely venue. The curriculum at Houston required poetry candidates to enroll in at least one fiction workshop. The same was true for fiction writers, who had to take a stab at making poems. These 'cross-over' workshops sought to break down barriers not only between writers in the program but also between genres and styles. Little did I realize that my cross-over workshop taught by Mary Robison would inspire me to help Critical Theory (traditionally the province of scholarly literary studies) 'cross-over' into the field of Creative Writing.

I chose Robison's workshop for the simple reason that I deeply admired two of her short stories, 'I Am 21' and 'Yours' (Robison, 2002), both of which I still teach in Creative Writing courses. I had no idea at the time that a brief comment made by her to one of my classmates would ultimately provoke me to dedicate a good deal of my writing and teaching life to studying the ways in which the ideas of Michel Foucault, Jacques Lacan, Jacques Derrida, and other so-called 'high theorists' could help maturing creative writers break new ground in their poems, stories, and dramatic works.

Generally, Robison was an approving and supportive workshop leader. As a poet required to test my hand at fiction, I tended to be treated not so much as an intruder but as a tolerable outsider – a novice in the craft who received friendly, but understandably truncated, guidance from a group of veteran tellers of tales. Mostly, the workshop found serious fiction writers talking seriously to each other about the finer points of structure, conflict, characterization, and narrative development. I listened. Closely.

Despite her supportive presence, Robison could be a stern taskmaster. Slack, baggy sentences were her pet peeve. At the appearance of one, Cy Twombly-like scribblings would cover her brow. I applauded and learned from her lessons in compression, immediacy, slick erasures. But Robison's greatest contribution to my future as a writer and writing teacher came one afternoon when she offered a pointed critique of a story submitted by a peer. In response to what she regarded as a cleanly written but ultimately unsuccessful piece, Robison cleared her throat, tied her lips in a knot, and pronounced: 'There's no Marx, no Freud, no Asia.' The workshop waited, but she said nothing more. She glanced at the clock, dismissed class.

Obviously, Robison wasn't suggesting that the student's story should be set in Cambodia, or overtly capture some kind of class struggle, or include a psychoanalyst as an integral character. She was passing judgment on the story's provincial attitudes, its failure to grasp the subtle power relations that function perennially in all private and public spheres. The story was insular. It lacked critical consciousness. But what of 'critical consciousness'? Did it have a legitimate place in the Creative Writing classroom? Couldn't it stifle the imagination by filling the mind with theoretical abstractions removed from the drama of language and human interaction?

These were the kinds of questions and concerns that I had heard repeatedly from writer friends. Moreover, most of the workshops I'd taken up to that point (at both Columbia and Houston) had operated under the assumption that creative writers should steer clear of analytical discourses. In his widely taught writing book *The Triggering Town*, Richard Hugo (1979: 7) sums up the general attitude in this way: 'The poem grows from an experience, either real or imagined ... Think small. ... If you can't think small, try philosophy or social criticism.' Susan Stewart, in the Winter 2004/5 issue of the *Chicago Review*, offers this: 'As any working artist knows, art practice that proceeds under the shadow of theory is doomed to be mere allegory' (Stewart, 2004: 300). The old standby principle 'Show more than tell' likewise emphasizes the need to depict actual behavior rather than ideas or ideals, to privilege concrete imagery over intangible concepts, to hold the reader inside a scene by foregrounding interpersonal conflict and foregoing philosophical speculation. It's no overstatement, then, to claim that critical theory has long been regarded in writing circles as a 'dangerous supplement' to the creative imagination.

Gradually, however, I have come along with Robison to believe otherwise. It may in fact be equally dangerous to separate ourselves and our students from theory, and it would seem that increasing numbers of writers – many of whom now hold PhDs – are less inclined to divorce critical theory from Creative Writing pedagogy. In an essay entitled 'Eight Rules for the

Poet/Critic,' which appeared in the Fall 2005 issue of *American Poet*, Linda Gregerson writes that:

> Poets need to be curious about the world. This includes the world of theory. ... The powerful questions, those that captivate the human spirit and the human art, are durable questions. Those which animate 20th-century semiotics also animated 8th-century Byzantine and 16th-century Reformation debates about the status of the sign ... Poets and critics alike need to be able to recognize the human story in high theory, to renew their relation to venerable conundrums by means of theoretical formulations that reveal these conundrums from new angles and lift them to new articulateness, to move among different levels of abstraction and concretion. (Gregerson, 2005: 17)

With the hope that this chapter might promote the spirit of curiosity described by Gregerson, and also cultivate a refined sense in students of 'different levels of abstraction and concretion,' I offer the following account of how I present some dominant critical theories in my Creative Writing courses. Throughout this chapter, I introduce theoretical concepts just as I might in the classroom, in language that deliberately avoids the 'alienating verbosity' (57) that Brazilian philosopher and educator Paulo Freire (1974: 57) eschews in his landmark study *The Pedagogy of the Oppressed*. Ultimately, I hope that these explanations can help students internalize and subtly express the practical Creative Writing equivalent of 'some Freud, some Marx, some Asia.'

Theory 101, or the Lesson of the Van Dyke

The roots of current theory (and the roots of all evil, some might say) lie in semiotics. This is where I begin my discussions with writing students. I tell students that without a thorough grasp of semiotics, none of the more complex theoretical approaches – including deconstruction, post-feminism, neo-Marxism, and Lacanian psychoanalysis – make a mote of sense. Then, in true Creative Writing fashion, I offer concrete examples in lieu of abstract explanations. I show more than tell.

The choice of signs doesn't much matter: the object is to select a meaning-filled cultural phenomenon that Creative Writing students can interpret with confidence and pleasure. Often, I ask students to decode the 'Van Dyke' beard, which continues to be sported by a relative minority of young men at my state university in the Bible Belt of the southern United States. Why, I ask the class, would a student wear this pointed, triangle-shaped facial hair that covers only the skin around the mouth and over the chin? What does this particular style of beard signify in contemporary American culture? With questions like these, we begin the semiotic unpacking of the sign.

Serving as guide, I lead the class though an unearthing of the Van Dyke's cultural associations and meanings. It doesn't take long before students suggest that this particular beard conveys 'rebelliousness,' 'malicious cunning,' 'the dark side of reality' (they note seeing frequent representations of Satan wearing a Van Dyke). As I chalk their responses on the board, they eventually point out that there also appears to be an 'intellectual' element inscribed in the sign: a Van Dyke connotes 'iconoclastic thinking,' 'taboo concepts.' Students also state that the Van Dyke signals a particular kind of anger – a smoldering, interiorized, misanthropic disgust with the world. The Van Dyke wearer is not a fighter; he destroys with his pen. He reads de Sade, listens to Coltrane, smokes Gauloises. And the Van Dyke, we decide, signifies 'Europe' – especially a European disdain for homespun American values. He and his sculpted beard embody 'youth,' as well – not the youth of the springy athlete but that of dangerous new ideas, the advance guard.

Group semiotic readings of this kind set the stage for further investigations into the cardinal principles of semiotic theory. After recording my students' excavations of the Van Dyke sign, I pose the question, 'From where do these associations arise?' I go on to explain that – at least according to semiotics – the meanings that they have just unearthed are not inherent in, or naturally connected to, the hair on the student's face. For the semiotician, I note, the links between the Van Dyke and its multiple meanings are arbitrary and culturally constructed; there are no fixed or eternal meanings of any sign. In fact, the student's Van Dyke only means 'Mephistophelean,' 'radical,' 'hip,' and so on, because his beard is _relative_ to other signs in present-day America's sign system of male facial hair. This system includes 'full beard,' 'clean-shaven face,' and 'moustache only.' The Van Dyke's meanings, therefore, are relational – not essential – part of a comparative system, not part of the beard itself or the student who wears it. I suggest that this particular beard can't 'exist' as a recognizable cultural artifact without related signs to give it meaning and value. It can't 'be' without, as semioticians say, 'difference.'

Thus, I add, the realities in which we find ourselves (and the realities in which we place our fictional characters and poetic speakers) arise from complex webs of endlessly interrelated linguistic associations. There's nothing intrinsically 'satanic' or 'rebellious' about the Van Dyke: it carries these significances only in conventional comparison to, for example, 'full beard,' which in American culture signifies 'respectable,' 'established,' 'earnest,' 'rational,' 'wise,' 'traditional,' and 'scholarly,' among other things.

Questions of (Author)ity

I follow this discussion of relationality with the observation that signs are never separate from intricate interplays of power. Meaning, I say, is not only relational in nature but is also connected to ideology. Such signs as the Van Dyke beard are always already 'political,' where politics is understood to mean not strictly the work performed in legislative bodies like the US Congress, but the more pervasive clashes – violent, moderate, and almost imperceptible – that perennially occur between differing ideological positions, value systems, and widely held assumptions often referred to as 'cultural myths.' To underscore the power-laden nature of signs, and thus of all knowable reality, I ask my writing students to look at who on campus wears the Van Dyke. Their answer is swift and definitive: students. I then inquire: 'What hidden ideologies does this beard suggest? How might this sign interrogate established power structures, even while unconsciously perpetuating them?' I remind them that, in the words of Jack Solomon and Sonia Maasik (2000: 19), 'cultural myths reflect the values and ideological interests of [a culture's] builders, not the laws of nature or logic.' Countermyths, I add, can point to a vast array of resistant ideological positions that may oppose a given culture's so-called 'master narratives.'

Ultimately, I hope to show students that the Van Dyke beard – like any sign – is a piece of language that relies on other signs for identity and meaning, and that also carries ideological baggage. It communicates political, moral, and ethical suggestions (whether the beard-wearer knows it or not). When a couple of students inevitably note that some faculty members also wear the Van Dyke – that it's not just a student phenomenon – this begs several questions: 'Which professors? Are they younger? What is conveyed ideologically when a professor wears a Van Dyke? Is he suggesting a resistance to traditional approaches to teaching? That he speaks the language of students, knows their music, understands them better than the old guard?'

More than a decade has passed since my classmate in Mary Robison's workshop submitted a story that showed little concept of the explicit and implicit, the flamboyant and subdued, the unapologetic and cleverly concealed, even unconscious, exercises of power that inform all human experience. And it is always with the memory of that uncomfortable yet illuminating workshop moment that I expand my discussions of the ideological nature of signs by referencing the nuanced sense of power that theorists such as Michel Foucault began to articulate in the 1960s and 1970s.

Power, stated Foucault, (1980: 60) 'isn't localized in the State apparatus'; there also exist countless 'mechanisms of power that function outside, below and alongside the State apparatuses, on a much more minute and everyday level.' Without a fine-tuned awareness of 'minute and everyday' expressions of power, as well as of larger authoritarian forces in culture (not to mention the continual commingling of the two), Creative Writing students may open their work to criticisms of parochialism. My fellow student at Houston received a sharp but crucial rebuke from a theoretically informed writer deeply sensitive to the fact that skillful authorship demands a keen perception of authority in its innumerable forms – from its most overt expressions in big business and government, to local-level yet no-less-complex exchanges between parents and kids, to 'everyday' (and often seemingly power-neutral) interactions with friends, lovers, and perfect strangers.

As Foucault (1990) argued in *The History of Sexuality Volume I,* power is not 'something that one holds on to or allows to slip away,' and its presence 'must not be sought in the primary existence of a central point.' Rather, it is a process always at work, and at stake, in human interactions. 'Power is everywhere; not because it embraces everything, but because it comes from everywhere.' It is frequently this vision of power that leads students to subtler works of fiction, drama, and poetry. It helps them avoid the narrow view that simply ignores the play of power, and the similarly limited vision that believes power to be located solely in institutions divorced from, and standing above, the 'everyday' (Foucault, 1990: 93–94).

The Eternally Missing Link

It is also important to emphasize for students that no guaranteed correlation exists between (a) the meaningful *signals sent* by a sign like the Van Dyke beard, and (b) any real-world action, belief, or identity on the part of the sign's sender. In other words, there's no way ever to know for certain if the student actually endorses the meanings his beard suggests semiotically and behaves in accordance with the politics inscribed in the sign. The student may wear a conventionally 'iconoclastic' beard with the utmost of outward pride, and yet hold boldly reactionary world views. No one (not even the student himself, contemporary theory would claim) can completely comprehend the relationship between the semiotic signals being disseminated and their source in the sender. Indeed, there can never be any perfect unity or conclusive correspondence between the two. To determine the student's character and politics – in short, to test the correspondence between the 'surface' significations of his beard and his so-called 'inner'

identity or self – we can only wait for additional signs from him: speech, actions, purchases, work, and so on.

Individual psyches, to summarize the French psychiatrist Jacques Lacan (2007), are composites of ultimately indeterminate signs. The student's 'being,' his 'essence,' his 'real self,' amounts to an infinite regress. The answer to 'who he is' will always recede, even from himself, just as the final meaning of any sign always escapes definitive analysis. In the end, it becomes impossible to distinguish between the student's surface significations (his beard, clothes, favorite phrases and music, and so forth) and his so-called 'inner' subjectivity. We are left with signs pointing to signs – a world in which the very notions of 'outside' and 'inside' begin to blur. Hence, significations can be highly 'performative.' (It may be fruitful to remind students that deceptions, ambiguities, and performative tinkerings at the level of the sign stir the conflicts and drive the plots in many a Shakespearean drama and many a TV sitcom.)

Such ideas, needless to say, have become self-evident – even passé – for most writers teaching in universities internationally. A great number of professors now hold doctorates in Creative Writing and have been exposed to the rigors of semiotic and high critical theory. But undergraduates of many stripes come to Creative Writing classes new to the notion of meanings as relational, contextual, cultural, historical, and political. They find it illuminating – even if it may be obvious to us – that place and power determine meaning, not inner truths and categorical essences. Most of those I teach at the undergraduate level tend to be surprised that the Van Dyke-wearing student may sometimes reflect the progressive politics encoded in his beard, even while unwittingly refracting those very politics in other circumstances. As is true for all of us, the student's actions and identity will correspond well with certain signs at certain times, and not so well at others.

My teaching experience at no fewer than five universities in the United States has shown me that, by and large, American students are simultaneously intrigued and deeply disturbed by the implications of semiotic theory on meaning, selfhood, and knowable reality. Right now, I work at an institution where numerous students hail from fundamentalist religious backgrounds that tend to emphasize essentialist and Manichean outlooks. The blow delivered by semiotic theory to such world views can be stress-inducing, but I would argue that such difficult encounters with contemporary thought are not only integral to a legitimate college education in general, but also deeply enriching for the creative-critical imagination and the making of fictions and poems.

Theory into Practice

What does all this theory talk have to do with the teaching and making of Creative Writing? In the remainder of this chapter, I suggest a handful of possible responses to such an inquiry. The following ideas and accounts hardly represent a panacea for the challenges that Creative Writing teachers face in helping students to avoid parochialism and to enlarge their creative-critical sensibilities. I can say, however, that many of my students take greater risks and lend greater complexity and philosophical rigor to their prose and poetry after being exposed to theoretically informed strategies like those described below.

Mining the gaps ...

It takes time – often a semester or more – before emerging writers can confidently fulfill the fundamental narrative requirement to make fictional characters behave with clear-cut motivations. Writers-in-training frequently neglect to create specific and subtle tensions, and to drive a plot in plausible yet non-formulaic ways, simply because they haven't adequately focused on their characters' particular needs and desires in concrete contexts. As a consequence, the writing can become static, overly interiorized, monological rather than dialogical. Creative Writing instructors constantly have to remind students to dramatize not only what their characters desire, but also what familial, social, occupational, psychological, and historical obstacles impede the fulfillment of those desires.

But maturing writers additionally need to realize and represent the fact that many characters don't always know exactly what they want, who they are, or why they behave in certain ways. The most interesting and well-rounded characters and poetic speakers are fundamentally divided between conscious and unconscious impulses and motivations, actions and understandings. These divisions profitably complicate characters as well as the craft of characterization, and to achieve success on the page, student writers must ultimately learn to 'mine the gap' between what, on the one hand, a character *knows* he or she desires and comprehends, and what, on the other hand, he or she remains unclear about wanting and recognizing. As postmodern theory reminds us, the selves of 'artificial' characters – like our own 'real' selves – remain open rather than closed, indeterminate and evolving rather than final and fixed. Their beings and meanings are, like ours, necessarily relational and contextual in nature.

The deft handling of this fissure in characterization poses one of the toughest challenges to developing writers. In effect, every complex character or speaker achieves legitimacy and believability in the gaps between known, as-yet-unknown, and ultimately unknowable desires and self-awarenesses. The selves we often hold as sacred entities – influenced by but ultimately separate from language – are in fact regarded by many contemporary theorists as vast, often contradictory agglomerations of signs that fall only tenuously under the umbrella signs 'self' or 'identity.' And for creative writers, this is exceedingly good news. Such a recognition can be extraordinarily empowering (especially in the early drafting and revision stages of the writing process) because it helps emerging writers de-essentialize their characters and destabilize formulaic plots.

What happens to a desire deferred?

I have briefly mentioned Jacques Lacan. With regard to refining the sense of 'gaps' in self-awareness and desire, there may be no better theorist to introduce to students. One the most oft-cited concepts in Lacanian theory suggests that the unconscious is structured like language. What does this mean theoretically, and what value might it have for Creative Writing students? For one, the concept has to do with *desire*. Lacan argues that desire is always in some way unconscious (never fully knowable), and also that desire is like language because both are always in motion, always deferred, with no stabilizing 'transcendental signified' – no sign that signifies all by itself, without relying for meaning on its differential relationships to other signs. Lacan asserts that human beings continually struggle toward a 'transcendental' grounding desire, a final completion of desire – yet they always fail, come up short, eternally 'lack' closure. Any object of desire, for Lacan, always points to some other object.

As stated, maturing creative writers face serious challenges in representing the motivations of their characters and speakers. To address this predicament, Creative Writing professors might take Mary Robison at her word and attempt to introduce 'some Freud' in the writing classroom. But I have found that Freudian theory has been so bastardized by general culture, with his thinking reduced to a collection of clichés – and also found so thoroughly wanting by feminist theorists – that Lacan, who has escaped popular appropriation and has actually been championed by many feminists, offers a useful alternative. Ultimately, though, with respect to nuts-and-bolts guidance, I find that the Lacanian notion of deferred desire can help students create characters whose motivations are less predictable, more open to surprise.

Lacanian theories about selfhood have a special force, as well, for student poets. At the onset, many students who wish to write poems proceed from myths of wholeness about the self. Students often write poems to voice what they take to be the essence of an inner being. They seek to capture some final, genuine truth about an allegedly unique emotion or experience. And these underlying assumptions often produce texts that reach for effect. Often misreading the confessional poets (who are perhaps our most sophisticated theorists of the self's radical incompletion rather than its inherent unity), student poets pour out the language of the stable self in despair or under duress. They try to out-Sexton Sexton. Having been culturally conditioned to assume that poems should represent the individual self in peril, these writers lack a model to help them distance themselves from widespread myths of the self as a unique and unified entity.

Lacanian theory can help students recognize not so much the fragmentation of an ultimately unified albeit imperiled self (a modernist conception), but the cultural/linguistic manufacture of the very idea of selfhood (a more postmodern assertion). Such a perspective gives students a different kind of freedom to adopt masks and to explore self-contradictions as generative rather than logically fallacious. Lacan can't help students completely shed the dominant fictions of culture (none of us can do that), but his thinking can encourage students to recognize and tamper with these assumptions in unexpected, artistically vitalizing ways. Students may in fact become more willing, after a little training in Lacanian theory, to let language (rather than a sense of stable selfhood) guide the poetic process. They may allow language to suggest unstable constructions of selfhood, flickers of desire, suggestions of unconscious strings of motivation. This can lead to stronger poems.

Greater linguistic play ...

If student poets can enrich their craft by considering the consequences of Lacanian theory and its demystification of the unified self perpetuated by Western culture, then they may gain additional practical benefits from a basic exposure to the semiotically grounded philosophies of Jacques Derrida. Like Lacan and Foucault, Derrida concentrated on the categorizing, essentializing tendencies of Western thought. He set out to show the instabilities inscribed linguistically in the foundational (often binary and hierarchical) assumptions of Western culture. Ultimately, Derrida sought to show that these root concepts unwittingly 'deconstruct' themselves by trying to repress the implications of semiotic theory.

In his famous essay 'Structure, Sign, and Play,' Derrida explains that the concept of a coherent structure containing a stable, organizing center is just that, a *concept* – a necessary fiction rather than a categorical reality or truth. Derrida (1978: 278–79) maintains that the process of giving any structure a 'point of presence,' where 'the permutation or the transformation of elements ... is forbidden,' creates boundaries specifically designed to circumscribe the contents of that structure, and, above all, to limit the scope of their play. The idea of a centered structure is for Derrida intrinsically illusive and reductive. It falsely posits 'a play based on a fundamental ground, a play constituted on the basis of a fundamental immobility and a reassuring certitude, which itself is beyond the reach of play' (Derrida, 1978: 279). Thus, the elements 'inside' any given structure may change shape and appear strange, but ultimately, they are bound and neutralized by a fictive schema with a synthetically secure and pristine center.

At the start of every term, I have to remind myself that, prior to entering the Creative Writing classroom, students have passed through years of critical-writing training that tends to privilege a 'center' of meaning. For better or worse, students are taught to write from a dominant theoretical claim, or thesis, that organizes an interpretative argument and lends coherence to a critical essay at large. Derrida's thinking calls this basic pedagogy into question, but I am less interested in challenging the operative discourses of the critical classroom. Instead, I try to show students how Derrida's thought can 'free' them from the 'tyranny of the central idea.' Such freedom frequently leads to greater flexibility in characterization, plot development, and language use. By not beginning with a main theme or idea, students avoid working predictably down the page.

In addition, I suggest that creative writers (poets especially, perhaps) tend to be unsatisfied with pre-established grids. They tend to want to let language itself bring about reconceptualizations and expansions of reality. To encourage this type of thinking, I perform an in-class brainstorm where students are asked to re-envision parts of reality and to simultaneously create language that 'produces' that reality. 'What's the sign for the space between stars?' I might ask. Students have fun throwing out suggestions: *nonstar, unglobe, ringblack*. What's the sign for the place where the trunk of a tree meets the soil? Answers: *woodsoil, rootstart, trunkseat*. Calisthenics like these don't necessarily lead to useable imagery (though sometimes they do in the most startling of ways), but they certainly build linguistic muscles, encourage students to play with sound and sense, and cultivate a spirit of expansion when it comes to the borders of language and thought. Obviously, this simple, 'playful' strategy is just one among many possibilities that arise from the implications of Derrida's thought. The main issue – as with Foucault, Lacan, and other significant theorists – is to show students that their creative practices can frequently benefit from exposure to complex theoretical paradigms.

Decades have passed since Roland Barthes and Michel Foucault pronounced, with varying emphases, the death of the all-knowing, God-like 'Author' who allegedly possesses profound and timeless insights into the human condition. Nowadays, critical theorists veer from claims about authorial genius, preferring instead to embed writers such as Shakespeare, Dante, and Dickinson in their historical moments, and to show how the texts of 'master' authors both reflect and refract various cultural and aesthetic ideologies. I am going to step out on a limb, however, and make a somewhat retrograde statement: 'Great authors are great semioticians.' Indeed, I make this claim on the day that I introduce contemporary critical theory, proceeding then with practical examples from two 'great' authors who, for me, represent the pinnacle of critical awareness and semiotic savvy.

My two favorite 'master' texts for examination in semiotic terms are the opening chapter of Don DeLillo's (1999) *White Noise* and Toni Morrison's breathtaking short story 'Recitatif' (Gale Group, 2002). Due to space constraints, I won't offer detailed comments here on the texts themselves, but simply note that both reveal a theoretical sensibility that I find not only worthwhile but imperative to cultivate in student creative writers. Both successfully avoid the polemical while still addressing issues of power and culture; both explore the complexities and contingencies of desire; and both continually test the resources of language in their willingness to 'play' with words. In these and other regards, DeLillo and Morrison show students that good writing emerges first from the writing strategies that we as a class have practiced in the opening half of the term: concrete vs. abstract language, grounding the writing in real-world experiences and specific places, avoiding discursive explanation, and so on (all of which are outlined beautifully in Hugo's *The Triggering Town* and similar writing manuals). But these two masters also signal a second component of strong creative writing – the critical consciousness that blurs the boundaries between author and semiotician, and that addresses the concerns that my teacher Mary Robison called for in that graduate workshop years ago. Creative Writing professors who decide to teach these texts will find models about which no reader could complain, 'There's no Marx, no Freud, no Asia.'

References

DeLillo, D. (1999) *White Noise*. Harmondsworth: Penguin Books.
Derrida, J. (1978) *Writing and Difference* (A. Bass, trans.). Chicago, IL: University of Chicago Press.
Foucault, M. (1980) *Power/Knowledge: Selected Interviews and Other Writings, 1972–1977* (C. Gordon, ed.). New York: Pantheon.
Foucault, M. (1990) *The History of Sexuality Volume I: An Introduction* (R. Hurley, trans.) New York: Vintage.

Freire, P. (1974) *The Pedagogy of the Oppressed*. New York: Seabury Press.

Gregerson, L. (2005) Eight rules for the poet/critic. *American Poet* 29 (Fall), 16–17.

Hugo, R. (1979) *The Triggering Town: Lectures and Essays on Poetry and Writing*. New York: Norton.

Lacan, J. (2007) *Ecrit: The First Complete Edition in English*. New York: Norton.

Gale Group (2002) *Toni Morrison's 'Recitatif': A Study Guide from Gale's Short Stories for Students*. Farmington Hills, MI: The Gale Group.

Robison, M. (2002) *Tell Me: 30 Stories*. Cambridge, MA: Counterpoint Publishing.

Solomon, J. and Maasik, S. (eds) (2000) Introduction. *Signs of Life in the USA* (3rd edn). Boston: Bedford/St Martin's.

Stewart, S. (2004) On the art of the future. *Chicago Review* 50 (2/3/4), 298–315.

Afterword

DAVID FENZA

Like the first classes in English composition, the first classes in Creative Writing were a reaction against the study of literature as most universities practiced it before 1900. After the Civil War, study in the Classics began to be supplanted by the study of philology. Philology was an effort to make literature the subject of a linguistic science; philology sought to define and anatomize literary works for intimations of a culture's meaning and order. Although philology opened academic study to literary works in English, and not just those in Greek and Latin, philology became specialized and limited. With each passing decade, it became more divisive as well.

The founder of *The American Journal of Philology*, Basil Gildersleeve of Johns Hopkins University, codified the practices of 'historico-philological science,' as he called it. His pronouncements illustrate a rift in academe that remains with us today. Professor Gildersleeve, in the 1920s, divided the study of literature into two camps: the scholars versus the aesthetes – the philologists versus the *littérateurs*. Gildersleeve likened the philologists to botanists; these were the real men of letters, scholars who defined, classified, annotated, and conserved literary wisdom. Those who were interested in studying a poem's music or a novel's aesthetic form – the mere *littérateurs* – Gildersleeve likened to florists.

The phrase 'creative writing' was, perhaps, first coined by Emerson in 1837. In his Phi Beta Kappa address 'The American Scholar,' Emerson referred to 'creative writing' and 'creative reading' as respites from 'the restorers of readings, the emendators, the bibliomaniacs of all degrees.' The advocate of a new culture for a new nation, Emerson became a famous detractor of received bodies of knowledge. For Emerson, America's enabling spirit was in its proclivity to add, to test, to revolt, and to innovate. Philology, as it was usually practiced and taught, thwarted these New World tendencies in an effort to conserve the past. Emily Dickinson, too, would write a poem ('Shall I take thee, the Poet said') that – obliquely, of course – criticizes philology for being spiritually inept.

The first classes in writing were offered by Barrett Wendell at Harvard

University in the 1880s, and such classes grew by steady increments thereafter. These early classes were, in part, a revolt against philology. These new classes in writing emphasized practice, aesthetics, personal observation, and creativity rather than theory, history, tradition, and literary conservation. In 1884, Professor Wendell offered his first course in advanced composition. A fusion of the study and practice of journalism, literary techniques, grammar, rhetoric, and aesthetic discernment, Wendell's 'educational experiment,' as he called it, was daring for its time. It was also wildly popular among students. Despite his requirement that the students submit daily writing exercises, 150 students enrolled for the course the following year. Le Baron Briggs taught, also at Harvard from 1889 to 1925, a class in the history and principles of versification. A former newspaper man, Charles T. Copeland, succeeded Briggs as a professor of Creative Writing. A few of the students of these teachers – Wendell, Briggs, and Copeland – would become professors themselves and offer similar classes, and some would become accomplished authors as well.

One of Barrett's former students, William Hughes Mearns, conducted an experiment of his own at a junior high school. Mearns found that 'creative writing' was an extremely effective means of motivating students to learn more and to write well. His classes emphasized motivation, active participation, creativity, and self-expression over discipline, historical study, memorization, and drills. Inspired by the progressive educational ideas of John Dewey, Mearns published what was, perhaps, the first anthology of student literary work; and his own books, *Creative Youth* (1925) and *Creative Power* (1929), made 'creative writing' a ubiquitous subject of interest among educators and young students.

After the 1920s, philology gave way to various practices of literary criticism that, despite their being various and more concerned with aesthetic discernment, still owed a great deal to philology and Germanic traditions of scholarship (the *wissenschaftlichte Methode*). Literary study continued to be retrospective and scientific in temperament. 'We study literature today,' Allen Tate remarked, 'as if nobody ever again intended to write any more of it. The official academic point of view is that all the literature has been written, and is now a branch of history.'

Scholars criticized the study of Creative Writing in return. Creative Writing classes, the scholars argued, showed an immoral disregard for great literary monuments; such classes were too intuitive and naive at best, and they were irrational and ignorant at worst – occasions for self-indulgence, confessional exhibitionism, etc. – hardly the stuff for the rigors of an academic discipline. At many institutions, scholars resisted and sometimes thwarted the efforts of writers to implement classes and programs in Creative Writing.

Today, Creative Writing classes have become among the most popular classes in the humanities. Many students, especially today's students, feel that the world is not of their making, and not theirs to form or to reform; but writing classes often demonstrate the efficacy of the human will – that human experience can be shaped and directed for the good – aesthetically, socially, and politically. In Creative Writing classes, students learn about elements of literature from inside their own work, rather than from outside a text; and this has motivated many to gain greater command of rhetoric and communication skills in general. In Creative Writing classes, students also analyze psychology and motives, the dynamics of social classes and individual, regional, and national beliefs. Students shape experiences into stories and poems. They order their lives and their world. In addition to advancing the art of literature, creative writing workshops exercise and strengthen the resourcefulness of the human will, and it is the exercise of will, not over others, but for others, as stories and poems are made as gifts for readers and listeners. The making and exchange of literary talents and gifts is, of course, a highly civilized and humane act; and appropriately, academe has accepted the practice and making of the literary arts along with study and scholarship in the literary arts.

Acknowledgement

David Fenza is Executive Director, The Association of Writers and Writing Programs (AWP). The Editors wish to sincerely thank David and the AWP for permission to use the above excerpts from *Creative Writing & Its Discontents* by D.W. Fenza (March/April 2000) and *A Brief History of AWP* by David Fenza (2007). Complete versions of these articles can be found online at http://www.awpwriter.org.

Index

AAWP 1
adult learners 127
Arvon Foundation 67, 68
Aurora Leigh 46
AWP 1, 67, 167

Bakhtin, Mikhail, 102-104, 105, 114 ff
Barthes, Roland 18, 139, 161
Bausch, Richard 67
Bishop, Wendy 66
Bloom, Harold 18, 95
Bradbury, Malcolm 67
Browning, Elizabeth Barrett 46-47
Butler Archive 41-47

Calvino, Italo 54, 63, 65
Carter, Paul 4
Carver, Raymond 131, 139, 141-150
characterization 159-160
Chekhov, Anton 142, 144, 145, 147, 149
chronology 54, 55, 64
Cixous, Hélène 48, 65
collaboration xiv, 121-124
Collins, Billy 84
Connolly, Cyril 141
Craig, David 70
craft 70, 71, 72, 82, 90, 91, 106, 107, 109, 112,
    123, 124, 130, 132, 142, 152, 159, 161
creative industries 8
critical analysis xiv, 1-2, 4, 6, 7, 9, 10, 12, 16,
    36, 37, 38, 39, 43, 45-47, 71, 72, 73, 77, 81,
    88, 89, 92, 93, 96, 101-104, 106, 109, 114 ff,
    120, 149- 150, 152, 159, 162
culture cult 63

'departmenalisation' 7
Derrida, Jacques 161-162
designer tribalism 63
Dewey, John 92, 166
Dillard, Annie 130-131
Doctorate xi-xiii, 10-14, 18, 36-39, 43, 45, 46,
    48, 67, 163 *Also see:* critical analysis,
    examination, knowledge, research
Doctor of Creative Arts *see* Doctorate

Doctor of Philosophy *see* Doctorate
domains of the writing process 15, 17
Doty, Mark 51, 65
dramatic writing 137

Eagleton, Terry 6
ego 16-17
Engle, Paul 67
English Literature 4, 22, 109
Evaristo, Bernadine 46
examination 10, 12, 14, 16
examiners *see* examination
exegesis/exegetical 10-14

Feminism 50-51, 58
Fleming, Keith 51
Foerster, Norman 67
Forster, E. M. 53, 54
Foucault, Michel 78, 152, 157, 161-162
Fowles, John 64, 65
funding 7-8

Gallagher, Tess 84
Garrett, Stewart 24
genius 119
Goldsworthy, Andy 21, 28, 34

Hughes, Langston 85-86

knowledge xii, 1-4, 6, 7, 8, 9, 11, 13, 19, 22,
    46, 57, 58, 62, 79, 90, 93, 99, 105, 107- 110,
    118, 120, 125, 128, 129 ff, 151 ff, 162 ff,
    165
Kolb, David 92
Kundera, Milan 53, 65

Lacan, Jacques 152, 158, 160-162
language 133
Lewis, Saunders 142
listening 30-31
Lodge, David 102

MA 37, 67, 98-99, 137
Madonna 50

marking 136
Masters of Arts *see* MA
Master of Fine Arts *see* MFA
Master of Philosophy *see* MA
Mayers, Tim 22, 71, 72
mentoring xiii
methodology 90
MFA 11, 67
models 123
Murray, Margaret 56
Myers, D.G. 66, 69, 99

National Association of Writers in
    Education (NAWE) 1, 68
National Writing Project 68
new media xii, 24, 118
New Writing 1
novel xiv, 10, 10-14, 18

O'Connor, Flannery 67
O'Connor, Frank 146
orientalism 60
Orpheus 34

Paglia, Camille 51
'Pearl of the Orient' 53, 54, 56
pedagogy xi-xiii 1, 2, 8-9, 17-19, 71, 72,
    88-89, 96-99, 101, 105, 107, 110, 120, 127,
    Also see: workshops
phases 125
philology 165
poesis 88, 91
poetics 22, 23
poetry 22, 28-34, 76, 82-86, 119, 152
Porter, Dorothy 44, 47
postcolonial 60, 61
practice 3-5, 116-128 *Also see:* praxis
praxis 88, 91-94, 96, 103-104
prison writing 134-135,
process 72, 80, 88, 89, 90, 92, 94-96, 97, 98,

    99, 101, 106, 125, 132, 133, 157, 160
Prose, Francine 58, 65
Proust, Marcel 70, 72

research xi-xiii, 1-9, 88 *Also see:* knowledge
Rice, Anne 51
Robison, Mary 152-153
Romantic 33, 68, 72
Roth, Philip 67, 69

Sebold, Alice 84
short story xiv, 141-150
Smiley, Jane 67
Sontag, Susan 63, 65
sound 24-27, 29
sun square moon: writings on yoga and writing
    64
Steiner, George 78
Stevens, Wallace 83
Strand, Mark 34, 35
supervisors xii 4, 10, 14-16

TEXT 1
Thompson, Hunter. S. 104-106
Thousand Plateaus, A 125-126
Tzara, Tristan 27, 28, 35

Van Dyke 154-157

Walcott, Derek 46, 47
White, Edmund 51
Williams, William Carlos 76, 79
workshops/workshopping xiii, 47, 67,
    77-81, 103, 139
Writer's Chronicle, The 1
Writing in Education 1

Yeats, William Butler 82

zeitgeist 56